CONCEIVING DESIRE IN LYLY AND SHAKESPEARE

CONCEIVING DESIRE IN LYLY AND SHAKESPEARE

Metaphor, Cognition and Eros

◆ ◆ ◆

GILLIAN KNOLL

EDINBURGH
University Press

For Ted Leinwand

Edinburgh University Press is one of the leading university presses in the UK. We publish academic books and journals in our selected subject areas across the humanities and social sciences, combining cutting-edge scholarship with high editorial and production values to produce academic works of lasting importance. For more information visit our website: edinburghuniversitypress.com

Edinburgh University Press Ltd
The Tun – Holyrood Road
12(2f) Jackson's Entry
Edinburgh EH8 8PJ

First published in hardback by Edinburgh University Press 2020

Typeset in 12/15 Adobe Sabon by
IDSUK (DataConnection) Ltd, and
printed and bound by CPI Group (UK) Ltd,
Croydon, CR0 4YY

A CIP record for this book is available from the British Library

ISBN 978 1 4744 2852 1 (hardback)
ISBN 978 1 4744 2853 8 (paperback)
ISBN 978 1 4744 2854 5 (webready PDF)
ISBN 978 1 4744 2855 2 (epub)

CONTENTS

ACKNOWLEDGEMENTS

Writing a book about metaphor has made me especially conscious of the metaphors we find in Acknowledgements pages. Like many authors, I have incurred debts, I have leaned on countless others for support, and this book has been a journey made richer by colleagues, students, friends and family who have helped along the way. This journey began at the University of Maryland, and it is my pleasure to acknowledge mentors and friends there who encouraged and modelled a creative approach to literary interpretation. First and foremost, I thank Ted Leinwand, to whom this book is dedicated, and who, to borrow Janet Adelman's metaphor, 'has been the only begetter of my ideas about Shakespeare (and much else) for several years'. Ted's presence is everywhere in this book, not only because of the careful attention he paid to the words on its pages but also because of the care and friendship he continues to bestow on its author. I am also grateful for Kent Cartwright's wise advice and thoughtful interest in this project, and for his exemplary scholarship on John Lyly. Others at the University of Maryland patiently read drafts and talked through ideas that sharpened my own. Among them are Theresa Coletti, Gerard Passannante, Brandi Adams, Christine Maffuccio, Adele Seeff, Karen Nelson, Michael Israel and Megan Monserez. I must also thank Rhona Gordon, who helped me 'think organised' throughout the many stages of this process.

Colleagues and students at Western Kentucky University have provided support in more ways than I can enumerate here. Their intelligence, energy and generosity continue to inspire me as a teacher and scholar. Valued conversations with Lloyd Davies, Alison Langdon and Alex Olson sparked new ideas that made this a better book. Others who offered a friendly ear or shoulder include Jess Folk, Wes Berry, Elisa Berry, Dale Rigby, Dan Liddle, Dawn Hall, Rob Hale and my other exceptional colleagues in the Department of English. My research and writing benefited from generous grants and fellowships at Western Kentucky University, especially the Department of English 2018–19 Wood Professorship, which supported the final stages of writing and revising *Conceiving Desire in Lyly and Shakespeare*. Travel grants from Potter College of Arts and Sciences made it possible to visit the Folger Shakespeare Library to conduct research and to participate in the 2017 Institute seminar on the Embodied Senses. The Folger has been an inspiring place to work and learn for many years, and I thank the library staff, especially Camille Seerattan, along with the congenial community of readers there. Others whose feedback and insights have enriched this book include Valerie Traub, Amy Cook, Ricardo Padrón, P. A. Skantze and many other participants at seminars and conferences where I presented earlier versions of this research.

I must also express my gratitude to Kevin Curran for approaching me about this series after hearing my quirky paper on Shakespeare's erotic metaphors and Aristotle's *Metaphysics* at the Renaissance Society of America conference in 2016. Each time I read Kevin's Preface, I feel privileged to count *Conceiving Desire in Lyly and Shakespeare* among the fine volumes in this series. Many thanks to Kevin and to Michelle Houston for their encouragement and support throughout this process.

An earlier version of Chapter 3 appeared as 'How to Make Love to the Moon: Intimacy and Erotic Distance in Lyly's *Endymion*', *Shakespeare Quarterly* 65, no. 2 (2014) and I am grateful to Gail Paster and Lars Engle for their generous feedback on that essay. A version of Chapter 4 appeared as 'Binding the Void: The Erotics of Place in *Antony and Cleopatra*', *Criticism: A Quarterly for Literature and the Arts* 58, no. 2 (2016).

Finally, I could not have written this book without the love and support of my family. I thank my wonderful parents, Anne and Fred Knoll, for their unflagging belief in me. And I thank my son Nathan, without whom this book almost certainly would have been published nine months earlier, for giving the title *Conceiving Desire* special significance when he came into the world. My deepest gratitude goes to Justin, who gives meaning to all the metaphors in my book. Together, Justin and Nathan teach me every day that love is a collaborative work of art.

SERIES EDITOR'S PREFACE

Picture Macbeth alone on stage, staring intently into empty space. 'Is this a dagger which I see before me?' he asks, grasping decisively at the air. On one hand, this is a quintessentially theatrical question. At once an object and a vector, the dagger describes the possibility of knowledge ('Is this a dagger') in specifically visual and spatial terms ('which I see before me'). At the same time, Macbeth is posing a quintessentially *philosophical* question, one that assumes knowledge to be both conditional and experiential, and that probes the relationship between certainty and perception, as well as intention and action. It is from this shared ground of art and enquiry, of theatre and theory, that this series advances its basic premise: *Shakespeare is philosophical*.

It seems like a simple enough claim. But what does it mean exactly, beyond the parameters of this specific moment in *Macbeth*? Does it mean that Shakespeare had something we could think of as his own philosophy? Does it mean that he was influenced by particular philosophical schools, texts and thinkers? Does it mean, conversely, that modern philosophers have been influenced by *him*, that Shakespeare's plays and poems have been, and continue to be, resources for philosophical thought and speculation?

The answer is yes all around. These are all useful ways of conceiving a philosophical Shakespeare and all point to lines of enquiry that this series welcomes. But Shakespeare is philosophical in a much more fundamental way as well. Shakespeare is philosophical because the plays and poems actively create new worlds of knowledge and new scenes of ethical encounter. They ask big questions, make bold arguments and develop new vocabularies in order to think what might otherwise be unthinkable. Through both their scenarios and their imagery, the plays and poems engage the qualities of consciousness, the consequences of human action, the phenomenology of motive and attention, the conditions of personhood and the relationship among different orders of reality and experience. This is writing and dramaturgy, moreover, that consistently experiments with a broad range of conceptual crossings, between love and subjectivity, nature and politics, and temporality and form.

Edinburgh Critical Studies in Shakespeare and Philosophy takes seriously these speculative and world-making dimensions of Shakespeare's work. The series proceeds from a core conviction that art's capacity to think – to formulate, not just reflect, ideas – is what makes it urgent and valuable. Art matters because, unlike other human activities, it establishes its own frame of reference, reminding us that all acts of creation – biological, political, intellectual and amorous – are grounded in imagination. This is a far cry from business-as-usual in Shakespeare studies. Because historicism remains the methodological gold standard of the field, far more energy has been invested in exploring what Shakespeare once meant than in thinking rigorously about what Shakespeare continues to make possible. In response, *Edinburgh Critical Studies in Shakespeare and Philosophy* pushes back against the critical orthodoxies of historicism and cultural studies to clear a space for scholarship that confronts aspects of literature that can be neither reduced to nor adequately explained by particular historical contexts.

Shakespeare's creations are not just inheritances of a past culture, frozen artefacts whose original settings must be expertly reconstructed in order to be understood. The plays and poems are also living art, vital thought-worlds that struggle, across time, with foundational *questions* of metaphysics, ethics, politics and aesthetics. With this orientation in mind, *Edinburgh Critical Studies in Shakespeare and Philosophy* offers a series of scholarly monographs that will reinvigorate Shakespeare studies by opening new interdisciplinary conversations among scholars, artists and students.

Kevin Curran

INTRODUCTION

Conceiving Desire

The eye of man hath not heard, the ear of man hath not
seen, man's hand is not able to taste, *his tongue to conceive*,
nor his heart to report what my dream was.

> (*A Midsummer Night's Dream* IV, i, 209–12,
> emphasis added)[1]

This is a book about tongues that conceive – tongues that
think, tongues that imagine, tongues that 'expound' (IV, i, 205)
and conceptualise, and thereby *bring into being* erotic
dreams and desires on the early modern stage. That Bottom
intends for 'Peter Quince to write a ballad of this dream'
(212–13) testifies to the capacities of language – and artistic language in particular – to 'conceive' his erotic, fantastic,
metamorphic midsummer night with Titania.[2] So, too, does
the innate wisdom of Bottom's synaesthesia affirm that
hearts can indeed 'report' experiences that 'hath no bottom'
(214). Because conceiving such bottomless experiences is
both a cognitive and a linguistic activity, this book analyses
the interplay of the heart, tongue and mind in creating erotic
experience. To 'conceive' desire is also to beget it, to give it
form and shape, as in Theseus's famous description in which
'imagination bodies forth / The forms of things unknown'

and 'the poet's pen / Turns them to shapes' (V, i, 12–13, 17). *Conceiving Desire in Lyly and Shakespeare* explores this generative potential of the erotic imagination, and the language it inspires, in plays by John Lyly and William Shakespeare.

Although Lyly and Shakespeare wrote for different types of theatres and only partially overlapping audiences, both dramatists created characters who speak erotic language at considerable length and in extraordinary depth. Their words do more than merely narrate or express eros; they *constitute* characters' erotic experiences. *Conceiving Desire in Lyly and Shakespeare* locates this constitutive power in metaphor. Metaphor, I argue, gives Lyly, Shakespeare, their characters, and us through them, *a way in*, a way of accessing experiences as formless and fleeting as ecstasy. Taking my cue from cognitive linguists such as George Lakoff, Mark Johnson and Mark Turner, I begin from the premise that the erotic imagination – indeed, that thought itself – is metaphorical.[3] Metaphorical language 'bodies forth' a character's cognitive interior, an inner erotic life that derives from such embodied experiences as physical struggle and spatial containment, violent restraint and turbulent motion. My approach to dramatic character aligns with cognitive literary studies such as Rafael Lyne's *Shakespeare, Rhetoric and Cognition*, which emphasises characters, rather than authors or texts, 'as the sites of represented cognition . . . because of a literary-critical conviction that Shakespeare's characters do not simply or readily recede in favour of a play-wide network of language'.[4] That Lyly's and Shakespeare's characters body forth profound human thoughts and imaginings, fantasies and feelings – that they desire – is a premise of this book. The metaphors by which they think and imagine and desire are, to borrow from George Lakoff and Mark Johnson, metaphors they live by.

Take, for example, Shakespeare's Troilus, eagerly awaiting the arrival of his beloved Cressida in the orchard. An

eponymous character in one of Shakespeare's most 'consciously philosophical' plays, Troilus is always thinking
through what it means to be in love.⁵ Technically, that is all
he does as he waits. But for Troilus, erotic imagining is filled
with drama. Thus Jean-Luc Marion writes of erotic anticipation, 'In the time in which I wait for something to happen,
and in which nothing happens, a whole host of things nevertheless happen.'⁶ Here we see a whole host of things happening to Troilus as he speaks:

> I am giddy. Expectation whirls me round.
> Th' imaginary relish is so sweet
> That it enchants my sense. What will it be
> When that the wat'ry palates taste indeed
> Love's thrice-repurèd nectar? Death, I fear me,
> Sounding destruction, or some joy too fine,
> Too subtle, potent, tuned too sharp in sweetness
> For the capacity of my ruder powers.
> I fear it much; and I do fear besides
> That I shall lose distinction in my joys,
> As doth a battle, when they charge on heaps
> The enemy flying.
>   (III, ii, 16–27)

As Troilus stands alone on stage, erotic language acts on him
and alters him. It even objectifies him: Eros is the subject of
his action verbs. 'Expectation whirls [him] round'; 'imaginary
relish . . . enchants [his] sense'; and his 'joys charge on heaps'.
Desire happens *to* Troilus, whose only 'I's' in this soliloquy
govern verbs of being ('I am giddy'), of feeling ('I fear') and
of loss ('I shall lose . . .'). It might be argued that he is merely
imagining future events, but his hectic imagining is unmistak-
ably a source of drama in the present. The prospect of future
pleasures creates not just present-tense fear ('I *do* fear') but
present-tense pleasure ('th' imaginary relish *is* so sweet / That
it *enchants*'). And there can be no question but that Troilus

is different at the end of his soliloquy from when he began. Speaking his desire changes him, and change is the surest marker of action.

Troilus's speech provides a telling example of the importance of cognition in creating erotic experience. As he details his fear of the sexual pleasures that await him, it becomes clear that he suffers from a kind of cognitive performance anxiety. He worries about sexual pleasures that are

> too fine,
> Too subtle, potent, tuned too sharp in sweetness
> For the capacity of my ruder powers.
>
> (21–3)

To which 'ruder powers' does Troilus refer? His sexual potency? His taste buds? His nerve endings? All of these connotations are available but chief among these receptive organs is the *mind*, the organ that makes sense of sensation. For Troilus, '*imaginary* relish' – the fantasy of sensation, rather than sensation itself – is powerful enough to 'enchant . . . my sense'. The double resonance of 'sense' (a familiar gloss is 'senses / power of reason') reflects the importance of both sensation and cognition in generating erotic pleasure.[7] While the 'poten[cy]' of his impending orgasm is the source of some trepidation, it is the acuteness of his pleasures that most unnerves him (his joys will be 'too subtle . . . too sharp') because he may not have the requisite perceptual and conceptual acuity to process them. It is as though his conceptual system is too coarse a sieve to capture the fine grain of the 'joys' that await him, dooming him to lose them forever. Throughout these lines, Troilus demonstrates that our ability to process erotic experience mentally completes our access to it: both contemplation and action are vital ingredients. The same set of physical acts can produce wildly different responses – from 'death' and 'destruction' to 'joy too fine' – because of the conceptualising mind, which makes eros happen by *making erotic meaning*.

As Troilus's fears become more pronounced, so do the connections he draws between cognitive and erotic experience. Erotic consummation is often imagined as 'death' or 'destruction', but Troilus begins to fear a different kind of loss in the final lines of his soliloquy:

> I do fear besides
> That I shall lose distinction in my joys
> As doth a battle, when they charge on heaps,
> The enemy flying.
>
> (24–7)

The prospect of such powerful sexual pleasures constitutes for Troilus both an ecstatic fantasy and a nightmare of 'los[ing] distinction'. At risk in this loss are, first, his cognitive ability to discriminate – to identify, isolate and define each joy – and second, his ability to remain distinct from Cressida amidst lovemaking.[8] For Troilus, it seems that the latter depends on the former. His individuality – his 'distinction' from Cressida – is a product of his capacity to conceive his pleasure, to distinguish joy from joy, drop from drop of 'Love's . . . nectar' (III, ii, 20). This temporal cause and effect relation of dependence is, however, at odds with the way that erotic experience demands that Troilus simultaneously maintain a strong cognitive presence (an ability to distinguish himself and his joys) and risk that 'distinction' by becoming vulnerable to his beloved. If such simultaneous vulnerability and self-possession is impossible in the event, it proves otherwise in Troilus's cognition and language. Contemplating pleasure, he opens himself to pleasure. Parsing his fears, he experiences fear. It is Troilus's '*cognition* / Of what I feel' (V, ii, 64–5, emphasis added) that distinguishes him as a lover. When he stops conceiving desire, which he tries to do when he learns of Cressida's betrayal of him later in the play, Troilus finally suffers the loss he fears. Trying to quiet his pain by vowing, 'I will not be myself nor have cognition / Of what I feel,' Troilus forsakes his 'distinction' as a lover.

Metaphor, Cognition and Eros

Troilus's declaration is a speech act – a vow – that forges an intimate connection between loving, thinking, feeling and speaking. And yet it is telling that the locus of Troilus's 'fear' and Bottom's doubt is the mouth, whether Bottom's speaking tongue or Troilus's 'palates'. Such misgivings about the tongue's capacity to conceive erotic experience correlate with longstanding philosophical questions about the relationship between linguistic representation and erotic desire, both on and off the stage, within and beyond the early modern period. Most theorists have framed this relationship in terms of lack, emphasising the gap between language and the erotic experience it struggles to name. As Judith Butler puts it, 'we can't trust language to give us a clear picture of desire, because they're bound up together. No exposition of desire can escape becoming implicated in that which it seeks to clarify.'[9] The failures of language to approximate or represent erotic desire lie at the core of the psychoanalytic narratives that have been the touchstone for several generations of scholarship on early modern desire.[10] More recent work on early modern sexualities, such as Valerie Traub's *Thinking Sex with the Early Moderns* and Jeffrey Masten's *Queer Philologies*, argues for what Masten calls the 'constitutive power' of particular words and phrases within early modern discourses of sex and gender. Although Masten's emphasis on the 'historical and cultural specificity' of those discourses differs from my own broader view of erotic language and cognition, we share a belief in the generative capacities of erotic language.[11] Importantly, this language need not be fixed or consistent in order to be constructive. As Valerie Traub demonstrates in *Thinking Sex with the Early Moderns*, the obscurities, instabilities and even failures of sexual language are themselves productive. Traub's impressive book on the history of early modern sexual knowledge 'pauses over those moments *when words fail*. Not fail to be erotic – eroticism can thrive on uncertainty, ambiguity, and contradiction – but fail in their *indexical function*.'[12] For evidence of Traub's observation about eroticism that thrives on contradiction, we need look no further than the proximity of Troilus's 'joys' to his 'fear'.

Conceiving Desire in Lyly and Shakespeare does consider some of the failures and contradictions of erotic language – failures that, as I have suggested, can generate pleasure and shape erotic identities – but I focus on its accomplishments. Both Bottom's integrating synaesthesia and Troilus's ecstatic giddiness reveal to us characters who *successfully* conceive their desires. With this in mind, it is important to stress that desire is understood differently in cognitive theory, which breaks away from Lacanian models in which desire is believed to be a product of the fragmentation of the self. Cognitive theorists such as Mary Thomas Crane argue that desire plays a fundamental role in the emergence and formation of the self:

> A cognitive approach emphasizes a feeling of presence (rather than lack) as the basis of the self . . . Desire is seen to be bound up with the emergence of both consciousness and thought . . . [r]ather than a Lacanian scenario of desire emerging from a sense of loss in the mirror stage that is intensified by the acquisition of language.[13]

In Lyly's and Shakespeare's plays, erotic language not only intensifies the 'feeling of presence . . . as the basis of the self' but, time and again, it makes present an absent beloved. Troilus brings Cressida into his (and our) consciousness when he indulges in 'imaginary relish', just as

Juliet presences Romeo on her balcony and Endymion conjures the moon entirely by means of imagination and desire.
For these characters, contemplative language builds erotic
identities and relationships. It fills the gaps that separate
them from a beloved. It shapes their 'shaping fantasies'
(*A Midsummer Night's Dream* V, i, 5).

It may seem odd or counterintuitive to consider experiences such as fantasy, desire or pleasure in cognitive terms.
Is eros really a cognitive event, something we 'conceive'
mentally? Given all of the body parts that are involved in
erotic experience, is the *mind* the place where love or lust or
desire is experienced? According to many of Shakespeare's
and Lyly's characters, yes, it is. Berowne tells Rosaline of
his 'wooing mind' (*Love's Labour's Lost* V, ii, 413). Helena
tells us in the opening scene of *A Midsummer Night's Dream*
that 'Love looks not with the eyes but with the mind' (I,
i, 234). Any number of Shakespeare's sonnets debate this
point.[14] Lyly's lovestruck nymph Telusa first feels the pangs
of erotic desire as 'new conceits' that 'breed in thy mind'
(*Galatea* III, i, 1–2).[15] Of course, the mind does not operate
in isolation from the body, particularly when we consider all
of the early modern notions of embodiment, according to
which the body and the mind relate dynamically, both to one
another and to the outside world. Scholarship on humoral
theory has illuminated the interpermeability of the early
modern body, mind and world, all of which were composed
of the same four humours. Connected at the most basic level
of material substance, the desiring body and mind were one
and the same. Gail Kern Paster describes this mind–body
connection as 'psychophysiological'; emotional, mental and
psychic experiences were inextricable from the physical body
and the world that contained them.[16] Love in particular was
understood in material terms, sometimes as a humoral imbalance, sometimes as a physical disease. Robert Burton devotes
the third of the three sections that comprise *The Anatomy*

of Melancholy to the subject of 'Love melancholy', detailing the physical causes, symptoms and potential cures for the illness.[17] Different medical tracts from the period locate lovesickness in various parts of the body (the liver, the eyes and the heart are among the most common), but most agree that the disease circulated throughout the body and brain, emphasising its power to afflict the mind.[18]

Although our understanding of the scientific underpinnings of the mind–body continuum has changed considerably during the last 400 years, their connection is still understood to be as rich and complex as it was in Lyly's and Shakespeare's day. The reciprocal relationship between body and mind also lies at the core of contemporary cognitive theory. Paster has noted the similarities between early modern humoral theory and more recent cognitive theories of the embodied mind: 'such an emphasis on the biological functionality of the passions sounds strikingly like the interest of modern cognitive science in the evolution of the emotions'.[19] According to Lakoff and Johnson, the first of the three major findings of cognitive science is that 'the mind is inherently embodied ... in such a way that our conceptual systems draw largely upon the commonalities of our bodies and the environments we live in'.[20] Cognitive linguists emphasise the role of our physical and spatial orientation in the world as a primary source for our cognitive patterning. When Troilus talks of anticipation as a force that 'whirls' him, he conceptualises erotic desire in physical and spatial terms. To experience erotic 'expectation' as a physical force that can send one's body into frenzied motion is to conceptualise desire as an action, and perhaps more significantly for Troilus's particular experience, it is to conceptualise oneself as a separate entity vulnerable to desire's whims and subject to its power.

Troilus's experience of erotic expectation arises from the basic conceptual metaphor 'Desire is a physical force', which can generate any number of simple and complex turns of phrase, from 'expectation whirls me round' to joys 'that charge on heaps'. George Lakoff draws a sharp distinction between metaphor and a metaphorical expression. The former is crucially not a feature of language. A metaphor is a way of conceptualising, not articulating, experience. Lakoff defines it as

> *a cross-domain mapping in the conceptual system.* The term *metaphorical expression* refers to a linguistic expression (a word, phrase, or sentence) that is the surface realization of such a cross-domain mapping (this is what the word *metaphor* referred to in the old theory).[21]

Take, for example, the 'argument is war' metaphor: the features of wars are mapped on to the experience of argument.[22] In this instance, war is the 'source domain' because it is being used to conceptualise, or 'profile', the more abstract 'target domain' of argument. Mapping across domains creates a whole host of entailments that allow us to generate novel metaphors about arguments as war (such as 'she attacked his thesis' and 'I had to defend my side'). According to Lakoff and Johnson, 'metaphor is pervasive in everyday life, not just in language but in thought and action. Our ordinary conceptual system, in terms of which we both think and act, is fundamentally metaphorical in nature.'[23]

Lakoff and Johnson emphasise the power of both the content and the structure of each source domain to inform our experience of the target domain. The skeletal structure of the source domain, according to Lakoff and Mark Turner, is known as a 'schema'.[24] Each schema has slots, which stand for participants in the schema, or elements that are waiting to be filled in. In the example of desire as a physical struggle, the slots would include an aggressor, a victim, a physical encounter, perhaps a weapon, some kind of motive and so on. Each of these slots profiles the participants of the desire domain.

The metaphor itself constrains us to assign particular roles (for example: aggressor, victim) and relations between the roles (for example: the aggressor attacks / destroys/ 'charge[s] on' the victim), even though these may not be necessary parts of the target domain or pertain to other metaphors. Desire as a journey does not have a 'victim' slot.

Research in cognitive science further suggests that lived, physical experiences produce our most basic metaphors. Joseph Grady identifies a special class of metaphor called 'primary metaphors', or deeply entrenched metaphorical patterns, which are based on experiential correlations.[25] Grady discusses the cross-cultural definition of 'coldness' as 'lacking in emotion'. Languages ranging from Latin to Chinese to Old Irish associate coldness with indifference. And this connection extends to the animal kingdom, according to primatologist Franz de Waal, who noted on the *Times Book Review* podcast that

> we say we get 'cold feet' when we're afraid, and that's literally true, we've tested it. It's true for rats, too – they get cold feet, and their tails get cold, when they are scared. What fear does is draw the blood from the extremities.[26]

There is, unsurprisingly, a similar association between heat or warmth and aroused emotion. Primary metaphors are based on our physical experiences, not on shared features between source and target domains. That is, we feel warm when we experience affection, or any extreme emotion such as love or anger. Moreover, extreme emotion *causes* the change in body temperature. While other instances of metaphor may be considered correlations, then, there is a class of primary metaphors that have causal relationships.

Because it is both abstract and physical, conceptual and experiential, erotic desire is a particularly fruitful subject for scrutiny using conceptual metaphor theory. Conceptual metaphor theory would have it that complex ideas and emotions are understood in terms of tangible, physically based source domains, such as temperature and motion. But temperature and motion, to name only two, are key ingredients in the experience of desire (especially the early modern caloric analysis of desire, according to which the heat generated during lovemaking made for a better chance of conception). When we feel erotic attraction, our body temperatures rise and our blood circulates more quickly. We get butterflies in our stomach (another metaphor) and our pulse accelerates. We sweat. Our mouths water (cf. Troilus's 'wat'ry palates'). Our bodies move, stiffen, swell. Hence the relationship between physical source domains and the target domain of erotic desire is especially complex. Sometimes we use a particular metaphor because of correlations or shared characteristics between the two domains. At other times, we rely on primary metaphors to elaborate an experience of desire, revealing how difficult it is to abstract desire from the physical sensations it generates in our bodies.

A growing body of scholarship has reinvigorated literary studies by bringing the fruits of scientific enquiry and cognitive linguistic analysis to bear on our understanding of early modern texts. Cognitive approaches to Shakespeare's plays alone probe subjects as varied as memory and forgetting, consciousness and character, distributed cognition, the embodied mind, early modern performance practices, social cognition and theory of mind, and more.[27] Among these studies are compelling analyses of Shakespeare's 'conceptual blends' by scholars such as Amy Cook and, most recently, Michael Booth, whose work draws from research on imaginative language and thought by Gilles Fauconnier and Mark Turner.[28] I have confined my methodology in *Conceiving Desire in Lyly and Shakespeare* to conceptual metaphor theory rather than blending theory, but both are useful tools for understanding the accomplishments of Lyly's and Shakespeare's erotic language. Cognitive linguists have noted that 'the two frameworks are largely complementary. The conventional conceptual pairings and one-way mappings studied within CMT [conceptual metaphor theory] are inputs to and constraints on the kinds of dynamic conceptual networks posited within BT [blending theory].'[29] *Conceiving Desire in Lyly and Shakespeare* focuses on conceptual metaphor theory rather than blending because my main subject is erotic language rather than the mental processes that produce such language. Eros is always my 'target domain'; thus, conceptual metaphor theory's 'one-way' and 'asymmetrical' mappings have special value.[30]

Missing from the existing cognitive studies of Shakespeare is a full-scale analysis of love, desire or sexuality on the early modern stage. Because cognitive linguistics emphasises the interdependence of linguistic structures, the embodied mind and lived experience, its tools have much to offer scholars of early modern sexuality. Conceptual metaphor theory in particular opens up new ways of understanding how language dramatises the inward and often invisible experience of desire. My book draws on a cognitive approach to desire in two ways. First, I treat language as constitutive of erotic desire, exploring the potential of words to create eros and conjure the beloved, rather than to mark lack, loss or absence. Shifting my emphasis from what Judith Butler calls the 'exposition of desire' to erotic desire understood semantically and performatively, I explore the creative, as opposed to the expressive, potential of words. Second, I aim to understand the way in which characters experience eros by analysing how they conceptualise it. Language, according to cognitive theory, is a product of cognition – thus, to study erotic speech is to probe how a character mentally 'conceives desire'. This book's literary and linguistic analysis of metaphor credits the role of cognition in erotic experiences from desire to pleasure.

For example, a character like Lyly's Phao makes almost no distinction between erotic language and action. Upon falling in love with Sappho, Phao tells himself,

> Let thy love hang at thy heart's bottom, not at the tongue's brim. Things untold are undone; there can be no greater comfort than to know much, nor any less labour than to say nothing. But, ah, thy beauty, Sappho, thy beauty! Beginnest thou to blab? Ay, blab it, Phao, as long as thou blabbest her beauty.
>
> (*Sappho and Phao* II, iv, 28–34)

Phao's astounding reason for holding his tongue is that 'things untold are undone'. The words 'untold' and 'undone' are increasingly problematic in the context of Phao's speech because, while he struggles over the question of telling Sappho his feelings, he is telling himself in this speech, and telling us. It seems, therefore, that he *is* 'doing' whatever it is that one does when 'blabb[ing]' these feelings. What does Phao mean by 'undone'? Is it his hope that keeping his feelings secret will make them untrue, or not real, for him, as well as for his beloved? But Phao does not say that things untold are un*true* – he says they are un*done*. What is clear from this line is that, for Phao, 'to say' is to do; he makes a powerful connection between saying and feeling, between 'blabbing' and loving.

The connection that Phao draws is representative of the erotic language in much of Lyly's drama. It is probably no exaggeration to say that the language of desire is spoken more exhaustively by Lyly's characters than by any other playwright's in the sixteenth century. Almost all of his plays are about erotic desire, and almost all of them have been described at one point or another as undramatic.[31] Traditional scholarship on Lyly's drama characterises his plays as largely allegorical: that is, interesting primarily for their commentaries on Elizabeth's court and for their euphuistic style, but generally lacking in dynamism.[32] Although seminal books such as G. K. Hunter's *John Lyly: The Humanist as Courtier* reveal the political reach and context of humanist writers, Andy Kesson points out that 'the phrase "Humanist as courtier" . . . does not capture anything unique about Lyly, and it has severely constricted our understanding of his work. It also seems to radically undervalue Lyly's role as a popular writer.'[33] Hunter is in accord with many other scholars when he argues that Lyly's comedies 'depend on a . . . static and passive mode of contemplating and analyzing the conflicting emotions of love'.[34] Contemplation and analysis do comprise a good portion of Lyly's drama but this book challenges the characterisation of these activities as 'static'. *Conceiving Desire in Lyly and Shakespeare* reveals that erotic contemplation, and even analysis, can be vibrant, frenzied actions on a stage.

Metaphors of anticipation and fantasy, insinuation and confession, permeate Lyly's plays and give rise to an equally broad range of erotic experiences. Lyly's *Campaspe* and *Sappho and Phao* stage the overpowering desires of monarchs who struggle to maintain control and authority when burdened by the oppressive weight of love. In *Galatea, Love's Metamorphosis*, *The Woman in the Moon* and *Mother Bombie*, Lyly explores the confusions and misdirections of erotic desire by dramatising disguised identities and changing attitudes toward chastity and sexuality. Lyly's *Endymion* is one of the few early modern plays that dwells and remains in the realm of erotic desire. It is not hard to see why David Bevington twice describes it as 'uneventful' in his introduction to the Revels Plays edition of *Endymion*, since, after five acts of so-called drama, the play ends more or less where it begins.[35] What, then, makes *Endymion* dramatic, besides the fact that it is, generically, a drama? What happens to Lyly's hero? Or to pose a more apt question, what does he *do* in the play? The answer must be that Endymion desires. He does not attain, he does not marry, he does not really even court or seduce. He solely, and fiercely, wants. Wanting is the main event, the protagonist's primary action, in Lyly's play. And, as in so many other of Lyly's and Shakespeare's plays, his desire is dramatised through speech.

My emphasis on the active properties of Lyly's erotic language builds on the work of scholars such as Kent Cartwright and Andy Kesson. 'Although Lyly's plays have been treated by modern critics as static and intellectual dramas of ideas,' Cartwright argues, '*Gallathea* generates emotional and visceral delight from not exactly ideas, but a pleasurable "confusion" that displays theatrical values one expects from popular plays.'[36] Our understanding of Lyly's 'theatrical values' has grown as a result of the online 'Before Shakespeare' project, which combines theatre history, performance workshops, and live productions of plays such as *The Woman in the Moon* to illustrate the dramatic vitality of Lyly's drama. Although *Conceiving Desire in Lyly and Shakespeare* is neither a history project nor an authorship study, it is indebted to this pioneering 'recovery' work. Andy Kesson's claim that Lyly's theatrical innovations made him 'the most famous writer of the period, during the period itself' warrants *Conceiving Desire in Lyly and Shakespeare*'s focus on what Lyly's language can tell us about the experience, and the theatricality, of erotic desire.[37]

Lyly and Shakespeare

To date, no full-length study has paired Shakespeare's and Lyly's plays. *Conceiving Desire in Lyly and Shakespeare* aims to fill this critical gap, and perhaps more importantly, my intention is to make use of the rich linguistic resources that each playwright brings to bear on the drama of erotic desire because such analysis alters our understanding of both playwrights. Ruth Lunney writes that 'Lyly's claim to critical attention has rested largely on his reputation as the playwright who introduced the comedy of love to the English stage, providing an example for Shakespeare and others to follow.'[38] Generally speaking, when scholars pair Lyly and Shakespeare together, the words 'example' and 'influence' make an appearance.[39] Critics have long suggested that Shakespeare turned to Lyly's comedies as models for his own early plays about love. There are a number of advantages to these studies of Lyly's creative influence on Shakespeare. For one, they credit Lyly's innovations in the development of early English professional drama. They also contextualise Shakespeare's dramatic language, and they bring Lyly's plays in closer relation with those of a conventionally 'popular' playwright, thus affirming Kent Cartwright's claim that Lyly's plays had popular theatrical value in their own right. A disadvantage to reading these two playwrights together is that, as Andy Kesson warns, 'the apparent neutrality of the title "Lyly and Shakespeare" operates within a critical discourse that valorizes one writer by denigrating another'.[40] When Lyly's plays are considered alongside Shakespeare's with influence in mind, Shakespeare becomes the destination and Lyly is reduced to just one, sometimes glorified, pit stop on the Bard Highway.

Still, I contend that the 'and' in *Conceiving Desire in Lyly and Shakespeare* is neutral. My reading Lyly alongside Shakespeare, Shakespeare alongside Lyly, is neither teleological nor strictly comparative. *Conceiving Desire in Lyly and Shakespeare* resists many of the norms and expectations of two-author studies. A somewhat queer couple, Lyly and Shakespeare quite simply dwell together in this book. Their plays were selected due to their linguistic potential for dramatising erotic experience, and it will be seen that they use the same fundamental metaphors to that end. Some of these metaphors pertain more to Shakespeare's plays than to Lyly's, while others are more emphatically Lyly's. At times, one playwright's language illuminates the metaphors of the other. Some of the sharper edges of Shakespeare's compact analytical soliloquies limn the metaphorical contours of Lyly's longer erotic speeches, and they, in turn, elaborate the interdependence of the 'how' and the 'why' in the erotic experiences of Shakespeare's characters. Thus, particular erotic metaphors have led me to some unconventional play pairings: for example, I analyse early Lylian comedy in tandem with late Shakespearean tragedy. I also have introduced secondary literature familiar in Shakespeare studies into my readings of Lyly's plays, uncommon though this is in most Lyly studies. Guided by the conceptual metaphors I study and the philosophical questions they raise, I turn to thinkers as diverse as Aristotle, Giordano Bruno, Emmanuel Levinas, Gaston Bachelard, Stanley Cavell and Jean-Luc Marion. Their ideas have given us ways to understand Shakespeare's plays, and I have found that they offer significant insights into Lyly's genius for staging the dynamic experience of erotic desire.

Conceiving Desire in Lyly and Shakespeare is organised into three parts, each of which analyses a conceptual metaphor – motion, space and creativity – that shapes erotic desire on Lyly's and Shakespeare's stages. Although the three metaphors I have selected are relatively simple, the words and experiences they generate are, in Bottom's words, 'most rare' (IV, i, 203). As Lakoff and Johnson note in *Metaphors We Live By*, 'new metaphorical ideas – that is, new ways of organizing and understanding experience – arise from the combination of simpler conceptual metaphors to form complex ones'.[41] I treat the organising metaphors in this study as points of entry into the nuanced erotic experiences of Lyly's and Shakespeare's characters. From Bottom's dream of his magical night with the queen of the fairies to Endymion's intimate erotic connection with the moon, these basic metaphors impart form, make meaning, and thus *make possible* the most elusive erotic experiences on Lyly's and Shakespeare's stages.

It goes without saying that a comprehensive list of Lyly's or Shakespeare's erotic metaphors will be long. But the three with which I work constitute significant building blocks for erotic experiences such as sensation and arousal (motion), intimacy and connection (spatiality), and lovemaking (creativity). As the book progresses, the metaphors progress as well, evolving from primary metaphors based in sensorimotor experience to subtler, self-consciously poetic metaphors. The motion and space metaphors that I discuss in Parts I and II become constituent parts of the more complex aesthetic and self-reflexive metaphor of erotic creation, or lovemaking, that is my subject in Part III. It turns out that this metaphor proliferates on Lyly's and Shakespeare's stages, where desire is always artful, always a made phenomenon.

Each of this book's three sections begins by exploring the underpinnings of its metaphor, drawing from a range of ancient, early modern and modern philosophical models. It quickly becomes clear that some of the most basic metaphors emerge from complex philosophical foundations and engage with abiding philosophical problems. Perhaps the book's simplest metaphor is its first one – physical motion and stillness – but Aristotle's metaphysical inquiries into movement, change and action reveal the profound connection between metaphors of motion and erotic agency. By keeping *Conceiving Desire in Lyly and Shakespeare*'s philosophical scope broad, even opportunistic, I have been able to marshal ideas from classical metaphysicians, early modern scientists and contemporary philosophers to expose the extraordinary breadth and depth of Shakespeare's and Lyly's erotic metaphors. For example, in Part II's analysis of spatial metaphors, I align the work of Gaston Bachelard and Gilles Deleuze with the writings of early modern cosmologists Giordano Bruno and Francisco Patrizi, who debated the existence of infinite space in the universe. *Conceiving Desire in Lyly and Shakespeare* employs a 'critically eclectic' approach, to borrow a phrase from David Schalkwyk, who writes in his recent book, *Shakespeare, Love and Language*, 'there is no single theory or view of love in [Shakespeare's] plays and poems. He is responsive but not subservient to the concepts of love and desire that he may have inherited from Plato' and others.[42] Needless to say, I argue that his claim extends to Lyly's erotic drama.

Part I of *Conceiving Desire in Lyly and Shakespeare* surveys sensorimotor metaphors of erotic desire as physical stasis and motion, and analyses the ways that such metaphors dramatise the dynamic features of erotic experience. I begin with Aristotle, introducing the different forms and degrees of motion (*kinesis*), potency (*dunamis*) and action (*energeia, entelecheia*) that structure a variety of erotic metaphors – idleness and lethargy, submission and passivity, giddiness and violence – on the early modern stage. Chapter 1 tracks these metaphors in Lyly's plays and focuses on idleness, an experience his characters conceive less as physical stasis than as movement without purpose or *telos*. Idleness has a peculiar, perhaps counterintuitive, feel to it in *Galatea*, a play in which cross-dressed maids find eroticism not in Aristotelian action or actuality, but in potentiality. Galatea, Phillida and the nymphs who fall in love with them discover the erotic potential of circuitous language that prolongs desire and defers closure. In Chapter 2, I study Shakespeare's metaphors of stillness and motion in *Measure for Measure* and *Othello*. While some of Shakespeare's characters are immobilised by erotic desire, others experience desire as a stirring, physically moving, experience. For Angelo, Claudio and Othello, it is both. Drawing on the work of Stanley Cavell and Emmanuel Levinas, I discuss the ontological and ethical consequences of such conflicting metaphors. At first, Othello's joy 'subdues' him but, in short order, the 'violent pace' of his sexual imaginings propels him into fits of frenzied motion.

Part II focuses on spatial metaphors of permeability and containment that dramatise erotic desire as a rupture between self and world. Such metaphors raise the stakes of erotic desire when intimacy requires characters to make themselves vulnerable. They compromise their personal and bodily boundaries but they also gain access to new forms of intimacy. These experiences are shaped by the container schema, a basic cognitive structure that allows us to conceptualise bounded regions in space by imagining an inside, outside and boundary. Chapter 3 analyses Lyly's *Endymion*, whose eponymous hero forges an erotic connection with the moon across the vast expanse of the night sky. Endymion's investment in Cynthia's strangest and most distant incarnation grants him access to a form of intimacy that emerges from erotic distance. His metaphors of permeability open Endymion to a mutual and profoundly intimate erotic relation with the moon. In Chapter 4, I take up the erotics of bounded place and of limitless space in *Antony and Cleopatra*. I begin with Edward Casey's philosophical history of place and space in order to consider the erotic implications of these two concepts. Antony and Cleopatra, I argue, eroticise the infinite void by imposing the sturdy boundaries of place on to vacant space. Binding the void allows the lovers to *present* this vacancy to one another, enabling pleasurable experiences of self-loss and self-forgetting.

In Part III, I study characters who conceive of desire as a dynamic process of mutual creation. Such erotic relationships often introduce a third entity – a filter, a buffer or an instrument – that mediates between the subject and object of desire. When Kenneth Burke writes about the role of instruments in daily life, he emphasises the instrument's ontological connection, its potential fusion, with the subject who deploys it. Chapter 5 explores this connection in Lyly's *Campaspe*, a play in which the painter Apelles and his model Campaspe employ creative instruments – easel and canvas, pigments and words – to *make* love. Like any object placed between two bodies in some kind of dynamic relation, these erotic instruments invariably generate friction and heat. Lyly's euphuistic language is, I argue, an erotic instrument in its own right. Providing the lovers with more than a vocabulary, it affords them a conceptual system that gives their experience of erotic desire its form, its medium and its meaning. In Chapter 6, I argue that the 'Desiring is Creating' metaphor in *The Taming of the Shrew* also depends upon the generative power of words as erotic instruments. For Petruchio and Kate, these words are fictions – often, they are outright lies – that Petruchio hopes will generate a privately constituted truth. But it can do this only if Kate consents and confirms his untruths. Petruchio may believe that he must 'tame' Kate if he is to secure her confirmation, but only their mutual erotic and affective experiences enable them to inhabit the shared reality that becomes their marriage.

Having emphasised the creative potential of erotic metaphor, I conclude by reflecting on some of its limits: specifically, the incapacities of any single metaphor to dramatise eros in all of its complexity. While Troilus considers his erotic limitations 'monstrous' (III, ii, 75), I probe the potential of limits – and metaphorical constraints in particular – to tether elusive erotic experiences to language and to the desiring body. For Troilus, as for so many of Shakespeare's characters, contemplative speech brings coherence to physically incompatible sexual scenarios, making erotic experience startlingly new.

Notes

1. All quotations of Shakespeare's plays are from *The Complete Pelican Shakespeare*.
2. A number of scholars have commented on the reach and wisdom of Bottom's synaesthesia. For a representative example, see Marjorie Garber: 'The inversion of "eye" and "ear" is a

structural parody of the Pauline original; that "tongue" should "conceive," however, is both more profound and more relevant to the interests of the play' (*Dream in Shakespeare*, 79).

3. Two foundational books are George Lakoff and Mark Johnson, *Metaphors We Live By*, and Lakoff and Mark Turner, *More Than Cool Reason*.
4. Rafael Lyne, *Shakespeare, Rhetoric and Cognition*, 27.
5. S. L. Bethell, *Shakespeare and the Popular Dramatic Tradition*, 98; L. C. Knights, *Some Shakespearean Themes*, 58, qtd in David Hillman, 'The Gastric Epic', 296.
6. Jean-Luc Marion, *The Erotic Phenomenon*, 33.
7. See Jonathan Bate and Eric Rasmussen's RSC Shakespeare edition of *Troilus and Cressida*, 77.
8. Daniel Juan Gil refers to a third meaning of 'lose distinction': that of losing dignity. See Gil, *Before Intimacy*, 80–2.
9. Judith Butler, 'Desire', 369.
10. Two foundational studies are Janet Adelman, *Suffocating Mothers*, and Valerie Traub, *Desire and Anxiety*.
11. Jeffrey Masten, *Queer Philologies*, 15.
12. Valerie Traub, *Thinking Sex*, 176–7.
13. See Mary Thomas Crane, *Shakespeare's Brain*, 95–6.
14. See, for example, Sonnets 27, 113, 114, and perhaps most famously 'the marriage of true minds' (1) in Sonnet 116.
15. All quotations of Lyly's plays are from The Revels Plays editions.
16. Gail Kern Paster, *Humoring the Body*, 19.
17. See Robert Burton, *The Anatomy of Melancholy*, especially the Third Partition, 'Love melancholy'.
18. Burton notes that 'the Symptoms of the minde in Lovers, are almost infinite, and so diverse, that no Art can comprehend them' (Ibid., 148). For a comprehensive study of lovesickness in the early modern period, see Mary Frances Wack, *Lovesickness in the Middle Ages*.
19. Paster, *Humoring the Body*, 18.
20. See George Lakoff and Mark Johnson, *Philosophy in the Flesh*, 3 and 6. According to Lakoff and Johnson, thoughts are embedded in our basic sensory experiences: 'An embodied

concept is a neural system that is actually a part of, or makes use of, the sensorimotor system of our brains. Much of conceptual inference is, therefore, sensorimotor inference' (20).

21. George Lakoff, 'The Contemporary Theory of Metaphor'.

22. See Lakoff and Johnson, *Metaphors We Live By*, for a more extensive discussion of the 'argument is war' metaphor and its entailments.

23. Ibid., 3.

24. See Lakoff and Turner, *More Than Cool Reason*, especially 'Part II – The Power of Poetic Metaphor'.

25. Joseph Grady, 'Primary Metaphors as Inputs to Conceptual Integration'.

26. De Waal, in Tina Jordan, 'Guilt, Jealousy, Empathy: Your Dog Has the Same Emotions You Do'.

27. Three representative examples include Mary Thomas Crane's foundational *Shakespeare's Brain*, Amy Cook's *Shakespearean Neuroplay* and Evelyn Tribble's *Cognition in the Globe*.

28. Michael Booth's *Shakespeare and Conceptual Blending* provides a more comprehensive account of this work, particularly Chapter 1 (1–14).

29. Joseph E. Grady, Todd Oakley and Seana Coulson, 'Blending and Metaphor'.

30. Ibid. Conceptual metaphor theory is also uniquely well suited to my philosophically oriented study of erotic desire. Unlike the input 'mental spaces' in blending theory, which Gilles Fauconnier and Mark Turner define as 'small conceptual packets constructed as we think and talk, for the purposes of local understanding and action' (*The Way We Think*, 40), the source domains in conceptual metaphor theory are broad and philosophically complex.

31. See, for example, Mary Beth Rose, in *The Expense of Spirit*, who describes Lyly's 'view of sexual love as abstract and impersonal, polarized, static, emotionally simple, and morally predictable' (35). For 'undramatic', see 26.

32. Earlier criticism of Lyly's work tends to focus more on his prose works than his drama, and it is mostly occupied with close formal analysis of allegory and euphuism in his drama.

For examples, see G. K. Hunter, *John Lyly: The Humanist as Courtier* and Michael Pincombe, *The Plays of John Lyly: Eros and Eliza*. Ruth Lunney's 2011 collection of essays on John Lyly (the first compilation of its kind) offers some useful categories for the types of scholarship typical of Lylian studies over the past half-century. She divides her edition into four parts, one of which focuses on desire. The other three sections study humanism, Lyly's courtship of the queen and theatrical performance. See Lunney, *John Lyly*.

33. Andy Kesson, *John Lyly and Early Modern Authorship*, 12.

34. G. K. Hunter, introduction to *Galatea*, 15. See also Kesson, *John Lyly and Early Modern Authorship*, 106, for a survey of similar comments on Lyly's static drama, from critics such as W. W. Greg and Michael Best.

35. See Bevington's introduction to the Revels Plays *Endymion*. First, the play is 'seemingly uneventful' (21) and then progresses to 'largely uneventful' (52).

36. Kent Cartwright, 'The Confusions of *Gallathea*: John Lyly as Popular Dramatist', 208.

37. See Kesson, *John Lyly and Early Modern Authorship*, 214. See also Andy Kesson, Lucy Munro and Callan Davies, *Before Shakespeare*. A number of early modern scholars, including Kesson, Valerie Traub, James Bromley, Simone Chess and Denise A. Walen, have identified Lyly's potential for drama-tising queer eroticism in particular. I study queer relationships in *Galatea* and *Endymion* in Chapters 1 and 3, respectively.

38. Lunney, *John Lyly*, xxiv.

39. See for example Leah Scragg, *The Metamorphosis of Gallathea: A Study in Creative Adaptation*.

40. Kesson, *John Lyly and Early Modern Authorship*, 13.

41. Lakoff and Johnson, *Metaphors We Live By*, 251.

42. David Schalkwyk, *Shakespeare, Love and Language*, 11–12.

PART I

MOTION

THE PHYSICS AND METAPHYSICS OF METAPHOR

'Properly a noun,' writes the poet Anne Carson, 'eros acts everywhere like a verb.'[1] Nowhere is this grammatical pliability more evident than in our metaphorical expression of eros. In modern phrases such as 'falling in love,' 'having sex' and 'making love,' the erotic noun couples with verbs that tell condensed stories about the relationship between erotic being and doing, passion and action.[2] 'Making' love tells a story of bodily arousal and mental provocation. In other metaphors, eros immobilises us: it points to a place into which we 'fall', or it stops us in our tracks or weighs us down. Even the most captivating, spellbinding erotic experiences 'move' us, blurring the distinction between emotion and motion (note that the transit from the former to the latter requires no more than the addition of a single letter).[3] Perhaps this linguistic intimacy explains why we feel physically moved by our emotions, and why we *make* a move or 'put the moves' on a beloved. From what Lucio, in Shakespeare's *Measure for Measure*, calls 'the wanton stings and motions of the sense' (I, iv, 59) to what Angelo describes as a force that 'subdues me quite' (II, ii, 185), eros has the capacity to catalyse and paralyse, sometimes at the same time.

Whether it is a source of action or an act in its own right, eros is always an event. Hence, this section argues that Lyly's and Shakespeare's characters process and experience the event that is erotic desire through the primary metaphor of motion. In the pages that follow, I explore the philosophical and conceptual underpinnings of this metaphor by way of Angelo's example. Drawing from the work of cognitive linguists George Lakoff, Mark Johnson and Zoltán Kövecses, I introduce the broad metaphorical structures that shape Angelo's erotic experience as both a passion and an action. Things happen within Angelo well before he 'acts out' his sexual pursuit of the novitiate Isabella. Further on, I consider the relationship between erotic potentiality and actuality in Aristotle's *Physics* and *Metaphysics*. In Aristotle's writings, as in Shakespeare's play, the boundary between potency and actuality is fluid rather than fixed. As a result, Angelo's metaphors dramatise the capacity of erotic potentiality to create drama. For him, as for so many of Lyly's and Shakespeare's characters, desire is itself a frenzied action.

In *Measure for Measure*, the language of physical stillness and motion cues metaphysical questions about causes, essences, actions and agency. When Isabella unwittingly arouses Angelo's lust, he asks himself, who is doing what to whom? In whom does erotic desire originate, in the lover who is moved or in the beloved who moves him? But first he poses the more metaphysical 'what':

> What's this? What's this? Is this her fault or mine?
> The tempter or the tempted, who sins most, ha?
> Not she, nor doth she tempt; but it is I
> That, lying by the violet in the sun,
> Do as the carrion does, not as the flower,
> Corrupt with virtuous season. Can it be
> That modesty may more betray our sense
> Than woman's lightness? Having waste ground enough,

Shall we desire to raze the sanctuary
And pitch our evils there? O fie, fie, fie!
What dost thou, or what art thou, Angelo?
Dost thou desire her foully for those things
That make her good?

(II, ii, 162–74)

Angelo's alarmed 'What's this?' is as broad in scope as it is
ambiguous in meaning and rich in interpretive potential. His
question is primarily an ontological one, an attempt to pin
down his stirring encounter with Isabella, to fix the flurry
of his sensations into a single and settled essence – a 'this'.
Angelo's speech evolves much as he himself does over the
course of the play, from a position of relative stasis toward
increasingly frenzied motion. Like Isabella, who asks for
'a more strict restraint' (I, iv, 4), Angelo begins Act I in a
static posture that seems to invite or demand activity. Both
Angelo and Isabella appear to others as implacable, unmovable and unmoving. Lucio admonishes Isabella for being 'too
cold' (II, ii, 56) and describes Angelo in similar language,
as 'a man whose blood / Is very snow broth' (I, iv, 57–8).
The Duke, too, notes that Angelo 'scarce confesses / That his
blood flows' (I, iii, 51–2). Angelo's cold rigidity, his humoral
froideur, is suspicious from the start, and when the Duke
puts him in charge, he does so partly to test the unfeeling
deputy by setting him in motion. Praising Angelo, the Duke
insists that he must mobilise his good qualities, telling him
that 'our virtues' must 'go forth of us' (I, i, 34–5).

What exactly transpires within Angelo as he delivers his
soliloquy? Although nothing is apparently happening on
stage, something is clearly happening at the level of language,
of body, of thought. Perhaps the actor who plays Angelo
is transfixed as he speaks, but his words pick up speed in
tandem with his sexual arousal. When he marvels that 'she
speaks, and 'tis / Such sense that my sense breeds with it'

(II, ii, 141–2), we hear his 'sense' unfold and multiply both metaphorically and semantically. Active verbs predominate when he confesses that he is '*going* to temptation' (158), which 'doth *goad* us on / To sin in loving virtue' (181–2, emphases added). Although he imagines himself slowly 'corrupt[ing]' like a 'carrion', in short order, the pace of his imaginings accelerates as he pictures himself 'raz[ing] the sanctuary / And pitch[ing] our evils there' (170–1). 'O fie, fie, fie!' (171), indeed: in ten lines, enquiry ('What's this?') and judgement ('who sins most?') yield to devastation.

Angelo's tacit question, 'why am I moved?', is rooted in basic sensorimotor experiences that structure our inner lives. In the conceptual metaphor 'desire as motion', which so often characterises sexual and emotional experience, the concrete source domain of physical movement is selectively mapped on to the more abstract target domain of desire. The fundamental metaphor that undergirds this conceptu- alisation of eroticism is what George Lakoff calls the 'event structure metaphor'. According to Lakoff, 'various aspects of event structure, including notions like states, changes, processes, actions, causes, purposes, and means, are charac- terised cognitively via metaphor in terms of space, motion, and force'.[4] Some of the basic entailments of the event struc- ture metaphor include conceptualising changes as move- ments, causes as forces, and difficulties as impediments to motion. Cognitive linguist Zoltán Kövecses has shown that much of our emotional life, in particular, is shaped by the event structure metaphor. We get 'carried away' and 'trans- ported' into and out of emotional states; our emotions 'run away with us' and sometimes 'weigh us down'.[5] Indeed, the conceptual link between motion and emotion is a product of our sensory experiences of emotion. Erotic attraction is an embodied event, and even when we are not physically in motion, things happen in desiring bodies: they move, swell, stiffen, soften. Kövecses notes that two of the most common metaphorical domains for lust – heat and hunger – originate in the biomechanics of the desiring body.[6] Desire has the effect of thickening the bodily interior by sharpening our awareness of it. It reminds us of our lower halves, forcing us to contend with the conflicting impulses within us and creating multiple agencies that dramatise eroticism as an event in its own right.

Cognitive linguists have shown that we conceptualise amorous emotions in multiple and often conflicting ways: as states ('falling *in* love'), as events ('she *conquered* him'), as actions ('she decided to *let go* of her feelings') and as passions ('she *attracts* me *irresistibly*').[7] Each of these aspects of event structure pertains to Angelo's desire for Isabella. At the most basic level, he interprets his new desires as an event – a 'this' – that has suddenly and unexpectedly happened *to* him. He wavers between experiencing erotic longing as an action and a passion, at first taking responsibility for his desires when he claims that he is the one who 'corrupt[s]' (167), but then imagining 'That modesty may more *betray our sense* / Than woman's lightness' (168–9). The latter construction is passive in form, even as Angelo claims to have control over his desire: he has been betrayed by 'modesty', apparently the real villain of the story. Later, he will imagine that the devil has 'bait[ed]' (180) him with Isabella in order 'to catch a saint' (179). Metaphorical entailments such as 'Difficulties are Impediments to Motion' frame these passive accounts of being baited, hooked and captured, whether by 'modesty', by Isabella or by the devil himself.

For 'saint' Angelo, then, the event structure metaphor provides a language and logic with which to exonerate and to castigate himself, creating an inner drama complete with antagonist, motive and method. Guided by what Kövecses calls the 'underlying master metaphor' of 'Emotion as Force', Angelo feels 'in my heart the strong and swelling evil / Of my conception' (II, iv, 6–7). The specific force metaphor in Angelo's heart, 'Emotion is Pressure inside a Container', raises complex questions of agency and blame. Angelo reinforces Isabella's innocence when he claims that his desire comes from within. But then he evasively splits himself into container and contents, identifying more with his nobly labouring heart than the 'swelling evil' it struggles to contain. Other instances of the 'Emotion as Force' metaphor create a similar narrative, in which Angelo is the protagonist and his lust the villain he is powerless to stop. When he tells Isabella, 'I have begun / And now I give my sensual race the rein' (II, iv, 158–9), he again experiences conflicting internal forces. Here, as with the metaphor of Angelo's 'swelling evil', his 'sensual race' appears to reside within him but is not quite coextensive with him. Is Angelo's desire – and the troubling actions he undertakes in its name – his own fault, or the fault of a greater 'evil' that he tries but fails to curb?

To bring to bear the event structure metaphor on Angelo's language is to reveal that Angelo's battle to control lust consistently prompts him to fracture himself into agonist and antagonist, angel and demon. This cognitive self-division produces Angelo's experience of eros as an opponent, a moving force against which he struggles and which victimises him, even as he heroically fights to preserve his former stable (and static) self. The event structure metaphor also elucidates Angelo's erotic drama *as* drama, especially in his solitary moments. Alone on stage, he is in motion. He fights a battle, whether against Isabella or modesty, 'virtuous season' or the carrion's corruption, his own 'sensual race' or 'the cunning enemy' outside him. Angelo's shifting perceptions of his own role in this process are less congruent or causal than kaleidoscopic. Angelo as 'carrion' fails to align with Angelo as 'angel' or as 'betray[ed]' or plainly 'evil'. Each metaphor remakes him into a slightly different character, leading Angelo to ask himself, 'What dost thou, or *what art thou*, Angelo?' (II, ii,

172, emphasis added). Reminding us, and himself, that doing and being are intrinsically connected, Angelo's Aristotelian question tethers actions to essences, verbs to nouns, metaphors to identities – even to his very name. He asks not only what he is doing but why he is *like* this. Was he prone to be aroused by a virtuous nun? Did he have this potential all along?

Angelo's potential to be moved answers to Isabella's potential to move, or specifically to 'move men' (I, ii, 83), as Claudio puts it. Although her brother claims that Isabella's 'dialect' is 'speechless' (182), her first scene with Angelo suggests otherwise. Not only do her 'moving graces' (II, ii, 35) apparently activate Angelo's lust, but her words themselves gain momentum as she 'put[s] . . . sayings on [him]' (II, ii, 133) with increasing force and intensity. Beginning with her tentative question, 'But can you [pardon Claudio], if you would?' (II, ii, 51), Isabella's 'if' and 'would' weave together the potential and the actual.[8]

> *If* he had been *as* you and you *as* he,
> You *would have* slipped like him; but he, like you,
> *Would not have been* so stern.
> (64–6, emphases added)

Isabella does more than ask Angelo to empathise with her brother. Her hypothetical language exposes the actual Angelo – not someone who *might* have 'slipped' in Claudio's place, but the Angelo who most certainly '*would* have slipped'. Isabella's words unlock the 'potency' (67) that rests within Angelo, a 'natural guiltiness' (139) that the Duke suspects early on. When Isabella implores Angelo to

> Go to your bosom,
> Knock there, and ask your heart what it doth know
> That's like my brother's fault,
> (136–8)

her metaphor mobilises Angelo's active inquiring self to go, to knock, to ask and proleptically to discover his quiet, sinful self, the erotic 'potency' lodged within his bosom.

What does it mean to possess this potency? Do all beings have it? Only animate beings? Only human beings? Are some of us more disposed to be moved than others? This string of questions underwrites the extended enquiry into the nature of movement and action in the *Physics* and *Metaphysics*. Aristotle's term for potential, or what Isabella calls potency, is *dunamis*. On the other end of the spectrum to which movement gives rise is *entelecheia*, which is typically translated as actuality. Although the relationship between *dunamis* and *entelecheia* is the subject of debate, philosophers often conceive of the two terms as points on a continuum:

━━━━━━━━━━━━━━━━━━━━━━━━━━━━▶

Dunamis	*Kinesis* →	*Entelecheia*
Potency / Potentiality	Movement	Actuality
Starting-point of change		Being-complete

Potentiality itself is a concept that has challenged thinkers as diverse as Aquinas, Heidegger and Agamben, but its rich philosophical history begins with Aristotle's definition of *dunamis* as 'a starting-point of change in another thing, or in the thing itself *qua* other'. Mark Sentesy's recent work on Aristotelian physics and metaphysics challenges this continuum by arguing for the 'positive' character of *dunamis*. Rather than conceiving of potentiality as the absence of activity, Sentesy points out that Aristotle's *dunamis* includes both active and passive capacities. Take, for example, the potency of heat, or temperature change in general: 'a stone has the power of heat because 1) there are things that can be heated by it, and 2) it can be heated'.[9] A hot stone has the same *dunamis* as a cold stone: both have the active power to heat and the passive power to be heated. Placing the stones side by side activates their potentialities and produces reciprocal change: the cold stone heats up and the hot stone cools. Although we tend to imagine heat transfer as unidirectional, the colder stone is just as significant to the action.

What happens, then, when two of Shakespeare's coldest stones meet in *Measure for Measure*? Chilly Isabella and icy Angelo are each selected for their particular tasks based on the potentialities that others see in them. Isabella's brother Claudio describes her potency, or *dunamis*, as a 'prosperous art' (I, ii, 183), and Lucio will encourage her to 'Assay the power you have' (I, iv, 76). Angelo, who wonders at Isabella's power and questions her role in arousing his lust, ultimately decides that his desire has sprung from his own power to be moved:

Not she, nor doth she tempt; but it is I
That, lying by the violet in the sun,
Do as the carrion does, not as the flower,
Corrupt with virtuous season.
(II, ii, 164–7)

Angelo locates greater power in the carrion and the violet, the objects, than in the sun, arguably the agent, the source of change. Yes, the sun's power is great, but whether we blossom or decay beneath its rays depends in good measure on our *dunamis*, our potentiality on the ground. Angelo's self-regarding interpretation of temptation, in which he sees his own potential for corruption as more powerful than Isabella's actions, provides a new context for the darker, ethically troubling power he activates while pursuing an illicit, non-consensual sexual relationship with the young nun.

Angelo's erotic experience demonstrates the volatility of sexual potential, especially its capacity to constitute erotic action. Aristotle sets this precedent when he writes that both *dunamis* and *entelecheia* involve movement, process and change. *Entelecheia*, as Aristotle describes it, is a type of motion in which the end or completion is always present; the Greek word translates literally as 'having the *telos*, or goal, *en* / in / inside'.[10] Aristotle contrasts entelechy with other forms of motion, or *kinesis*, in which beings may be moving towards a goal but have not yet arrived. Ordinary *kinesis*, writes Aristotle, may be exemplified by the process of weight loss, in which body parts move toward thinness but are not yet thin. As an incomplete process, this is not an action. Entelechy, which denotes processes 'in which the end is present', pertains to happiness, understanding, seeing and thinking: 'at the same time we are seeing and have seen, are understanding and have understood'.[11] We might define 'entelechial desire' as erotic desire that nourishes itself, like Hamlet's image of his mother's 'increase of appetite' for his late father, which 'had grown / By what it fed on' (I, ii, 144–5). Entelechial desire strengthens as it ebbs, intensifies rather than abates as it reaches a *telos* of pleasure or satisfaction or possession. And sometimes its *telos* is desire itself, as when characters pursue the pleasures of delay, indulging in erotic fantasy and contemplation rather than pursuing sexual gratification.

The relevance of cognitive linguistics to Aristotle's conceptualisation of entelechy is evident when we notice that the latter is itself guided by the event structure metaphor. The primary metaphor 'Causation Is Action to Achieve a Purpose' lies at the core of our most basic experiences of teleology. According to George Lakoff and Mark Johnson, 'Aristotle . . . took this metaphor as a truth. Causes conceptualised according to this metaphor are what Aristotle called *final causes*, that is, causes constituted by purposes, either the purposes of a person or purposes conceptualised as being in nature.'[12] The event structure metaphor is as true for Aristotle as for any number of Lyly's and Shakespeare's lovelorn characters. The different qualities and degrees of motion (*kinesis*), potency (*dunamis*) and action (*energeia*, *entelecheia*) in Aristotle's *Metaphysics* form the basis of erotic metaphors such as idleness and lethargy, submission and mastery, giddiness and violence.

Chapters 1 and 2 consider how such metaphors constitute erotic experiences for Lyly's and Shakespeare's characters. In Chapter 1, I survey Lyly's metaphors of erotic idleness and then focus on *Galatea*, a play in which characters conceptualise idleness less as physical stasis than as a particular quality of motion – movement without purpose, or *telos*. In the play's principal love relationship, the cross-dressed maids Galatea and Phillida find eroticism less in Aristotelian actuality than in potentiality, in idle and circuitous language that prolongs desire. Chapter 2 analyses metaphors of stillness and motion in *Measure for Measure* and *Othello*. Both of Shakespeare's plays dramatise the high ontological and ethical stakes of erotic stillness and movement. Like Angelo's desires, which first 'subdue' (II, ii, 185) him but soon prompt him to aggression, Othello's joy 'subdues' (I, iii, 249) him before the 'violent pace' (III, iii, 457) of his sexual imaginings propels him into fits of frenzied motion.

For all of Lyly's and Shakespeare's desiring characters, eroticism is an event, replete with Aristotelian potentialities, causes, agencies and *teloi*. Because the event structure metaphor maps causes, changes and purposes as types of physical motion (causes as forces; changes as movements into and out of bounded regions; achieving a purpose as reaching a desired location), characters who deploy and are deployed by it experience erotic desire as drama. Even when their desires stymie them completely – when they are passive, subdued or immobilised – eros is still an action. It is a struggle, whether against a beloved, one's own competing impulses or love itself. And it is a journey, slow and meandering or a headlong rush. Lyly's and Shakespeare's erotic metaphors never operate in isolation from one another; they collide, interweave and collapse, they overflow and spill into entelechial action.

Notes

1. Anne Carson, *Eros the Bittersweet*, 63.
2. Valerie Traub notes the early modern origins of 'making love', which 'was used as early as 1567 to mean "to pay amorous attention; to court, woo," but apparently did not allude to engaging in sexual *acts* until 1929'. See Traub, *Thinking Sex*, 147.
3. The first two of the *Oxford English Dictionary*'s three entries for 'emotion' feature words that cue motion: movement, agitation, disturbance. See 'emotion, *n.*', *OED Online*. January 2018. Oxford University Press. Available at: <http://www.oed.com/view/Entry/61249?isAdvanced=false&result=1&rskey=jyhsnq&> (last accessed 30 January 2018). The third entry captures the term's popular modern association with inner 'feelings'. The earliest instance of this usage, according to the *OED*, dates back to 1602.
4. George Lakoff, 'The Contemporary Theory of Metaphor', 220.
5. Zoltán Kövecses, *Metaphor and Emotion*, 51–60.
6. Shakespeare frequently taps into these metaphors, as when Angelo longs to 'feast upon' (II, ii, 178) Isabella's eyes, instructing her to 'fit thy consent to my sharp appetite' (II, iv, 160).
7. Kövecses, *Metaphor and Emotion*, 27, 51–60. Kövecses catalogues a robust sample of love and lust metaphors in his chapter on 'Metaphors of Emotion' (see especially pp. 26–32). Representative examples include 'Love is Fluid in a Container: She was overflowing with love,' 'Love is a Physical Force: I was magnetically drawn to her' and 'Lust is a Natural Force: He was drowning in his own desire.'
8. In her opening encounter with Angelo (II, ii), Isabella repeats 'if' five times and 'would' six times.
9. Mark Sentesy, 'On the Many Senses of Potency According to Aristotle', 67, 78.

10. English translations for Aristotle's *entelecheia* are the subject of some debate among scholars of Aristotle's metaphysics. A sample of recent scholarship illustrates this point: Charlotte Witt translates *entelecheia* as 'actuality', Jonathan Beere as 'being-in-fulfillment', Mark Sentesy as 'being-complete' and Joe Sachs as 'being-at-work-staying-itself'. See Beere, *Doing and Being: An Interpretation of Aristotle's* Metaphysics Theta; Sachs's translation of *Aristotle's Metaphysics*, li; and Witt, *Ways of Being: Potentiality and Actuality in Aristotle's Metaphysics*. Unless otherwise noted, all translations of Aristotle's works are from *The Complete Works of Aristotle: The Revised Oxford Translation* (1984).

11. Aristotle, *Metaphysics*, IX.6 1048b 22–3.

12. George Lakoff and Mark Johnson, *Philosophy in the Flesh*, 218. Lakoff and Johnson devote a chapter of their study to the metaphorical underpinnings of Aristotle's philosophy – his metaphysics and also his definition of metaphor. See Chapter 18, 'Aristotle', 373–90.

CHAPTER 1

THE EROTIC POTENTIAL OF IDLENESS IN LYLY'S DRAMA

It may seem odd or counterintuitive to study metaphors of motion in plays that have been characterised as 'static and passive'.[1] What can John Lyly, a playwright routinely criticised for his lack of stage action, possibly show about the 'event' of erotic desire? By consistently refusing to subordinate eros to other actions that characters might undertake in its name, Lyly confirms that desire itself can be the main event, making good on Anne Carson's assertion that 'eros acts everywhere like a verb'. In Lyly's drama, desire moves, especially when characters do not.[2] As Andy Kesson notes, 'Lyly exploits the considerable dramaturgical power of a character who is still as they speak, making them what Janette Dillon calls "a centre of contained activity-in-stillness".'[3] Struck and immobilised by Cupid's arrows, or by the beauty of a beloved, or by their own longings, even the slumbering bodies of Lyly's characters rouse and stir from the erotic dreams that captivate them. Stock-still and caught in love's idleness, Lyly's lovers move by means of metaphor, which Angus Fletcher describes as 'a figure of instant animation [that] lifts the mind to a fervour of aesthetic activity. Metaphor as a structural principle generates restless shift and flexing of sense.'[4]

Restless shifts make eros new for Lyly's characters, many of whom are themselves new to eros. Among Lyly's favourite dramatic subjects are moments of sexual awakening – the very instant of erotic change – 'moments' that he is prepared to stretch across five acts of drama. For Aristotle, as for Zeno, the instant was a paradox of stillness and motion: an instant, or a 'now', is a fixed point and yet a series of instants comprises a sequential, moving experience of time.[5] Lyly knew that a moment of erotic awakening is like Zeno's arrow, which, at any particular instant, is apparently at rest but which also is moving, 'shift[ing] and flexing', over a sequence of instants. Whereas Shakespeare's Angelo effectively stops wrestling with his desires and moves on to blackmailing Isabella for sex by the end of Act II, Lyly's characters spend the better part of a play wrestling. Or they analyse, they fantasise, they dream, they confess. From Sappho to Endymion and Alexander the Great, they experience erotic change instant by instant.

This chapter considers the role of potentiality, what Aristotle calls *dunamis*, as both the source of erotic change and its medium. I survey metaphors of motion and stillness that dramatise subtle erotic changes in Lyly's plays, culminating with *Galatea*, a work that explores alternatives to the fast-paced, teleological movement typically associated with sexual pursuit. Curiously, the role of action in both Aristotle's and Lyly's writing has been misunderstood. Aristotle's *dunamis* is often imagined as a dormant trait when potentiality is understood as the absence of activity. But when Mark Sentesy calls attention to the longstanding philosophical bias against potentiality, he notes that

> potency has often, in the history of philosophy, been degraded into possibility, a kind of bare logical possibility, a faint reminder that things could still be otherwise, a sense which Aristotle subordinates to the robust sense of potency in Met[aphysics]. IX.4.8.[6]

It is this 'robust sense of potency' that I focus on in Lyly's erotic drama. Because Aristotle defines *dunamis* as a source of change either 'in another thing, or in the thing itself *qua* other', potentiality not only entails movement but can unite two separate beings through movement. According to Sentesy,

> potency as the capacity to change other things requires *others*. Put another way, when one thing moves another, the two already have or come to have something in common; the mutual movement of things is a way that being is one.

Sentesy points out that Aristotle illustrates the rich concept of potentiality through the example of a teacher and student drawn together in a single action or movement:

> Multiple sources are required in a movement: the learner needs a potency for being changed, and the teacher needs the potency to change the learner . . . The being-at-work [activity / *energeia*] of the learning student is at the same time precisely the activity of the teacher in the student . . . This teacher does not need to be learning, but the motion of learning is this teacher's being-at-work in this student (*Physics* III.3 202b6–25).[7]

The one who moves (teacher) and the one who is moved (student) are united in a single process of change that mobilises their combined potentialities. In the earlier example of the hot stone that warms the colder one, the two stones share the same potency for temperature change. Both are potentially hot and potentially cold at the same time. Just as 'too cold' Isabella possesses the capacity to thaw and heat Angelo, the frosty deputy is always potentially hot. What unlocks this potential is the language of potentiality itself – Isabella's unwitting 'what if'. If Shakespeare probes the erotic power of this language, John Lyly makes it the primary source of erotic heat in his plays. No other early modern playwright so fully commits to a dramaturgy of contemplation and fantasy. Erotic potentiality unites the most distant of his characters in shared processes of motion and change.

On Lyly's stage, physical stasis always entails motion. Lylian 'activity-in-stillness' often discloses itself as idleness, but the relationship of idleness to eros can be confused, even paradoxical. The women in Lyly's *Midas* at first identify love as the remedy for idleness, and then immediately change their minds and decide that love is its cause: 'there are other things to keep one from idleness besides love; nay, that there is nothing to make idleness but love' (*Midas* III, iii, 25–7). Caused and cured by love, static and moving, idleness in Lyly's *Endymion* is represented as a staggering, physically felt event. When the lovestruck Corsites realises he cannot lift the sleeping Endymion, he asks:

> Have my weak thoughts made brawnfallen my strong arms? Or is it the nature of love or in the quintessence of the mind to breed numbness, or litherness, or I know not what languishing in my joints and sinews, being but the base strings of my body? Or doth the remembrance of Tellus so refine my spirits into a matter so subtle and divine, that the other fleshly parts cannot work whilst they muse?
>
> (*Endymion* IV, iii, 19–26)

Corsites's experience is far from peaceful or soothing; neither is it perfectly still. His suspicion that his arms are 'made brawnfallen' by his desire for Tellus suggests that his desire feels more like a downward pull than total stasis. His numbness, too, entails motion, since love 'breed[s]' it throughout his body. Idleness and atrophy are eventful in Corsites's account: they languish, they breed, they muse, they fall. In short, these stilled and passive experiences of desire are dramatic in their own right. Not so much the staged action of trying to lift his sleeping friend as Corsites's *language* dramatises the force of his 'weak thoughts' as they bear down on his 'strong arms'.

Erotic language has similar dramatic force in Lyly's *Sappho and Phao*, another play in which slumbering bodies are charged with sexual intensity and potential. When the ladies of Sappho's court recall their recent dreams for each other and their queen, their talk reignites the erotic energies that once coursed through their sleeping bodies. Telling a dream is a confession, as well as a potentially erotic act in its own right, especially when it reveals a fear of excess or a monstrous desire beyond one's control. In the first of these accounts, Mileta's dream of desire portends her death in graphic and violent imagery:

> I dreamed last night – but I hope dreams are contrary – that, holding my head over a sweet smoke, all my hair blazed on a bright flame. Methought Ismena cast water to quench it; yet the sparks fell on my bosom, and, wiping them away with my hand, I was all in a gore blood, till one with a few fresh flowers stanched it. And so, stretching myself as stiff, I started; it was but a dream.
>
> (IV, iii, 28–35)

Mileta's dream is anything but static in its linguistic depiction of sexual desire, pleasure and pain. Besieged by flames, the signifiers of femininity on Mileta's body – her hair and bosom – are ravenous, dreadfully unquenchable, spinning out of control. Although the end of the dream figures her body in death, stretched stiffly beneath 'a few fresh flowers', this seemingly static final tableau surprisingly causes Mileta's slumbering body to move. Her physical body 'started', jostling back to life at the very moment that she dreams of lifelessness.

This entire scene from *Sappho and Phao* might feel static, since it stages nothing more than a conversation. But in sharing their frenzied, sometimes even terrifying, erotic fantasies and fears, the women experience them anew, reliving them with a difference. Do the women fan the flames of each other's desires by telling, hearing and interpreting each other's fantasies? What exactly is Mileta's friend Ismena doing in her dream, and why is she the one to offer an interpretation in this scene? Decoding its images of seductive smoke, flames and water as primarily linguistic phenomena, Ismena raises the possibility that the women's conversation itself can ignite desire: 'It is a sign you shall fall in love with hearing fair words. Water signifieth counsel, flowers death. And nothing can purge your loving humour but death' (IV, iii, 36–8). As Ismena parses the significance of each image, she unfolds a story largely shaped by the event structure metaphor. Language figures centrally in Ismena's interpretation – not just the desire for 'fair words' but also a friend's words of counsel. Thus, words fill multiple roles in the event of Mileta's dream. To 'fall in love with hearing fair words' suggests that 'hearing fair words' is both the object of love and its medium. A dream that seems to be about the physical, sensory and emotional experience of passion becomes, in Ismena's analysis, a dream about the heat of erotic language.

Like Corsites's eventful idleness, Mileta's report of her provocative dream voices the dramatic potential of erotic captivation. Dreams and fantasies are vehicles for exploring erotic *dunamis*: eros as a source of change. Visions such as Mileta's can spark new feelings, change attitudes, stimulate the physical body, awaken the imagination. When Mark Sentesy argues that potency and actuality are compatible rather than opposing, he considers what happens to potential when a being undergoes 'change that leads not to a reduction or disappearance of potency, but to its strengthening':

> A thing can move when its *dunamis* is increasing instead
> of being removed or left behind: learning, for example, is
> a movement in which the ability to think increases, not a
> movement in which this ability is destroyed.[8]

In Mileta's dream, her desire grows without end. Rather
than shifting from potentiality to actuality, her potential to
be moved only increases as flames consume her and rouse her
slumbering body to wakefulness.

When her friend Favilla relates her dream of uncontrollable heat – this time, a stone that does not cool after it has
been exposed to heat – she too reminds us that erotic potentiality is a source of action that can increase as it is realised:

> I saw one playing with a round stone . . . which being once
> hot would never be cold. I, forgetting myself, delighted
> with the fair show, would always show it by candlelight,
> pull it out in the sun, and see how bright it would look
> in the fire, where catching heat, nothing could cool it: for
> anger I threw it against the wall, and with the heaving up
> of mine arm I waked.
>
> (IV, iii, 87–97)

Favilla's dream prompts Mileta to warn that 'women's hearts
are such stones, which warmed by affection, cannot be cooled
by wisdom' (98–100). The stone's potential for heat does not
fade once it is actualised, and its heat catalyses Favilla's slumbering body, setting it in motion 'with the heaving up of mine
arm'. Each of the women's dreams is an event – a struggle
against desire – that moves their bodies and ignites their language as they console, provoke and perhaps also excite one
another in this intimate scene.

Erotic potentiality and actuality converge in Lyly's
Galatea, a play premised on 'what if'. Based loosely on Ovid's
tale of Iphis and Ianthe in the *Metamorphoses*, *Galatea* follows the passionate love between two young women, Galatea
and Phillida, whose fathers disguise them as boys to avoid

their being taken as virgin sacrifices by the monster Agar, sent by Neptune. As the two women fall in love, Cupid's arrow pierces Diana's nymphs and they, too, dote helplessly on the disguised maidens. For all the women of the play, new sexual longings generate profound experiences of personal change, perhaps most significantly the gender transformation that Venus promises to perform at the end of the play. That Lyly's metaphors of motion aptly capture such change may derive from one of the basic entailments of the event structure metaphor: 'Changes are movements.' In Lyly's day, writes Angus Fletcher, 'change is always a matter of movement . . . For the Renaissance period, the general economy of motion needs to be understood as the essential problem for all theories of change.'[9] Hence the contemporary preoccupation with Aristotelian theories of change dependent on movement toward an innate *telos*. Just as an acorn moves toward its *telos* of a tree, a young girl is said to move toward the *telos* of a woman. The woman, in this view, exists as prior to the girl – ontologically, she precedes the girl. What kind of movement or activity is available, then, to the young maidens in Lyly's play, one of whom will become male in order to marry the other?

Motion in *Galatea* rarely takes a straight path; as a number of scholars have observed, the play's erotic terrain is decidedly queer. Simone Chess summarises some of this work:

> The play has been read in many ways: as lesbian, showing love between two female characters through the often-ineffective veil of their male disguises [Walen, Jankowski, Traub, Shannon]; as gay, showing love between two boy actors, dressed as boys, through the often-ineffective veil of the fact that they are meant to be playing women [Billing]; as straight since the resolution appears to seek heterosexual closure; and as queer, because the characters' heterosexual closure is elusive, unstaged, and cannot undo the erotic work of the play's body.[10]

Movement along the play's queer landscape will obey different rules from those governing Aristotle's acorn. For the two
principal maidens and the throng of Diana's nymphs who fall
in love with them, eros reverberates and hovers in the air;
it moves back and forth rather than advancing inexorably
forward. Playful and mimetic, their desires swerve and loop
back on one another, and their language follows suit.[11] In
asides and hypotheses, 'contraries' (III, i, 1–2) and 'riddles'
(III, i, 38), the women unfold their longings to each other
and to themselves. Their circuitous language resists the forward press of time, the movement towards closure or *telos*.
In this respect, the play's temporality is itself queer.[12] But the
play's resistance to teleological movement does not deplete it
of action or drama. Idleness may be the charge that Neptune
levies against the women at the end of the play – 'an idle
choice, strange and foolish, for one virgin to dote on another'
(V, iii, 139–40) – but Lyly's drama credits the pleasures of
idleness, its potential as an erotic means and an end.

With origins in the Old English *ídel*, meaning empty and
worthless, idleness might look like stasis or laziness, as when
Diana calls her lovestruck nymphs 'prentices to idleness' (III,
iv, 54). But even as she scolds her nymphs, Diana's phrase
implies that idleness is a learned art or craft, and certainly
an activity. For the nymphs, as for the disguised maidens,
the pleasures of idleness are felt in the body but they originate in the mind. Hence Diana's nymph Telusa asks, 'What
new conceits, what strange contraries, breed in thy mind?'
(III, i, 1–2).[13] Like Angelo's 'sense', which 'breeds' when Isabella speaks, Telusa's mind is a breeding ground for 'new'
and 'strange' desires. The metaphor of breeding is apt not
only because of its sexual connotations but also because it
reflects the mingling of opposites – 'contraries' – in the newly
desiring body and mind. In Cupid's description of love as
'a heat full of coldness, a sweet full of bitterness, a pain full
of pleasantness' (I, ii, 18–19), Lyly's love language brings

together 'contraries' but never quite resolves them. Sweet and bitterness neither merge completely in Cupid's account, nor do they neutralise one another. Instead, each new paradox adds and depletes, advances and emends, generating a rhythm that moves forward, only to pull back. Time and again, Lyly's prose opens for us a moment that feels like a caesura – a dream or a fantasy, a soliloquy or an aside, idleness or absence – and reveals it to be anything but a break from eros. Like drama, love happens in time, and its syncopated rhythms carry lovers forward.

Lyly's Cupid is not alone in his efforts to define love; nor is he the only character in *Galatea* to suggest that to define love is to constitute it. Although Diana's nymphs struggle to name the erotic sensations they share, each one seems to recognise her own experiences in the group's collective efforts to express them. The women come closest to describing or defining desire when, paradoxically, they identify with each other's inability to 'know' it. Eurota tells her friends that she is in love, 'yet swear that I know not what it is' (III, i, 51–2), only that she is 'myself in all things unlike myself' (III, i, 55). To what exactly do 'am' and 'is' refer when Telusa responds, 'Thou hast told what I am, in uttering what thyself is' (III, i, 57)? Desire, we learn from the nymphs' shared language of indirection, consists of negation and self-comparison. Their relations with one another depend on their signal failures to know desire; indeed, they become these failures (Telusa = Eurota = 'unlike myself'). Anne Carson describes the complex relationship of desire and identity as self-consciousness with a difference:

> Eros' ambivalence unfolds directly from this power to 'mix up' the self. The lover helplessly admits that it feels both good and bad to be mixed up, but is then driven back upon the question, 'Once I have been mixed up in this way, who am I?' Desire *changes* the lover . . . The change gives him a glimpse of a self he never knew before.[14]

What is so remarkable about this scene in *Galatea* is the nymphs' collaborative *success* at glimpsing their changed selves by means of the others' mixed-up language. As Telusa acknowledges, Eurota has, in fact, 'told what I am' by (however imprecisely) 'uttering' her own experience.

Rather than arriving at a stable or static definition of love, or of themselves as lovers, Diana's nymphs mobilise each other as they describe and confess, layering one metaphor upon the next. Ramia recognises the erotic power of telling and hearing one's desires when she explains, 'If myself felt only this infection, I would then take upon me the definition, but being incident to so many I dare not myself describe it' (III, i, 86–8). Once Telusa and Eurota share their desires with one another, they hunger for more words: 'How did it take you first, Telusa?' (III, i, 61); 'But how did it take you, Eurota?' (64–5). Eurota's response, 'By the ears, whose sweet words sunk so deep into my head' (66–7), conveys the power of language to move and change the hearer, saturating her erotic imagination. The nymphs' greed for more words is sexually suggestive, as is their volley of questions and answers, and even the subtle metaphor, 'how did it take you', which evokes a kind of rapture in its own right. The erotic power of hearing one's own desires shaped in another's language is perhaps most evident at the end of the scene, when Eurota helplessly cries, 'Talk no more, Telusa; your words wound' (III, i, 119). Now it is her friend's language that penetrates, rather than the 'sweet words' of love that first 'sunk so deep'.

Note that it is not the lover's language of flirtation and seduction that we hear in this scene. The nymphs' goal is ostensibly to understand or locate desire – in themselves and each other – but the impasse to understanding curiously generates an erotic energy in its own right, itself becoming the object of knowledge and desire. Here is Valerie Traub on such blockage: 'The epistemological orientation enacted here derives not only from hitting up against such impasses, but from intuiting that these structures of occultation and unintelligibility *are also the source of our ability to apprehend and analyze them.*'[15] The opacity of the nymphs' desires is substantive; it is less a gap or lack than a thick fog. Moving between lovers is an erotic *some*thing – an 'it' that can 'take you', compounded of 'new conceits' and 'strange contraries', of shareable and therefore knowable images, felt experiences, sounds and syllables, each one as obscure as the next. Within this erotic gap – 'the interval between reach and grasp', writes Anne Carson – 'desire comes alive'.[16] But what Lyly's plays, in particular, remind us is that this interval is neither static nor empty. What Carson characterises as a present absence or a lack for the women of *Galatea* teems with words that move.

Lyly represents the fullness and the dynamism of this interval – its capacity to accommodate erotic activity and change – by means of the imprecise, yet strangely effective, quality of the nymphs' conversation. In the nymphs' confessions, as elsewhere in *Galatea*, Lyly finds ways of dramatising, if not defining, desire. As Robert Y. Turner has noted, Lyly's indirect dialogues about love consist of 'conversations not about love but conversations that dramatize love'.[17] Turner claims that Lyly is the first English playwright to do this, the first to negotiate the delicate balance between action and language successfully. But this balance is subtle and difficult to sustain. If it tips to the side of action, Turner observes, 'love' can be dramatised as a series of chivalric feats; if it tips too much to the side of language, love becomes lyrical and therefore undramatic. 'Lyly avoided both extremes of direct statement and irrelevant action', Turner writes, 'by creating dialogues which contribute to the plot while still expressing the emotions of love.'[18] Such is Lyly's art of indirectness. Characters who are in love talk around the topic or, to put it in cognitive linguistic terms, they use different domains to elaborate their experiences of desire. In *Campaspe*, Apelles and Campaspe use the metaphor of painting; in *Sappho and Phao*, the eponymous characters deploy the language of disease to express love.

Like the nymphs, Galatea and Phillida glimpse their changed selves (changed by disguise but also by *eros*) in one other's ambiguous language, what Phillida calls their 'doubtful speeches' (III, ii, 31). Together, the maidens generate an erotic movement that follows Cupid's rhythm of adding and depleting, advancing and emending. Their language reaches toward knowledge – of the other's disguise, of the other's desires, of their own metamorphosed selves – but pulls back, often at the very edge of revelation. 'Edging', as it happens, is our contemporary word for the psycho-physical version of this, for the sexual practice during which a person deliberately evades orgasm in order to explore the pleasures of indirection, foreplay and delay.[19] Time moves slowly in the scenes between Galatea and Phillida, often because their conversations are spliced with more asides than lines of actual dialogue. As stylised and fanciful as Lyly's language can be, there is something uncannily real and familiar about the erotic rhythm generated in the maidens' dialogue: it dips in and out of real time, in and out of fantasy. Although Galatea and Phillida hardly ever direct their speech at one another in their opening scene, they none the less seem to hear and, strangely, to connect with each other.

When the cross-dressed Galatea and Phillida first meet, they fall in love instantly but are unable to reveal their desires because of their male disguises. Their first conversation hardly qualifies as a dialogue, since almost every line appears to be spoken in an aside:

> *Gal:* I would salute him, but I fear I should make a curtsy
> instead of a leg.
> *Phill:* If I durst trust my face as well as I do my habit,
> I would spend some time to make pastime; for say

what they will of a man's wit, it is no second thing to
be a woman.

Gal: All the blood in my body would be in my face if he
should ask me (as the question among men is common),
'Are you a maid?'

Phill: Why stand I still? Boys should be bold. But here
cometh a brave train that will spill all our talk.

(II, i, 25–35)

This 'dialogue' of alternating asides is cut off by the entrance
of Diana and her nymphs. Although it does not appear that
the girls have actually spoken a word to each other, Phillida
worries that the intruders 'will spill all our talk' (II, i, 35).
Perhaps Phillida is acknowledging that their 'talk' exists only
in their minds (precisely where Telusa locates the experience
of desire later in the play), and the intrusion of the nymphs
will cause their thoughts to 'spill' out and be heard. Phillida's
metaphor conveys the intensity of their speaking silence and
the fullness of the erotic potential that moves between them.
Kent Cartwright observes that the dramatic energy and dynamism of the scene come from the women's deferred acknowledgement of what they know to be true: that they are, in fact,
both women in disguise. 'For the two girl-boys,' Cartwright
notes, 'pleasure and titillation arise from unknowing, postu-
lating, guessing, hypothesizing – that is, deferring certainty.'[20]
Not only does this conversation dramatise love's indirection,
but, as Cartwright points out, it dramatises the pleasures of
desire as well.

Through their indirect speech and disguised bodies, Galatea
and Phillida sustain erotic potentiality while actualising it,
thereby drawing ever closer together; their 'language of erotic
similitude' gives rise to what Valerie Traub calls the couple's
'mirroring resemblance'.[21] Poised between their grammatical
symmetries, the women's veiled language and bodies open
up a small space of difference. Linguistically, this difference
often takes the form of simile. The disguised maidens are 'like'

and 'as' each other: 'he is as I am' (III, ii, 44). Each syllable, each 'like' and 'as', brings them into relation but also stands between 'he' and 'I', subject and predicate, and thus delimits each maiden with a boundary or an edge. For Anne Carson, the movement of eros 'defin[es] one certain edge or difference': 'Its action is to reach, and the reach of desire involves every lover in an activity of the imagination.'[22] Galatea and Phillida activate this 'reach of desire' across their increasingly opaque erotic language, from parallel dramatic asides to hypothetical speech, repeated words, and phrases that echo one another with a difference. Moreover, structurally and dramaturgically, their scenes' edges and gaps kindle erotic potential. Their shared scenes end without really ending; Galatea and Phillida repeatedly plan to 'wander into these [offstage] groves' (IV, iv, 34) to continue whatever it is that they have been doing. It is as if Lyly punctuates their dialogue with ellipses rather than a full stop. Perhaps the play's most memorable resistance to closure is Phillida's suggestive invitation to Galatea, 'Come, let us into the grove, and make much of each other, that cannot tell what to think of one another' (III, iii, 62–3). Since the women's activities in the grove are never staged – how exactly does one stage 'mak[ing] much?' – Lyly invites the audience to participate in the 'activity of the imagination' that both fills and extends the space of erotic potential. Imagining Galatea's and Phillida's offstage activities – and with them, the boy actors' backstage activities – can open at least as many erotic possibilities for audiences as for Lyly's characters. With his ellipses, Lyly takes them all to the edge.[23]

At the edge that joins sound and sense, the women of *Galatea* make much of their erotic gestures of reaching out and making space. Take Galatea's punning confession of her love for Phillida:

> *Telusa.* Saw you not the deer come this way, he flew down
> the wind, and I believe you have blanched him.

Galatea. Whose dear was it, lady?
Telusa. Diana's deer.
Galatea. I saw none but mine own dear.

(II, i, 41–5)

In the mingling of two senses in one sound, Galatea unfolds multiple potentialities – that Phillida is both her prey (deer) and her beloved (dear), that Phillida is 'mine own' and no one else's, that Phillida is all she can see. 'Like eros,' Carson writes, 'puns flout the edges of things. Their power to allure and alarm derives from this.'[24] Both alluring and alarming is the erotic slippage that Galatea's pun makes audible between eros and violence, beloved and prey, loving subject and desired object. Puns such as deer / dear and as hart / heart play with sameness and difference in much the same way that the disguised maidens do. Galatea and Phillida seem, sound, look the same – each hears herself echoed in the other – but the edges and gaps that differentiate their language remind them (and us) that they are not the same, they can never be the same, and perhaps most importantly, they do not really want to be completely the same. Theirs is an erotics of reaching, as their puns reach across the space they create with their language, patterned in the added vowel that extends 'hart' to 'heart'. Puns that are spoken on stage demand more imaginative activity than when they are written; in the theatre, we write the words in our minds, trace their edges, see twoness in one.[25]

Language, then, is Lyly's perpetual motion machine. The maidens' indirect addresses keep them always reaching out, always moving towards one another, closing in without achieving closure. Even in soliloquy, Galatea and Phillida experience desire as an event. Phillida's first speech after meeting the disguised Galatea is replete with stops and starts, dramatising the conflicts in her mind. She wavers as she tries to decide if she should go into the woods to follow the disguised Galatea: 'I will – I dare not. Thou must – I cannot. Then pine in thine own peevishness. I will not – I will. Ah, Phillida, do something – nay anything, rather than live thus' (II, v, 8–11). Phillida's soliloquy is a call to action, spoken in what Christian M. Billing calls 'the tantalisingly orgasmic language of yes, no, stop, go eroticism'.[26] From stop to go, Phillida begins by conceptualising love as a state (pining '*in* thine own peevishness') and ends by 'do[ing] something' instead, finally deciding to 'go' (II, v, 12) into the woods after her love. Galatea's soliloquy probes a more passive form of activity. She too resolves to do something instead of pining away – 'Let me follow him into the woods' (II, iv, 13) – but instead of going on her own, Galatea 'follow[s]' the disguised Phillida with Venus as her 'guide' (II, iv, 14). Although Galatea is not the subject of her sentence (she places the authority to 'let me follow him' in the hands of the fates), still she chooses, she follows. Moved by Phillida and moving after Phillida, Galatea experiences erotic *dunamis* as action.

Galatea's passive erotic activity contrasts with the rigid binary of Diana's chaste stasis on one hand and Cupid and Venus's amorous motion on the other. When Cupid plans to pierce Diana's nymphs with his love darts, he declares,

> Let Diana and her coy nymphs know that there is no heart so chaste but thy bow can wound, nor eyes so modest but thy brands can kindle, nor thoughts so staid but thy shafts can make wavering, weak, and wanton.
>
> (II, ii, 2–6)

The 'staid', chaste hearts of Diana's maids, heretofore fixed in their virtue, Cupid will set in motion. And so it is that the nymphs describe themselves as 'unstayed' (III, i, 53) and 'unbridled' (III, i, 58) once they are launched into the sexual scene. Although Diana chastises them, admonishing that 'the more [your thoughts] are assaulted with desires, the less they should be affected' (III, iv, 25–6), the women are still moved by desire. Against Diana's call for stillness and impassivity, Venus provokes lively, if unwieldy, thoughts and speech. Diana accuses Venus of having 'untamed affections' (V, iii, 44), complaining, 'your tongue is as unruly as your thoughts, and your thoughts as unstayed as your eyes. Diana cannot chatter; Venus cannot choose' (V, iii, 59–61). Unruliness is metaphorised as both physical motion and verbal activity, or 'chatter'. In the binary relation between Diana and the goddess of love (one that Venus appears to accept), desire is a moving force that only Diana can resist. Venus describes her nemesis as 'she that hateth sweet delights, envieth loving desires, masketh wanton eyes, stoppeth amorous ears, bridleth youthful mouths' (V, iii, 31–4). Venus sets things in motion. Diana retards motion. Where Diana argues that love is a scar, Venus corrects her, saying that love causes 'bleeding wounds' (V, iii, 50–1), ever fresh and in motion.

While the fixed-chastity / moving-desire binary runs throughout the play, the metaphor of hunting complicates the nature of mobility in *Galatea*. Although Cupid is conceptualised as a hunter constantly on the move, Diana and her company of chaste nymphs are themselves huntresses. Moreover, even though Lyly's lovers often conceive their desires as immobilising, they use the metaphor of hunting to do so. The nymphs, once pierced by Cupid's darts, find their 'conquering modesty [turned] to a captive imagination' (III, i, 3–4). Their thoughts are free and suddenly 'unbridled' but they also feel imprisoned by desire. Hunting metaphors allow Lyly to interrogate the quality of desire's mobility. Both Diana and Cupid hunt, pursue and attack. Both are mobile. Yet Diana's mobility contrasts sharply with Cupid's. Cupid is described as 'wander[ing]' (V, iii, 86) by Venus, and 'idle' (IV, ii, 64) by the nymphs. Love's arrows, according to Diana, merely 'drib . . . up and down Diana's leas' (III, iv, 6–7). His appetites are 'loose and untamed' (III, iv, 77). In short, Cupid's movements are notable for their laziness, carelessness, sloppiness.

When Cupid first meets one of Diana's nymphs, he assumes that she has 'strayed' (I, ii, 1) from the group, and now 'wander[s] solitarily' (I, ii, 2), solipsistically describing the nymph in language that characterises his own movements. The nymph responds that 'these woods are to me so well known that I cannot stray though I would' (I, ii, 4–5). Diana's nymphs are incapable of drifting because their aim is sure and their movements deliberate. Later in this scene, Cupid describes love to the nymph and asks her if she will yield to it. She replies,

> I have neither will nor leisure, but I will follow Diana in the chase, whose virgins are all chaste, delighting in the bow that wounds the swift hart in the forest, not fearing the bow that strikes the soft heart in the chamber.
>
> (I, ii, 25–9)

Anything but idle, this is movement with a purpose. We might say that Diana's movements have a *telos*, whereas Cupid 'straggleth up and down these woods' (III, iv, 7), seemingly without a goal. But Cupid does have a goal, one he proclaims early in the play: 'to so confound [the nymphs'] love in their own sex that they shall . . . practice only impossibilities' (II, ii, 7–10). Of course, if the women's loves are indeed 'practice[d]', they are not quite impossible. As Valerie Traub writes, 'Lyly makes clear that to practice impossibilities is . . . possible.'[27] Cupid's self-proclaimed *telos* is less an endpoint than it is a 'practice' or process, though perhaps paradoxically so.

What happens to this process as the play reaches its own *telos*? In the play's final scene, the dynamic ambiguity of the women's erotic language must contend with what is often seen as the static determinism of comic endings. While there is something final about the revelation of Galatea and Phillida's true identities at the end of the play, the marriage plot raises as many questions as it answers, perhaps most memorably the lingering question of which maiden will become male in order to marry the other. As the gods intervene in the women's plight, Neptune mocks the objects of their desires, calling their love '[a]n idle choice . . . to imagine a constant faith where there can be no cause for affection' (V, iii, 139–41). The language of 'constant faith' signals that whatever 'unstayed' affections were at work must now stabilise with marriage. The word 'constant', derived from the Latin *constare*, to 'stand together', indicates a stasis in desire, a standing still. Venus picks up on Neptune's language when it is time for her to decide whether she will change one of the maidens into a boy, asking the pair, '[i]s your loves unspotted, begun with truth, continued with constancy, and not to be altered till death?' (V, iii, 145–7). The goddess of love, who was described as 'unruly' and 'unstayed' less than one hundred lines earlier in this scene, now insists that the girls' love is 'not to be altered till death'. Does the necessary resolution of Venus and Diana's inaugural quarrel mean that errant desire must reconcile itself to permanence? Given that 'constant' (Venus's 'constancy') was often used to describe motion, and given that 'change is always a matter of movement' in early modern philosophy as in conceptual metaphor theory, Lyly's metamorphic ending suggests that constancy and change may be more compatible than Venus, Diana or Neptune is willing to admit.[28]

The word 'constancy' crops up one last time in the play, in Galatea's epilogue addressed to the women in the audience, when she implores them '[y]ield ladies, yield to love, ladies' (5). Galatea notes that 'Venus can make constancy fickleness, courage cowardice, modesty lightness' (2–3). The *telos* that was almost at hand has receded for a final time: yet again, 'constancy' is 'fickleness' under Venus's government. And fickle love is necessarily in motion – it 'lurketh under your eyelids while you sleep and playeth with your heartstrings while you wake' (5–7). Even though, then, Galatea instructs lovers (and ladies in particular) to 'yield' to Cupid and '[c]onfess him a conqueror' (10), and even though the language of yielding and conquest implies stasis and resolution, the play as a whole demonstrates that yielding is an event. It is a process or 'practice' – now meandering, now idle or playful – that unfolds over five acts and ostensibly beyond. Love's 'sweetness *never* breedeth satiety' (7–8, emphasis added), Galatea tells the ladies in the audience. Absent satiety, love is kept sweet . . . and at arm's length.

Lyly does not deny that to be forever reaching is to risk solipsism or alienation. And at times, the women of *Galatea* do seem more invested in their private experiences of love than in a particular beloved. In Cupid's scheme to pierce the nymphs, when he boasts that 'while they aim to hit others with their arrows, they shall be wounded *themselves* with *their own* eyes' (I, ii, 35–7, emphases added), his reflexive pronouns suggest that love is a solitary enterprise: instead of relating to 'others', the attentions and aims of the nymphs will turn inward. But the nymphs' inward turn is only the first part of their story, and in the end, their erotic experiences exceed Cupid's either / or logic: they relate to each other *by means of* the very inwardness he inflicts on them. As the nymphs 'dare . . . describe' (III, i, 88) their private desires, each sends flashes of recognition through the others. To describe and to confess, to listen and confirm, are all 'dar[ing]' acts that connect the nymphs as they share in erotic experiences that are both common and particular. Language is shared; it always 'aim[s] to hit others'. It moves and reaches, even when the women feel trapped by what divides them.

Neither does Lyly deny that Galatea and Phillida do feel trapped – by disguise, deceit, desire – starting with their first 'dialogue' of asides and continuing throughout much of the play. Whereas Romeo and Juliet compose a sonnet together upon their initial encounter in a crowded room, Galatea and Phillida, all alone on stage, can hardly exchange a single word. But in their alternating asides, the women hear each other. Galatea seems to answer Phillida's 'he might' (II, i, 21) with 'I would' (II, i, 25), to which Phillida offers 'If I' (II, i, 27), followed by Galatea's 'if he' (II, i, 32). It is as though the maidens are singing separate melodies, half-knowing that they are in nearly perfect harmony. Perhaps this unwitting duet is an instance of 'making much'. As the layers of their disguises peel back over the course of the play, their duet of asides, puns, parallel phrases and subjunctive verbs becomes increasingly opaque: 'Admit', proposes Galatea, 'that I were as you would have me suppose that you are' (III, ii, 25–6). This is the dizzying language of erotic potentiality. Through the sequence 'admit . . . I were . . . suppose . . . you are', Galatea manages both to stir Phillida's imagination and to conjure their actual situations as disguised women. Here, as elsewhere in their exchanges, the actual exists alongside the possible without depleting the erotic charge of potentiality, of 'what if'. Aristotle's definition of *dunamis*, 'a source of change in oneself or another', might seem to characterise Venus's role as metamorphoser rather than the women who are metamorphosed by love. But the women's language moves and changes them well before Venus intervenes. From 'deer' to 'dear', from 'admit' and 'suppose' to 'I am' and 'you are', the women of *Galatea* reach out, make space and imagine what is possible, thereby enriching what is real.

Notes

1. G. K. Hunter, 'Introduction', in the Revels Plays edition of *Galatea*, 15.
2. Carson describes eros as a 'dance' in which 'the people do not move. Desire moves' (*Eros the Bittersweet*, 17).

3. Andy Kesson (*John Lyly and Early Modern Authorship*, 121) quotes from Janette Dillon, *The Language of Space in Court Performance, 1400–1625*, 56.

4. Angus Fletcher, *Time, Space, and Motion*, 11.

5. See Richard Sorabji and Norman Kretzmann, 'Aristotle on the Instant of Change'.

6. Mark Sentesy, 'On The Many Senses of Potency', 73. Well-known scholars of Aristotle's *Metaphysics*, such as Jonathan Beere and Charlotte Witt, argue that *dunamis* and *energeia / entelecheia* (action / actuality) are incompatible, opposite or mutually exclusive ways of being. (See Beere, *Doing and Being*, and Witt, *Ways of Being*.)

7. Sentesy, 'On The Many Senses of Potency', 79.

8. See Sentesy, 'Are Potency and Actuality Compatible in Aristotle?', 248.

9. Fletcher, *Time, Space, and Motion*, 7, 10.

10. Chess calls *Galatea* an 'undoubtedly queer play' (Chess, *Male-to-Female Crossdressing in Early Modern English Literature: Gender, Performance, and Queer Relations*, 147, 148).

11. Valerie Traub notes that Galatea and Phillida's 'linguistic symmetry' conveys 'the mimetic nature of their mutual desires'. See Traub, *The Renaissance of Lesbianism in Early Modern England*, 328. Although Traub confines her analysis to the two main characters, her observation might well extend to Diana's nymphs, who also display linguistic symmetries, albeit differently from those of the principal pair.

12. For more on queer temporalities, which are broadly defined by their privileging of narrative gaps and disordered chronology, see Elizabeth Freeman, *Time Binds: Queer Temporalities, Queer Histories*. See also Heather L. Love's essay on teleoscepticism in *Macbeth*, 'Milk', in Menon, *Shakesqueer: A Queer Companion to the Complete Works of Shakespeare*, 201–8.

13. G. K. Hunter glosses 'conceits' as 'thoughts, fanciful notions' but a related linguistic sense is present as well. Lyly uses the word 'conceit' in *Euphues* to denote a speech act (Philautus plans to 'flap Ferardo in the mouth with some conceit'). Leah

Scragg glosses Philautus's line as 'tell Ferardo some story'. (See John Lyly, *Euphues: The Anatomy of Wit* and *Euphues and His England*, 60.) The word 'conceit' has a complex history that weaves together cognitive senses (as in 'conceive') with linguistic ones (deriving from the Italian *concetto*). The *OED* cites Lyly's *Euphues* to illustrate the entry: 'a fanciful or ingenious action or practice; an affectation of behavior or manner. Also: a trick' (see 'conceit, *v.*' entry, III.10a).

14. Carson, *Eros the Bittersweet*, 37.
15. Valerie Traub, *Thinking Sex*, 4.
16. Carson, *Eros the Bittersweet*, 30.
17. Robert Y. Turner, 'Some Dialogues of Love in Lyly's Comedies', 276.
18. Ibid., 277.
19. According to the International Society for Sexual Medicine, edging 'usually follows this pattern:

    • A person is stimulated almost to the point of orgasm ('the edge').
    • Stimulation is then reduced, so that the person does not actually climax.
    • Stimulation increases, bringing the person to the edge again.'

    This sexual practice, which might qualify as queer in its decentring of orgasm, follows the same contours as Lyly's erotic language, with its 'strange contraries' and the 'doubtful speeches' that bring lovers to the edge ('What Is Edging and Why Might It Be Employed?').
20. Kent Cartwright, *Theater and Humanism: English Drama in the Sixteenth Century*, 179.
21. Traub, *The Renaissance of Lesbianism*, 328–9. Traub identifies Lyly's use of *isocolon* and *parison* in particular.
22. Carson, *Eros the Bittersweet*, 69, 63.
23. On the eroticism of the boy actor, see Peter Stallybrass, 'Transvestism and the "Body Beneath": Speculating on the Boy Actor'. Evelyn Tribble challenges generalisations about boy actors as erotic objects in her essay, 'Pretty and Apt: Boy Actors, Skill, and Embodiment': 'the arousal of erotic

impulses on the part of spectators was an element of this theatre, but such moments might be seen as themselves skilled and canny displays' (629).

24. Carson, *Eros the Bittersweet*, 35.

25. G. K. Hunter notes the difference in performance when he glosses the deer / dear exchange: 'The puns made evident to the reader by spelling must be understood in the theatre by intonation and gesture' (47).

26. Christian M. Billing, *Masculinity, Corporality and the English Stage, 1580–1635*, 68.

27. Traub, *Renaissance of Lesbianism*, 327. Traub notes the many senses of *confound* in the *OED* that were available to Lyly, including 'to throw (things) into confusion or disorder' and 'to mix up or mingle so that the elements become difficult to distinguish or impossible to separate' (328). In Cupid's plan to 'confound their loves', he imagines a frenzied and chaotic form of motion.

28. Fletcher, *Time, Space, and Motion*, 7.

CHAPTER 2

THE 'RAGING MOTIONS' OF EROS ON SHAKESPEARE'S STAGE

If Lyly probes the directionality of erotic desire, Shakespeare gauges its intensity. We have seen that Lyly's is an art of potentiality – time and again, his characters are moved less by the actual than the possible – and although Shakespeare explores this form of eroticism, his characters are typically less content to linger there. Raising the stakes of motion and stasis, Shakespeare amps up his metaphors such that escape and imprisonment, chaos and death prevail. Armado wants to 'take desire prisoner' (*Love's Labour's Lost* I, ii, 57) with his sword; Demetrius and Chiron rape Lavinia with 'their worse-than-killing lust' (*Titus Andronicus* II, iii, 175); Proteus is 'yoked' (*The Two Gentlemen of Verona* I, i, 40) by the fool Love; Juliet 'should kill [Romeo] with much cherishing' (*Romeo and Juliet* II, i, 227). These metaphors charge motion with turbulent force and stasis with paralysing tension, prompting Shakespeare's characters to test the power of desire and offering them a means to test their own power over it. Whether casting themselves as captors or as victims, characters find agency on both sides of the verb. Take, for example, Shakespeare's Helena, as she navigates the formidable currents of desire in *A Midsummer Night's Dream*. Desire is never a static business in the forest, where lovers shift their attentions as quickly as they shift their gazes. And yet Helena, feeling stuck, laments her helplessness. She begs Hermia to 'teach me how you look, and with what art / You sway the motion of Demetrius' heart' (I, i, 192–3). For Helena, desire is something that can be controlled, directed through particular actions, or 'art', as she puts it.

Needless to say, the play itself is less confident. Even in Helena's metaphors of motion, she ascribes agency elsewhere. She wants to learn Hermia's seductive 'art', but in her speeches to Demetrius, Helena admits her powerlessness:

> You draw me, you hard-hearted adamant,
> But yet you draw not iron; for my heart
> Is as true as steel. Leave you your power to draw,
> And I shall have no power to follow you.
> (II, i, 195–8)

Shakespeare's magnetism metaphor complicates the play's account of erotic action and stasis. Is Demetrius's magnetism the same as action? Following Aristotle's example, Kenneth Burke distinguishes action from motion, defining the former as deliberate and purposive motion.[1] But intentionality is difficult to ascertain, particularly when it comes to magnetism. Helena seems to confer all agency on Demetrius: he has the 'power to draw' her. If he relinquishes this power, she will 'have no power to follow' him. What does it mean to have the 'power to follow' someone who draws you? Does the one who follows a magnetic pull not submit passively to the force of attraction? Is this a case in which motion develops into action? If to follow Demetrius's pull is to act, then even as she casts herself as a pure object of desire, Helena cannot quite cancel out her agency.

The agency that Helena finds on her side of the magnet corresponds with Aristotle's notion of passive power. Aristotle's ontology accounts for two types of *dunamis*:

the power to cause a change in something else and the 'power of suffering' a change. The latter, which Charlotte Witt describes as 'the power of being perceptible', applies to Helena's relation to Demetrius.[2] Throughout the play, Helena wields passive power in order to be perceived and acknowledged by Demetrius. She famously demands that Demetrius

> spurn me, strike me,
> Neglect me, lose me; only give me leave,
> Unworthy as I am, to follow you.
>   (II, i, 205–7)

Here, her authority and abjection collide. To insist that Demetrius spurn and beat her – to command him to command her – is to affirm Helena's 'power of suffering'. Her passive power falls in line with Aristotle's example in *The Metaphysics*: 'For that which is oily is inflammable, and that which yields in a particular way can be crushed.'[3] The power to yield or be crushed is Helena's *dunamis* in the play; it abets her pursuit of Demetrius in the forest. Hence, for Shakespeare, submission – a mix of action and stasis – is always a form of erotic agency. Characters acknowledge the loss of control that is part and parcel of erotic desire; they submit to desire, instead of being overcome by it. They choose.

Like Helena's language of active submission, many of Shakespeare's erotic metaphors draw from the domains of both stillness and motion, which often converge at the height of desire. Stasis can beget motion, as it does for Angelo in *Measure for Measure*, but for Othello, who obsessively longs for 'satisfaction', movement produces stasis. Set in motion by his erotic imaginings and unable to cope with Desdemona's sexual agency, Othello ends up eroticising the image of her 'monumental alabaster' stillness: 'I will kill thee / And love thee after' (V, ii, 5, 18–19). In both *Measure for Measure* and *Othello*, Shakespeare's metaphors trace the fine line that separates the extremity of erotic motion (chaos, convulsions, compulsivity) from the extremity of stasis (death, violent restraint). If, over such extremes, Shakespeare's characters have little control, they none the less struggle to understand desire, and attempt to exert some degree of agency by using 'reason to cool our raging motions' (I, iii, 329–30), as Iago puts it. I begin this chapter with a close analysis of one such attempt: Claudio's short but dense speech about sexual scope and restraint in *Measure for Measure*. In this passage, as elsewhere in Shakespeare's corpus, cool reason gives way to 'raging motion'. Claudio's layered and conflicting metaphors generate a dangerous logic of extremes, a logic that, it turns out, governs erotic experience from one of Vienna's 'dark corners' (IV, iii, 157) to the next. A similar logic underwrites Othello's conception of his relationship with Desdemona. But Desdemona's metaphors of motion may open up a *via media*, raising the possibility that erotic scope can 'increase' (II, i, 191) and 'grow' (192) endlessly. I conclude by analysing several other Shakespearean dramas of what, following Aristotle, I call 'entelechial desire'.

Metaphors of illicit sex and desire shape fundamental questions about erotic agency in *Measure for Measure*, a play in which characters are hard at work analysing the aetiology and significance of their lustful impulses. Desire in *Measure for Measure* is both physical and metaphysical, launching characters into the most scrupulous Aristotelian inquiries into the nature of being. We have already seen Angelo probe ontological questions of essences ('what dost thou, or what art thou, Angelo?' [II, ii, 172]), causes ('is this her fault or mine?' [162]) and teleology ('what is't I dream on?' [178]). In his attempts to understand both desire and his own desiring self, Angelo imagines eros as constitutive of his own being (indeed, of all human being). But in *Measure for Measure*, the metaphors that govern these analytical speeches are often incompatible. While such incongruities can expand the ambit of erotic experience, as they do for Lyly's lovers in *Galatea*, the rigid sexual climate of Shakespeare's Vienna cannot tolerate this ambiguity. The causes, essences and purposes of eroticism are various and multiple, but this multiplicity fractures rather than broadens erotic identities and possibilities in *Measure for Measure*.

Analytical, often reproachful, speeches crop up early in Shakespeare's play, structured by metaphors that obscure rather than illuminate the origins and *telos* of erotic desire. A particularly rich example is provided by Claudio, who has just been sentenced to death for the crime of fornication. On his way to prison, he explains to Lucio that his 'restraint' comes 'from too much liberty' (I, ii, 105). To describe the nature, causes and consequences of this sexual liberty, Claudio draws from a series of conflicting domains of experience:

> As surfeit is the father of much fast,
> So every scope, by the immoderate use,
> Turns to restraint. Our natures do pursue,
> Like rats that ravin down their proper bane,
> A thirsty evil; and when we drink, we die.
>   (I, ii, 106–10)

In these lines Claudio weaves together several different stories of what has happened to him, and more generally, what happens to any of us when we fall prey to erotic desire. In the sequence, structure and entailments of his metaphors, Claudio discloses the subtle tensions between unlawful sex and illicit desire, frenzied motion and purposive action, volition and compulsion, which he assumes animate erotic desire in all of us (hence 'we', '*every* scope' and '*our* natures').

In the first half of this passage, Claudio files sexual liberty under 'every scope', then imagines it as 'a thirsty evil'.

Each metaphor – of sex as scope, sex as thirst and sex as evil – comes with entailments that answer to conflicting rules governing lust and sex: Who or what calls the shots? What choices are available? What role does necessity play? What role ethics? Embedded in his metaphors are similes (overeating, fasting, drinking poison) that elaborate the target domains of illicit sex, desire and prohibition. By mapping the features of concrete domains (eating and drinking, animals and poison, kinship and death) on to experiences like desire or restraint, Shakespeare produces something of an elucidation effect. But in Claudio's case, each simile, each new source domain, takes us further from the discrete object that is desire. Broadening the target domains of sex, desire and prohibition, Claudio reveals new roles and new relations between them. Like a camera that keeps pulling back, Claudio's story gradually widens our field of vision at the cost of blurring the focus within the frame.

In lines 106–8, Claudio considers causation. Does sexual scope (motion) cause restraint (stillness)? Does surfeit cause fast? Below I emphasise the relationship terms that connect the two parts of Claudio's extended simile:

> As surfeit *is the father of* much fast,
> So every scope, by the immoderate use,
> *Turns to* restraint.
>
> (I, ii, 106–8)

Claudio begins by using a metaphor of kinship, cued by the word 'father', to describe how 'surfeit' causes 'much fast'. Surfeit, in Claudio's account, begets fast just as a father begets a child. According to Mark Turner, this is a 'causation as progenation' metaphor.[4] In order for Claudio's simile to match up with the experience it profiles, scope ought to be the 'father of' restraint. But it is not. Claudio says that scope 'turns to' restraint because of 'immoderate use'. Instead of *begetting* a separate entity, a child, as surfeit begot fast, scope here *becomes* restraint by engaging in an action (immoderate use). This is a 'causation as action' metaphor, which Turner defines as 'someone directly manipulating some pre-existing objects from one state into another state'.[5] Father and child also share essential features, but in the end, they are ontologically separate. In the 'causation as action' metaphor, however, scope and restraint are the same entity. At different points in time, sexual indulgence and repressive self-control are experienced within – and come to define – the same person. It turns out that scope and restraint have more in common than a shared lineage. In *Measure for Measure*, both are forms of erotic excess.

As we have already seen, Angelo is a case in point. 'A man of stricture and firm abstinence' (I, iii, 12), he becomes (or was he already?) the man who 'give[s] [his] sensual race the rein' (II, iv, 160). Likewise, Isabella's zeal for 'a more strict restraint / Upon the sisterhood' (I, iv, 4–5) is a testament to the scope of her abstinence. Katherine Eisaman Maus has observed that 'the concepts of restraint and transgression, discipline and capitulation . . . profoundly structure the experience of desire in *Measure for Measure*'.[6] Thus, Angelo conceptualises his attraction to Isabella as a 'desire to raze the sanctuary' (II, ii, 175). Thus, in the habit of a friar, the 'duke of dark corners' (IV, iii, 157) arranges a sexual tryst. Thus, Isabella sadomasochistically 'thrills to the idea of wearing "th'impression of keen whips . . . as rubies" and stripping herself "to death as to a bed / That longing have been sick for"' (II, iv, 100–2).[7] And thus Claudio seems to cling to his chains, even as he is being carted off to prison; he notes how 'just' (I, ii, 122) his punishment is, how even 'to speak of [his offence] would offend again' (I, ii, 136). And yet Claudio does continue to speak of his offence, however obliquely, in the lines that follow.

In the second part of Claudio's speech, metaphors of rats, poison, and death mark a shift in both agency and intensity.

The stakes of fasting and restraint are high, but they pale in comparison to 'thirsty evil' and death:

> Our natures do pursue,
> Like rats that ravin down their proper bane,
> A thirsty evil; and when we drink, we die.
> (I, ii, 108–10)

Here Claudio tells us that our sexual natures compel us to pursue evil – an evil that is somehow 'proper' to us and that kills us. If the first part of Claudio's speech interrogates causation, the second part asks questions about volition and agency. The players in the first part of Claudio's speech are abstractions: scope, restraint and so on. No person surfeits, no person 'uses' immoderately. Claudio depicts volitional acts but omits performative human beings. Even as his next sentence strips away free will, it introduces rat-like human agents. Where there is no obvious human agency there is volition, but where there is something akin to human agency there is compulsion. It appears that Claudio, like many of us, can conceive of controlling erotic desire only in the abstract.[8] When his abstractions become vivid dramatisations – when potentiality becomes actuality – he ratchets up from tidy sententiae to graphic, grotesque bodily metaphors. Cool reason yields to raging motion when Claudio devolves from a father to a rat. The puritanical deputy who 'scarce confesses / That his blood flows' (I, iii, 51–2) turns into a sexual predator who actively pursues a 'strong and swelling evil' (II, iv, 6).

Still more is going on in Claudio's story than a shift from abstract volition to embodied compulsion. In the breath between his first and second sentences, erotic compulsivity acquires action verbs. Initially, abstractions are joined by linking verbs. Surfeit 'is' the father of fast, and then scope, immoderate use and restraint are joined by another linking verb, 'turns to'. Something transpires but it does so in a notably passive, and static, fashion. But suddenly, all of us are said to 'pursue', 'ravin' and 'drink'. 'And when we drink, we die.' This is especially dynamic; it takes place at a specifiable moment (Claudio does not say, for example, '*if* we drink, we die') and it depicts a surprisingly clear chain of action. What accounts for this shift? If we trace the progression of Claudio's metaphors across all five lines, we discover that each new source domain introduces a new character, or role, that must be mapped on to the target. Beginning with only two roles (surfeit and fast), he makes his way toward the source domain of ratsbane, which tells its own, much more complicated, story.

Ratsbane, after it is ingested, induces unquenchable thirst. Rats typically die from overhydration; the water that they compulsively drink to slake their thirst eventually causes their bodies to burst. While the ratsbane domain entails four roles – the rat, the poison, the water and death – it is clear only that the rat profiles us and that death profiles 'restraint'. Poison and water are more difficult to map. Instead of consuming a single substance that would clearly profile illicit sex, the rats glut themselves on both poison and water. Both substances have a hand in killing the rat. Although the poison is ultimately responsible for the death, Claudio tells us 'when we drink [water, presumably], we die'. Claudio's metaphor adds depth and complexity to the story of sex and restraint, since he opens up a new slot (poison or water) to be filled in the target domain. What, then, might poison and water profile? Water, a natural and essential substance that fuels life, is tainted by the ratsbane that then corrupts the judgement of the one who drinks it. The rats, no longer able to calibrate how much water is too much (they 'surfeit'), are never satisfied, and effectively kill themselves under the misapprehension that they are nourishing themselves. Water, then, seems to profile sex, since both (in moderation) are natural and essential, promoting life. Apparently something else (something 'proper' to us) beguiles us before we drink, something that both poisons our relation to what might otherwise have been healthy and infects our judgement.

What, then, precedes sex and ruins it for us? What poison did Claudio 'ravin down' before bedding Juliet? As Angelo marvels after his first encounter with Isabella, 'What's this' (II, ii, 167)? In Angelo's case, the poison seems to be a kind of original sin. In his opening soliloquy, he decides that Isabella is not at fault for his lust:

> Not she . . . but it is I
> That, lying by the violet in the sun,
> Do, as the carrion does, not as the flower,
> Corrupt with virtuous season.
> (II, ii, 169–72)

For Angelo, the 'proper bane' is his own carrion nature. And if this is the *dunamis* that condemns him to rot, then perhaps Claudio's rat nature condemns him to chase 'thirsty evil'. Although Angelo's metaphor has a starting-point different from Claudio's – the carrion is already poisoned – their metaphors run a similar course. Angelo and Claudio conceive of their natures as both contaminated and contaminating. The sunshine, another natural and life-promoting substance, only deepens the effects of the poison, 'corrupt[ing]' Angelo as water destroys rats. For both Claudio and Angelo, ratsbane profiles erotic desire. Their desires are toxic; they lead to unreason, surfeit and perversion. And yet, if the first part of Claudio's speech details causal relationships, it never specifies a prior cause or assigns agency. Not until we arrive at ratsbane do we encounter desire in the form of a thirst-inducing poison that propels us toward painful, gluttonous but 'proper' death.

Claudio's metaphors sharply illuminate the difference between abstractions and dramatisations, stasis and action. Once human agents enter the metaphorical field, action verbs follow. Yes, ratsbane plays an important role, but words like 'pursue' and even 'thirsty' in the second half of Claudio's speech signal intention and motive. It is as if Claudio's abstract, analytical language of surfeit and fast invites the frenzied, dramatic actions that follow. So, too, does Angelo's analytical soliloquy set in motion his 'sensual race' (II, iv, 160). Try as they may to conceive of erotic desire cognitively, Angelo and Claudio conceive it actually, and so animate it. Here, and elsewhere in his plays, Shakespeare dramatises the interdependence of erotic potentiality and actuality. Imagination and contemplation ignite a fever of activity that causes us again and then again to pursue the imagined relief of sex until it kills us. Over desire that moves in this way – from apparent stasis to compulsive action and back to the stasis of death – we have no control at all. Passivity may afford *A Midsummer Night's Dream*'s Helena a modicum of power but nothing like this is available to Claudio or to Angelo.

The ratsbane metaphor, like the hunting metaphor in *Galatea*, also interrogates the quality of desire's mobility. If desire is an action in *Measure for Measure*, what is its *telos*? Claudio's lines suggest that our preoccupation with, and our inability to understand, our *telos* undo us. Scurrying along the path of survival, relief and satisfaction, we guzzle our way to the gluttonous demise that we have coming to us ('proper'). Like rodents on a wheel, we revolve assiduously from thirst to drink to thirst to drink. For Angelo, erotic desire is a 'fall' (II, i, 18). For Mariana, it is an unquenchable, uncontrollable thirst. Angelo's 'unjust unkindness, that in all reason should have quenched her love, hath, like an impediment in the current, made it more violent and unruly' (III, i, 238–41). Mariana's unruly desire for Angelo is conceptualised as motion along a path, and his rebukes as impediments to motion. According to the event structure metaphor, such an impediment should slow her down, but Angelo's 'unkindness' only strengthens Mariana's 'violent' love.

Thus, the metaphors of sexual scope and restraint in *Measure for Measure* tell a paradoxical story of eros. Two logically opposing forces – scope and restraint, stillness and motion, potentiality and actuality – are, in their extreme form, one and the same. Restraint consistently increases the velocity of desire in the play. Where we expect to see characters immobilised by desire, they move like frantic rats. Angelo's lust for Isabella both 'stirs [his] temper' (II, ii, 189) and 'subdues [him] quite' (II, ii, 190). Later in the play, when Angelo prays, the metaphors of stasis and motion again collide. His 'invention . . . [a]nchors on Isabel' (II, iv, 2–3) and yet his heart surges with the 'swelling evil / Of my conception' (II, iv, 6–7). Although he tells us that his 'invention' is held captive and weighed down, we have seen that nothing can be further from the truth. Angelo might locate his 'evil' in his 'conception' but original sin is too facile an explanation for the pace and force of his desires. It is no accident that the man who 'scarce confesses / That his blood flows' (I, iii, 51–2) soon surrenders his self-control by declaring 'Blood thou art blood' (II, iv, 15). Angelo's 'evil', as he calls it, originates less in his blood than in his unwillingness to 'confess' that it flows. The desire for control, toxic and intoxicating in its own right, is what produces the 'swelling' violence of the sexual release that follows it.

Of course, Angelo is not the only Shakespearean character who feels subdued by erotic desire. The word 'subdue' appears six times in *Othello*. In its first two appearances, aggression is emphasised: Brabantio furiously orders the guards to 'subdue' (I, ii, 81) Othello, who is soon accused of 'subdu[ing]' Desdemona's 'affections' (I, iii, 112). Thereafter, 'subdue' is a marker of conjugal generosity and affection. But like Othello himself, the word can never shake off the contentious resonances that accrue in the play's opening scenes. Being subdued by love always entails a measure of violence, as when Desdemona proclaims that 'My heart's subdued / Even to the very quality of my lord' (I, iii, 249–50).[9] A subdued heart suggests a quiet stillness, preferable to both the 'raging motions' of lust described by Iago (I, iii, 325) and the 'chaos' that Othello predicts will 'come again' (III, iii, 93), when he falls out of love with Desdemona. Othello imagines the unruly energy of chaos as an agitating force opposed to the subduing counterforce of marriage or love.

Desdemona's heart may be subdued, but the other parts of her body resist subjection, as Othello himself acknowledges. Initially, he appears to accept and even celebrate Desdemona's agency. He encourages the senators to send for Desdemona and 'let her speak of me' (I, iii, 116) in her own voice. Meanwhile, he recounts her enthusiastic responses to 'the story of [his] life' (I, iii, 129):

> These things to hear
> Would Desdemona seriously incline
> . . . and with a greedy ear
> Devour up my discourse
> (I, iii, 144–5, 148–9)

On the one hand, Desdemona is said to have been a submissive listener. On the other hand, she 'seriously incline[d]' to hear his stories, assuming a posture that Iago will recall later in the play, when he refers to 'th'inclining Desdemona' who is 'most easy . . . / to subdue / In any honest suit' (II, iii, 327–9). Stephen Greenblatt has noted that Desdemona's love has 'a quality . . . that unsettles the orthodox schema of hierarchical obedience and makes Othello perceive her submission to his discourse as a devouring of it'.[10] As Othello recounts for the senators '[h]ow I did thrive in this fair lady's love' (I, iii, 125), he alludes to the active, even aggressive and excessive quality of Desdemona's amorous response. Her 'subdued' heart competes with her hungry ear, which has the capacity to overwhelm what Othello feeds it.

Although Othello takes pride in Desdemona's 'greedy ear' early in their courtship, he cannot cope with her sexual agency for long. Nor, if we seriously incline our ears to his metaphors of marital confinement, does he appear to be able to cope with his own:

> For know, Iago,
> But that I love the gentle Desdemona,
> I would not my unhousèd free condition
> Put into circumscription and confine
> For the sea's worth.
> (I, ii, 25–9)

Between his 'unhousèd free condition' and 'circumscription', Othello can find no middle ground. Are eros and marriage necessarily inhospitable to 'unhousèd free[dom]'? Is there no 'free[dom]' within the bonds of matrimony? For Desdemona, yes; but for Othello, metaphors of movement and change prove ominous. Having arrived at Cyprus after enduring a storm at sea, he tells his wife that he would be 'most happy' (II, i,189) to die now. His soul is absolutely content with the way things are. Things being as good as they get, his life could end here. Desdemona responds,

> The heavens forbid
> But that our loves and comforts should increase
> Even as our days do grow.
> (II, i,192–4)

For Othello, love and desire are bounded experiences; for Desdemona, they are crescive. He is happy to die now because his content is 'absolute' (190); it can only have peaked. 'It stops me here,' he tells Desdemona, 'it is too much of joy' (196). Greenblatt notes the contrast between the chaos of the tempest that Othello has just endured and the calmness that follows it:

> The 'calmness' of which [Othello] speaks may express grat-
> ified desire, but, as the repeated invocation of death sug-
> gests, it may equally express the longing for a final *release*
> from desire, from the dangerous violence, the sense of
> extremes, the laborious climbing and falling out of control
> that is experienced in the tempest.[11]

What Greenblatt calls 'gratified desire' and '*release* from
desire' is the fantasy of stasis, of release from Desdemona's
unknowability and unboundedness. Iago repeatedly calls this
release 'satisfaction'.[12] Derived from the Latin *satisfacere*,
'to make enough', satisfaction – intellectual, sexual, psychic
or any other kind – implies a completion that falls in line
with Othello's desire for 'stops', and which is at odds with
Desdemona's commitment to 'increase'. In the temptation
scene, a now familiar Othello demands certain knowledge
of Desdemona by means of a satisfying truth that only Iago
possesses.[13] This kind of knowledge, according to Stanley
Cavell, is often metaphorised as a kind of ownership or a
violence that Othello wishes to exact on his wife in response
to the dominion that he fears she has achieved over him.[14]

As if in response to *Othello*, Jean-Luc Marion argues
that erotic relations require us to forsake the static goals of
attainment, satisfaction and certain knowledge – indeed, any
knowledge at all – of both the beloved and ourselves. 'The
lover is', according to Marion, fundamentally 'opposed to the
cogitant', who directs his or her thoughts to grasping objects
in the world.[15] Unlike static objects of knowledge, lovers in
Marion's account are always in motion. Their receptivity to
one another means that each will move endlessly towards the
other:

> I start off out of balance and I only avoid the fall by length-
> ening my stride, by going faster, in other words by adding
> to my lack of balance. The more I do to avoid falling, the
> more I advance without any hope of return. For even if I

reach the other, this does not give me possession, precisely because I only touch her and open an access to her by the impact that I provoke . . . [T]he other does not stop me like a wall or an inert and delimited lump, but offers herself to me like a path that opens, always continuing in proportion to my entry forward; the advance thus requires a permanent fresh start.[16]

There is plenty that is chaotic about the movement Marion calls 'the lover's advance' but this chaos need not lead inexorably to stasis or death, as Claudio, Angelo and Othello imagine it must. In Marion's final image of 'a permanent fresh start', we have another instance of the convergence of Aristotelian activity (*entelecheia*) and potentiality (*dunamis*). To start fresh is to imagine what is possible; to do so 'permanent[ly]' is to remain in process, to act again and again.

Like Marion's advancing lover, Desdemona's 'inclining' posture signals both movement and the potential to be moved. And like the lover who 'offers herself . . . in proportion to my entry forward', Desdemona imagines that their 'loves and comforts should increase' in proportion to time, apparently without end. This form of heightened erotic activity, which Marion describes as 'an act without term, without end, in short the accomplishment of an act insofar as it remains without accomplishment', comports well with Aristotle's writings on entelechy.[17] Entelechial desire does not exclude 'accomplishment' or 'satisfaction' so much as it reframes these *teloi* as part of a process, rather than mere products, of desire. For Desdemona, as for Juliet, love is dynamic.[18] Unlike Othello, Desdemona can imagine or anticipate the future (*telos*) without crushing the present.

What is responsible for Othello's 'stops'? Male anxiety in the face of female sexuality is frequently adduced as 'the cause' for Othello's uneasiness.[19] When Iago hatches his plan to 'abuse Othello's ears', his ambiguous pronouns encourage Othello to identify with Cassio as a defiler of Desdemona. Iago plans to mislead Othello into believing 'That *he* [Cassio? Othello?] is too familiar with his wife' (I, iii, 388, emphasis added). For Greenblatt, 'the dark essence of Iago's whole enterprise . . . [is] to play upon Othello's buried perception of his own sexual relations with Desdemona as adulterous'.[20] Edward Snow follows Shakespeare's lead, characterising Othello's anxiety via metaphors of stillness and motion. His Othello has 'released the sexual flow in her, and transformed her from a chaste object of desire into a sexually demanding woman'.[21] Having awakened what he perceives to be Desdemona's overpowering, sometimes even repulsive sexuality, Othello resorts to metaphors of stillness (subduing, stopping, satisfying) to staunch the chaos of Desdemona's 'increase'. Yet even as Othello is committed to stasis, he too is set in motion by the sexual anxieties that he has unleashed in himself by (presumably) deflowering his wife.[22] The man who was once ready to 'die now' soon falls into a fit described as both 'a trance' and 'an epilepsy' (a physiological manifestation of stillness and motion combined), and then barrels toward the play's murderous conclusion.

Set in motion by his own anxieties and suspicions, Othello is also propelled by Iago's insinuations. Twice in ten lines, Iago perceives that Othello has been 'moved' by talk of Desdemona's adultery ('But I do see you're moved' [III, iii, 217], 'My lord, I see you're moved' [III, iii, 224]). As Othello denies these charges, his agitation grows and, in short order, his thoughts are indeed violently in motion:

> Like to the Pontic Sea,
> Whose icy current and compulsive course
> Ne'er feels retiring ebb, but keeps due on
> To the Propontic and the Hellespont,
> Even so my bloody thoughts, with violent pace
> Shall ne'er look back, ne'er ebb to humble love,
> Till that a capable and wide revenge
> Swallow them up.
>   (III, iii, 453–60)

The 'compulsive course' of Othello's bloody thoughts contrasts starkly with his earlier 'stops' of joy with Desdemona,
just as the 'violent pace' of the temptation scene disturbs what
Iago calls 'dilatory time' (II, iii, 360), time that unfolds slowly
and expands steadily. Patricia Parker has argued that Iago's
insinuations in this scene are examples of rhetorical dilation;
he offers glimpses of a narrative, which prompt Othello to
flesh out a fuller story of Desdemona's infidelity.[23] Dilation
and 'dilatory time' are responsible for the dramatic progression of much of the play, its expansiveness recalling Desdemona's desire, which also steadily 'increase[s]' with time. But
there is nothing slow or steady about the 'violent pace' of
Othello's sexual imagination, which runs riot and culminates
in an epileptic fit. In a speech full of 'stops' ('Handkerchief –
confessions – handkerchief! – ' [IV, i, 37]), Othello first
'tremble[s]' (IV, i, 39), then 'shakes' (IV, i, 41) and finally falls
into a trance. Undone by the wild pace of his own thoughts,
Othello's body endures the chaos of his mind.

It would seem to have been the function of the play's noto-
rious handkerchief to subdue both father's and son's chaos into
love. As Othello tells Desdemona, "Twould . . . subdue my
father / Entirely to her [my mother's] love' (III, iv, 62–3). The
quality of being subdued (somewhat captured by the modern-
day idiom 'settled down') is crucial to Othello's conception of
his marriage. But when he begins to suspect Desdemona of
infidelity, he imagines her in motion, ceaselessly changing:

> she can turn and turn, and yet go on
> And turn again; and she can weep, sir, weep;
> And she's obedient, as you say, obedient;
> Very obedient.
>   (IV, i, 250–3)

These lines are prompted by Lodovico's request that Othello
call his wife back to speak with them. What begins as a test
of Othello's power to 'make her turn' (IV, i, 249) ends as

an image of Desdemona spinning out of control. The metaphor 'Changing Is Turning', a special case of the event structure metaphor, shapes Othello's experience of Desdemona's changing affections as a kind of physical turning.[24] Othello paradoxically imagines Desdemona's very obedience – her willingness to be subdued in their marriage – as motion that prompts her to 'go on / And turn' without his bidding.[25] Yet again, stillness and motion collide.

When the play arrives at its 'bloody period' (V, ii, 357), violent action and stillness coincide one last time in the act of suffocation. Othello appears to endorse static love when he pleads, 'Be thus when thou art dead, and I will kill thee / And love thee after' (V, ii, 18–19). This is to stop her life, only to set things in motion again by loving her 'after'. What can it mean that Othello gives equal rhetorical weight to the verbs 'kill' and 'love', and what can it mean that the former must precede the latter? Othello's necrophiliac fantasy suggests that loving Desdemona is an act of violence similar to 'knowing' her in Cavell's account, where knowledge is conceptualised as an act of conquest, possession or assimilation. Emmanuel Levinas, who defines knowledge similarly, observes that human beings are never able to know one another.[26] For Levinas, knowledge falls within the provenance of 'Sameness' because it is an act of totalisation by which we try to possess ideas, to synthesise the universe, to claim the outside world as our own. But the provenance of (erotic) relations between human beings is the 'Other', wherein such relations are 'non-synthesisable'. The Other is always infinite, wholly separate and therefore unassimilable.[27] This jibes with Stanley Cavell's observation that Desdemona is 'everything [Othello] is not', and that the two of them 'together form an emblem of human separation' that is too much for Othello to bear.[28] Othello's inability to assimilate or to know Desdemona prompts a crisis marked by both sexual and epistemological anxiety, a crisis that ultimately gives rise to Othello's necrophiliac fantasy of total erotic assimilation. If Desdemona is an object in the world, not a lover whose 'face alone signifies to me, in speech or in silence, "Thou shalt not kill"', then Othello can possess her as if she were indeed made of 'monumental alabaster' (V, ii, 5).[29]

Othello's desire for possession, his desire to know Desdemona with certainty, and especially his desire not to desire ('Would I were satisfied!' [III, iii, 390]), are all conceptualised by the metaphors of motion and stillness that govern erotic desire throughout the play. As we have seen, Othello is in his element either when he is stopped or when he moves at a 'violent pace'. Iago's slowly unfolding 'dilatory time' and Desdemona's steady 'increase' are uncongenial to Othello's psychology of 'honorable stop[s]' (II, iii, 2). According to Edward Snow,

> 'Killing' Desdemona (either again and again or once and for all) is a way of extinguishing what threatens to turn her from a passive object of desire into an actively dangerous lover; at the same time it is a displaced means of killing the feelings that threaten to engulf his own inner being.[30]

Othello's vulnerability in the face of female sexuality is hardly unique in Shakespeare's plays, and it has been much commented on.[31] Enobarbus's famous pronouncement that Cleopatra 'makes hungry / Where most she satisfies' (II, ii, 247–8) captures a paradox similar to the one Othello finds in Desdemona's erotic agency. Where Enobarbus describes Cleopatra as both stimulating and allaying, Othello imagines Desdemona both turning and obeying at the same time. Desire itself is 'a paradoxical structure', writes Emmanuel Levinas, in language reminiscent of Enobarbus's speech about Cleopatra: 'Desire in some way nourishes itself on its own hungers and is augmented by its satisfaction . . . Desire is like a thought which thinks more than it thinks, or more than what it thinks.'[32] Such satisfaction can be both a *telos* and a source (*dunamis*) of desire.

Hence desire can be entelechial, both in its capacity to accomplish itself in process and in its emphasis on 'making' (*facio*, *facere*), rather than 'enough' (*satis*). The word 'satisfaction' and its variants appear more frequently in *Othello* than in any other Shakespeare play, but its most famous instance in Shakespeare's corpus is arguably Juliet's 'What satisfaction canst thou have tonight?' (II, ii, 126). Her suggestive question reminds Romeo (and us) that there is more than one way to imagine, and to experience, erotic satisfaction. Satisfaction can be a *telos* and it can be a point of origin for a process that keeps repeating, fuelled by a desire that strengthens as it ebbs:

> boundless as the sea,
> My love as deep; The more I give to thee,
> The more I have, for both are infinite.
> (II, ii, 133–5)

Edward Snow argues that Juliet's erotic metaphors are 'extravagantly metamorphic' and 'overflowing'. Her experience of desire is correspondingly active and in motion: 'Juliet's images exist in an urgently desired future, and are charged with an erotic energy that makes the experience they invoke present and actual in her imagination.'[33] Juliet's erotic imagination, capable of crossing the grammatical boundaries of tense and mood, conjures the future in the present. For Levinas, that future is the temporal equivalent of the Other in its mystery and its resistance to assimilation through knowledge. The erotic relation, according to Levinas, is always a relation with the future: 'It is neither a struggle, nor a fusion, nor a knowledge . . . It is the relationship with alterity, with mystery, that is, with the future, with what in the world where there is everything, is never there.'[34]

It makes sense, then, that such a relationship with the future would be conceptualised through metaphors of perpetual, if paradoxical, motion. Entelechy crosses logical boundaries, so it is unsurprising to find that its metaphors often take the form of paradox, overturning the basic physical principles of the domains they elaborate: hunger does not succeed satisfaction, at least not within the domain of eating. Basic, primary metaphors cannot account for Levinas's 'thought which thinks more than it thinks' or Marion's 'permanent fresh start'. Neither can they structure the kinds of erotic activities Juliet experiences (having in giving) and that Cleopatra inspires (hunger in satisfaction).[35] Janet Adelman describes paradox in *Antony and Cleopatra* as a poetic form that 'demands an act of faith' to give it credence.[36] Such a requirement is especially well suited to conceptualisations of erotic love, which is itself an act of faith. Desdemona 'inclines' toward the future because her faith and belief in Othello are aspects of her entelechial desire, which typically occurs in the subjunctive mood and in the present tense. Such belief implies an acceptance and anticipation of the future in the present, and it presents an alternative to the violence of erotic knowledge – the 'satisfaction' that Iago proffers and Othello craves. Juliet's fear that she 'should kill [Romeo] with much cherishing' (II, i, 227) is her acknowledgement of (and a sign of her attraction to) this violence. To cherish Romeo is to keep him, to possess or assimilate him in Levinas's terms: that is, to force him into Sameness rather than to preserve his Otherness.

This is not to say that entelechial desire is gentle or 'subdued', to use the *Othello* word.[37] Juliet's fear of erotic violence does not protect her from its allure, from experiencing desire in all its acuteness and intensity. In her fantasy of ensnaring Romeo, 'lur[ing] this tassel-gentle back' (II, ii, 160) like a falconer, and later of 'cut[ting] him out in little stars' (III, ii, 22), Juliet experiences the 'violent delights'

(II, vi, 9) of endlessly nourishing eroticism. Within Desdemona's unabating 'increase', there is the comparable potential for violence of a 'greedy' and 'devour[ing]' ear. The difference between Othello's and Desdemona's erotic experiences, then, does not derive from force or aggression. Rather, it has to do with their capacities to tolerate – even welcome – the changes that are part and parcel of 'unknown fate' (II, i, 190), a certain *telos* of any erotic relationship. To set one's sights on this unknown and unknowable *telos*, which can never be grasped, is to engage in the kind of erotic reaching modelled in Lyly's *Galatea*. This is where erotic potentiality and actuality most fruitfully converge.

The metaphors of stillness and motion that I have explored in this section reveal the interdependence of erotic potentiality and activity. These two erotic 'ways of being', as *dunamis* and *entelecheia* are often understood in scholarship on Aristotle's metaphysics, not only coexist but can mutually constitute one another.[38] This is a radical shift from the way in which we typically understand the relation of potentiality and actuality. In modern-day physics, for example, potential energy has an inverse relationship with kinetic energy: we lose potential as we actualise it. With this in mind, I raise Mark Sentesy's compelling question: 'If being potentially hot is incompatible with being actually hot, what happens to the potential to be hot?'[39] For many of Lyly's and Shakespeare's characters, potential strengthens as it is realised. Cleopatra does not appear to lose her erotic potency upon actualising it. Neither does Desdemona; nor does Othello if we credit Desdemona's stunning declaration, 'I saw Othello's visage in his mind' (I, iii, 252). To see him in *his* mind – the potential Othello – and actively to 'consecrate' (254) herself to that vision (her vision *of his vision*) is to make him possible and thereby real. Juliet's erotic imagination has a similar actualising, entelechial force. When she tells Romeo that 'This bud of love, by summer's ripening breath, / May prove a beauteous flow'r when next we meet' (II, ii, 121–2), her metaphors of growth indicate that her desire will flourish even in Romeo's absence.[40] Juliet does not even need him to be around to experience her desire for him as process, growth, action. For Juliet, as for the women in Lyly's *Galatea*, the actual and the possible enrich one another. Juliet's fervent anticipation and her ability to experience the full force of her love by herself on her balcony are evidence that her desire is comprised of both hunger and fulfilment; it contains its *telos*.

Metaphors of mobility – ripening, increase, bounty, scope – can dramatise erotic experiences at one moment as rich and nourishing, and at the next as toxic and confining. Claudio's ratsbane metaphor, Desdemona's devouring ear and Cleopatra's hunger-inducing satisfaction canvas the dream and nightmare of perpetual desire. As metaphors, they draw simultaneously upon multiple domains of experience, many of which are incompatible. For Othello, they evoke dissonance, what he calls 'chaos'. For Juliet, metaphors of ungovernable change are integrating. They splice the future in the present, the infinite in finite acts. Infinity, the term that Levinas assigns to the Other and that, for him, exemplifies erotic relations, crops up again and again in Shakespearean metaphors of desire. Troilus's 'will is infinite' (III, ii, 75), Juliet's bounty and love 'both are infinite' (III, ii, 135), Cleopatra's 'variety' is 'infinite' (II, iii, 248). For Aristotle, infinity 'consists in a process of coming to be'.[41] Metaphors of infinity reach for what they can never grasp but each of the above examples nevertheless points to an accomplishment, 'a process of coming to be' that spans the fullness of the Aristotelian continuum with which I began. To stage such a process is to contend with the tensions between stasis and motion, potential and actual, present and future, which are fundamental to the experience of erotic desire and, as P. A. Skantze reminds us, to theatre itself:

At the heart of artistic endeavor is the preoccupation of creating an aesthetic work that will last forever while offering its power and vision again and again, without growing stale. Like Cleopatra the art of representation and crafted language seeks a timeless stability, 'age cannot wither it,' but neither can it be lifeless in its repeated display, for then might 'custom stale its infinite variety.'[42]

That Skantze finds a language for these aesthetic tensions in the paradoxical description of Cleopatra's erotic power reveals the power of this language itself to dramatise the still and moving experiences of erotic desire.

Notes

1. Kenneth Burke writes of the 'motion–action ambiguity' in his discussion of the 'Pathetic Fallacy', which typically assigns agency to things that move because we 'empathetically move them with our imagination' (*A Grammar of Motives*, 233).
2. See Charlotte Witt, *Ways of Being*, 20. See also Witt's discussion of terminology and translation of *dunamis* as the 'power of suffering' a change (126); and Aristotle, *Metaphysics*, IX.1 1046a 10–14.
3. Aristotle, *Metaphysics*, IX.1 1046a 20–5.
4. Kinship metaphor is the subject of Mark Turner's *Death is the Mother of Beauty: Mind, Metaphor, Criticism*. One of Turner's claims is that the kinship metaphor is essential to our understanding of metaphor itself: 'We explain metaphor to ourselves in terms of what we know about *family*' (12); hence Aristotelian metaphor is defined in terms of relations and resemblances.
5. Ibid., 141.
6. Katherine Eisaman Maus, *Inwardness and Theater in the English Renaissance*, 160.
7. Theodore Leinwand cites Isabella's lines to illustrate that 'the play is interested in her aspirations toward Catholic martyrdom *per se* but equally in their proximity to sadomasochistic fantasy' (Leinwand, 'Shakespeare against Doctrine').

8. Cf. desire and sex, which are subjected to Vienna's 'most biting laws' (I, iii, 19), and which in turn presume that, because erotic desire is volitional, citizens may be held accountable. Of course, the law at the beginning of *Measure for Measure* has been 'dead to infliction' (I, iii, 28), merely an abstract threat with no practical consequence. When a human agent actually enforces it, he degenerates like Claudio's rats.

9. In the 1622 Quarto, Desdemona says 'utmost pleasure' instead of 'very quality'. I cite from the Folio text as it appears in *The Complete Pelican Shakespeare* and I fall into line with 'most editors and textual scholars [who] have agreed that F is the superior text'. (See Russ McDonald's Introduction to the play in *The Complete Pelican Shakespeare*, 1400). Quarto Desdemona's line reads as a sexual submission, whereas 'very quality' has both social (profession, status, militarism) and inherent valences (natural gifts, essence, character).

10. Stephen Greenblatt, *Renaissance Self-Fashioning from More to Shakespeare*, 240.

11. Ibid., 243.

12. Patricia Parker describes Othello's repeated demands for satisfaction ('Would I were satisfied!' [III, iii, 390]) as evidence of his 'impatient and even compulsive rushing to end or conclusion' (Parker, 'Shakespeare and Rhetoric: "Dilation" and "Delation" in *Othello*', 66).

13. Cf. Iago's persistent queries: 'You would be satisfied?' (III, iii, 398), 'how satisfied, my lord?' (III, iii, 299), 'Where's satisfaction?' (III, iii, 406).

14. Cavell refers to Heidegger on the 'violence in human knowing' since Heidegger's philosophy has always 'conceived of knowledge under the aegis of dominion, of the concept of a concept as a matter, say, of grasping a thing'. See Stanley Cavell, *Disowning Knowledge in Seven Plays of Shakespeare*, 9. Cavell later notes that 'Desdemona's acceptance, or satisfaction, or reward, of [Othello's] ambition strikes him as being possessed' (10).

15. Jean-Luc Marion, *The Erotic Phenomenon*, 28. Marion begins *The Erotic Phenomenon* with a critique of metaphysics as an

insufficient mode for understanding eros. The study of Being, in which existence can be known or understood by a dominating Cartesian *ego cogito*, is ill equipped to account for the saturated experience of love. Breaking from Descartes, Marion focuses on the *ego amans*.

16. Ibid., 83.
17. Ibid., 131.
18. Edward Snow notes the similarities between Desdemona and Juliet, and Othello and Romeo, with regard to absolute content and increase. Romeo's (and Othello's) 'tendency to think of love as moments of satisfaction rather than a process of growth, and hence to experience happiness within it against a backdrop of apocalyptic loss, is something Romeo shares with the male protagonists in Shakespeare's darkest treatments of love and sexual desire'. See Snow, 'Language and Sexual Difference in *Romeo and Juliet*', 172–3.
19. Among others, see Greenblatt, Snow and Edward Pechter, '"Have you not read of some such thing?": Sex and Sexual Stories in *Othello*'.
20. Greenblatt, *Renaissance Self-Fashioning*, 233. Stanley Cavell also discusses Othello's suspicion that he has contaminated himself and his wife: 'The torture of logic in his mind we might represent as follows: Either I shed her blood and scarred her or I did not. If I did not then she was not a virgin and this is a stain upon me. If I did then she is no longer a virgin and this is a stain upon me. Either way I am contaminated.' See Cavell's 'Othello and the Stake of the Other', in *Disowning Knowledge*, 125–42, 135.
21. Snow, 'Sexual Anxiety', 392.
22. Pechter (208–10) discusses the play's grotesque evocations of Desdemona's sexuality: 'a cistern for foul toads / To knot and gender in' (IV, ii, 63–4) and 'the slime / That sticks on filthy deeds' (V, ii, 155–6), as well as her 'nasty smell'.
23. Othello's jealousy, which causes him to inflate the intensity and the frequency of Desdemona's adulterous encounters with Cassio, 'is also founded on a principle of enlargement'. (See Patricia Parker, 'Shakespeare and Rhetoric', 64.) Parker

quotes Iago's 'Trifles light as air / Are to the jealous confirmations strong / As proofs of holy writ' (III, iii, 322–4).

24. George Lakoff and Mark Johnson, *Philosophy in the Flesh*, 207.

25. Snow points out that once Desdemona starts to turn, Othello believes that she will 'turn again', exercising the autonomous sexuality he has unleashed and which is now 'beyond his capacity to satisfy'. See Snow, 'Sexual Anxiety', 398.

26. See Emmanuel Levinas, *Totality and Infinity: An Essay on Exteriority*. Also see Chapters 6 and 7 in Levinas, *Ethics and Infinity: Conversations with Philippe Nemo*.

27. Levinas defines desire as antithetical to knowledge or assimilation. In *Ethics and Infinity*, he writes, 'the relation to the Infinite is not a knowledge, but a desire' (92).

28. Cavell, *Disowning Knowledge*, 136, 142. According to Cavell, it is the realisation of Desdemona's Otherness that tortures Othello: 'He cannot forgive Desdemona for existing, for being separate from him, outside, beyond command, commanding, her captain's captain' (136).

29. Marion, *The Erotic Phenomenon*, 100. Marion writes that the act of killing a beloved can occur only after objectifying her. Levinas, too, acknowledges the ethical power in the 'non-violent transitivity' of the Other's face. (See Levinas, *Totality and Infinity*, 51.)

30. Snow, 'Sexual Anxiety', 394.

31. See especially Janet Adelman, *Suffocating Mothers*, 38–75.

32. Levinas, *Ethics and Infinity*, 92.

33. Snow, 'Language and Sexual Difference', 176.

34. Emmanuel Levinas, *Le Temps et l'autre* (Montpellier: Fata Morgana, 1979), 81, qtd in *Ethics and Infinity*, 68. Like some of Shakespeare's male characters, Levinas characterises infinity, alterity, futurity, mystery or 'Other' as feminine. His philosophy was received with a great deal of scepticism and elicited many objections from feminists, most famously in Simone de Beauvoir's footnote in *The Second Sex*, in which she charges Levinas with 'deliberately tak[ing] a man's point of view, disregarding the reciprocity of subject and object'.

See Simone de Beauvoir, *The Second Sex*, xxii. For examinations of Levinas's relationship to feminism, see Tina Chanter, *Feminist Interpretations of Emmanuel Levinas*.

35. In terms of conceptual metaphor theory, a paradoxical metaphor may be defined as, first, a metaphor that does not adhere to the constraints of the source domain, or second, a metaphor whose entailments are incompatible.

36. Janet Adelman, *The Common Liar*, 113. Adelman describes Cleopatra's Egypt in entelechial terms: 'Everything here is in process . . . everything is becoming' (144). Entelechial language can characterise the kinds of mental activity associated with paradox, which Anne Carson describes as 'a kind of thinking that reaches out but never arrives at the end of its thought' (*Eros the Bittersweet*, 81).

37. Here I follow Melissa E. Sanchez's persuasive critique of feminist scholarship that diminishes or softens the sexual agencies of female characters in early modern texts. See Sanchez, '"Use Me But as Your Spaniel": Feminism, Queer Theory, and Early Modern Sexualities' and '"In My Selfe the Smart I Try": Female Promiscuity in *Astrophil and Stella*'.

38. A representative example is Charlotte Witt's *Ways of Being*.

39. Mark Sentesy, 'Are Potency and Actuality Compatible in Aristotle?', 258.

40. Snow compares these lines to Romeo worrying that his evening with Juliet will fade into a dream after she leaves. Whereas she is capable of sustaining and developing her desire in Romeo's absence, he fears that it will fall apart altogether, once she is out of his sight. See Snow, 'Language and Sexual Difference', 178–80.

41. Aristotle, *Physics*, III.6 206a 25-b3. For a fuller account of Aristotle's (much debated) definition of infinity, particularly its relationship with actuality and potentiality, see John Bowin, 'Aristotelian Infinity'.

42. P. A. Skantze, *Stillness in Motion in the Seventeenth-Century Theatre*, 17.

PART II

SPACE

INTRODUCTION

IN LOVE

'I love you, but I'm not in love with you.' An online search for this sentence produces over four million results, including its very own page in the Urban Dictionary. But there, as elsewhere, writers do not quite agree on what being *in* love means. According to Bustle.com, 'the largest premium publisher reaching millennial women', being 'in love' is a deep and abiding state in which we 'can't live without' that special someone.[1] But a *Huffington Post* column tells an opposite story, in which 'being in love' is a fleeting 'infatuation', marked by 'surface feelings' that distinguish it from 'true love'.[2] That neither of these two columns pauses over the implications of its terminology is unsurprising – their metaphors of surface and depth, stasis and motion, inner and outer, are commonplace – but their conflicting evaluations of 'being *in* love' might give us pause. Is love a place, and if so, do we want to be there? Why does being in love signal a lack of control and helplessness for some, but stability and permanence for others? The answer lies in how we conceptualise spatial metaphors of love. If love is a container, its dimensions matter. A tight circumference and sturdy walls make for a strong and secure place, but what if it 'hath no bottom' (*A Midsummer Night's Dream* IV, i, 214) or if it 'hath an unknown bottom' (*As You Like It* IV, i, 194–5), as

Rosalind tells her cousin Celia? For Rosalind, who uses the phrase 'in love' no less than thirteen times, love is beyond understanding and control; neither she nor Celia can 'know how many fathom deep I am in love' (IV, i, 193). Love as a container can be narrow but deep; it can be suffocating or perhaps porous. Or it can be 'bottomless', as Celia jokes, 'that as fast as you pour affection in, it runs out' (IV, i, 196–7). Each spatial orientation captures new erotic possibilities and invites different forms of action. Whereas height and depth might prompt us to 'fall in love', a snug fit invites us simply to 'be in love'.

Because love as a place is a matter of boundaries, the spatial metaphors I survey in Part II often dramatise erotic desire as an erosion of the border that separates inner and outer, self and world. Take, for example, Valentine's soliloquy as he mourns his banishment from Milan, and more importantly, from his beloved Silvia. Forced outside Milan's city limits, he questions the boundaries in his life, those that separate him from Milan, from his lover and even from death:

> And why not death rather than living torment?
> To die is to be banished from myself.
> And Silvia is myself; banished from her
> Is self from self, a deadly banishment.
> What light is light, if Silvia be not seen?
> What joy is joy, if Silvia be not by?
> Unless it be to think that she is by
> And feed upon the shadow of perfection.
> Except I be by Silvia in the night,
> There is no music in the nightingale;
> Unless I look on Silvia in the day,
> There is no day for me to look upon.
> She is my essence, and I leave to be,
> If I be not by her fair influence
> Fostered, illumined, cherished, kept alive.
> I fly not death to fly his deadly doom:

Tarry I here, I but attend on death,
But fly I hence, I fly away from life.
>   (*The Two Gentlemen of Verona* III, i, 170–87)

At first, Valentine draws on the metaphorical domain of banishment to conceptualise death and separation; but not for
long. Apparently, this domain's clear delineation of inside,
outside and the boundary between them is too rigid to
accommodate Valentine's relationship to Silvia, who constitutes both his inner self and the world outside it. 'Silvia is
myself' (172) but she is also Valentine's place, the light in
his world, the 'day for me to look upon' (181). Craving her
nearness, he reiterates three times in four lines his need to be
'*by* Silvia'; yet somehow she also is his 'essence' (182), inex-
tricably part of or inside him. Although the famous questions
in *The Two Gentlemen of Verona* are '*Who* is Silvia? *What* is
she' (IV, ii, 39, emphasis added), Valentine himself turns out
to be preoccupied with the question, *where* is Silvia? Is she
outside or is she inside him?

Where do our lovers exist for us? When characters such
as Valentine conceptualise their lovers as place, they con-
form to a tendency that Kenneth Burke recognised when he
observed that characters can be 'treated as scenic conditions
or "environment," of one another'.[3] In these introductory
pages, I consider different philosophies of place pertinent
to the dynamics of desire in Lyly and Shakespeare, focus-
ing in particular on *Two Gentlemen of Verona*. While, at
first glance, this may seem like bloodless cartography, it will
become obvious that the stakes of erotic desire shift when we
open ourselves to the beloved as place. When our boundaries
are so fiercely compromised, we risk displacement from our
own secure sense of self. To become vulnerable to a lover's
'fair influence' is to contend not just with possibilities for
betterment but with the frightening, downright ontological
prospect that we might 'leave to be' in his or her absence. Of

course, the prospect of 'leav[ing] to be' can be enticing for some; it can cue ecstasy, or being 'beside oneself', another experience structured by metaphor. Valentine's longing to flee himself in Silvia's absence is shaped by the 'Divided-Person metaphor',

> according to which, [Lakoff] explains, a person is under-stood as an 'ensemble' containing the Subject (the locus of consciousness, rationality, and subjective experience) and the Self (the bodily and functional aspects of a person, including emotions, a past history, social roles, and more), with the Subject normally 'either inside, in possession of, or above the Self.[4]

For Valentine, the distance that separates him from Silvia extends to his own divided person. His erotic displacement widens the gulf between subject and self – but since 'Silvia is myself' *and* she is also Valentine's world, he is doubly displaced in her absence.

Valentine's struggle to locate Silvia either in himself or out in the world exemplifies what Kenneth Burke calls 'the paradox of substance'. Philosophically, substance is an onto-logical word, one that refers to the intrinsic quality of beings. Substance is the stuff of which we are made, and as such it defines us. But etymologically, as Burke points out, substance is an extrinsic and therefore a scenic word: 'Literally a person's or a thing's sub-stance would be something that stands beneath or supports the thing.'[5] Since substance refers to both the thing itself and what is outside the thing (what it is *not*), this term presents what Burke calls an 'unresolvable ambigu-ity' that illustrates the interdependence of the intrinsic and the extrinsic.[6] Even the most basic distinctions between self and world – or what Burke calls 'agent' and 'scene' – must contend with this paradox. Burke's 'scene–agent ratio', which maintains that the nature of agents should be consistent with the nature of the scene, both depends on and subverts the distinctions between agents and scenes that make the ratio useful. So too with Valentine, who is not so much consistent with his scene as he is conflated with it. In the throes of erotic desire, he embodies the paradox of substance. In Burkean terms, his desire renders him an agent suddenly and acutely vulnerable to his scene.

Although critics such as Stanley Wells have charged *The Two Gentlemen of Verona* with 'organic deficiencies' with regard to putatively authentic characterisation and genuine erotic experience (George Eliot was famously 'disgusted' with the ending), it is noteworthy that Valentine's speech often is cited as an exception.[7] Charles Hallet's critique of the play's many 'reversals' softens when he considers the 'touching sentiment' of Valentine's soliloquy. 'Though the process of reversal lacked credibility,' he writes, 'Shakespeare's Valentine feels its effects deeply.'[8] Inga-Stina Ewbank proposes that this credibility is a result, somewhat paradoxically, of the formal features of Valentine's speech, 'in which verbal patterning is functional and central'. Familiar poetic conventions that take on new meaning for Valentine lead Ewbank to hear 'a genuine ring of agony as the metaphors in Valentine's speech stop being conceits and become live reality'.[9] The authenticity that Ewbank identifies is an effect not of an overwrought poetic metaphor, but of a conceptual metaphor that emerges from Valentine's lived experience.

Valentine's confusion about where he ends and the world begins raises the at once alluring and frightening probability that lovers inhabit one another and the world at the same time. He wrestles with this prospect when he declares that

> She is my essence, and I leave to be,
> If I be not by her fair influence
> Fostered, illumined, cherished, kept alive.
> (182–4)

Valentine equates Silvia with himself ('She is my essence'[10]), only immediately to conceptualise her as a source of life and sustenance outside himself, using the metaphorical domains of maternity and astrology. Because both of these domains elide the paradoxical potential of the scene–agent divide, they offer Valentine alternative ways to conceptualise Silvia's place in (or out of) his world. Verbs such as 'fostered,' 'cherished' and, to a lesser extent, 'kept alive' draw from the metaphorical domain of maternity, by which Valentine conceives himself as a part of Silvia but not coextensive with her. Likewise, the words 'illumined' and 'influence' tap into the domain of astrology, specifically the power of the stars to affect beings under their sway.[11] These source domains, like erotic desire itself, threaten Valentine's integrity as an individuated self, but they also allow him to imagine various relationships with Silvia that range in their degrees of interdependence, separateness and power.

When Valentine abandons the metaphor of banishment in favour of more permeable metaphorical domains that obscure, or perforate, the boundary between scene and agent, he raises questions about how erotic desire changes our relation to the world around us. For Valentine, Silvia does not even have to be physically present to him in order to be his world. If she 'be not by' (175), he would be satisfied simply 'to think that she is by / And feed upon the shadow of perfection' (176–7). In this instance, metaphors of eating put pressure on the borders between agent and scene. Disquieting here is the possibility that Valentine might consume Silvia or, at least, her shadow.[12] The metaphorical domain of cannibalism extends and perverts the nourishment of a mother's 'foster[ing]' care but, however perversely, Valentine activates a primary metaphor when he conceives of his lover as a meal to be eaten. Erotic activity, from kissing to nibbling to oral sex, entails physical ingestion of a part of our lovers. Claude Rawson notes that the overlap between gastronomic and erotic metaphors, exemplified in the Ovidian kiss, signals a desire for the 'amorous intermerging' of lovers.[13] But all-consuming, total incorporation would prove a 'deadly banishment' indeed.

Valentine's experience of 'deadly banishment' is shaped by the 'container schema', which structures our most basic conceptualisations of ourselves and our relationship to the world.[14] This schema belongs to a category of primitive conceptual structures called image schemas, which emerge from our sensorimotor experience and orient us in space. The container schema allows us to conceptualise bounded regions in space via inside, outside and boundary, and it plays a central role in erotic experience. It shapes some of the most pervasive erotic metaphors (such as 'Love is fluid in a container,' 'Lust is pressure in a container'), along with the many metaphorical expressions they generate: being or falling in love, being in a relationship or a marriage, being 'into' someone or learning that 'he's just not that into you', being in a frenzy, and so on.[15] Valentine's fear of being 'banished from myself' (171) tells us that he conceptualises himself both as the boundary and as the entity that breaks through it – the container and its contents.

The container schema is such a powerful cognitive structure because it draws on our most fundamental embodied experiences. 'Our bodies are containers', write Lakoff and Johnson,

> that take in air and nutrients and emit wastes. We constantly orient our bodies with respect to containers – rooms, beds, buildings. We spend an inordinate amount of time putting things in and taking things out of containers. We also project abstract containers onto areas in space, as when we understand a swarm of bees as being *in* the garden.[16]

If the body as a container is abundantly familiar on the primitive level that Lakoff and Johnson point out, it has special significance in light of early modern notions of embodiment. The early modern body is a container of humours but it is permeable through the eyes, ears and mouth. Gail Kern Paster describes humoral bodies as 'earthly vessels defined by the quality and quantity of liquids they contain'.[17] As for their permeability, Paster conceives of 'the passions and the body that houses them in ecological terms – that is, in terms of the body's reciprocal relation to the world'.[18] For Paster, the study of emotion is the study of how early modern bodies inhabited the phenomenal world. Vulnerability and permeability characterise much of our embodied experience in and of the world, especially for those who are 'in the throes of strong feeling'.[19] The reciprocity to which Paster calls our attention runs throughout the opening lines of Valentine's soliloquy. Contemplating his banishment from Milan prompts Valentine to place himself in all three slots of the container schema – inside, outside and the boundary itself – rather than just outside the city walls. Ecologist of desire that he is, Valentine collapses the distinctions of the container schema, only to reconstruct them with Silvia at the centre. If 'Silvia is myself' (III, i, 172), then she both inhabits him and contains him.

Hence Valentine's conception of Silvia as scenic is, after all, Aristotelian, but in Irigarayan terms.[20] Whereas Aristotle sees place as an opaque and solid container, Irigaray insists on the sort of reciprocity that Paster describes. For Irigaray, who has famously written, 'as for woman, she is place', the porousness and permeability of woman-as-place is made possible by erotic desire.[21] The female body is always open and yet also able to contain and envelop her lover. Edward Casey compares Irigaray's complicated definition with Aristotle's: 'place as enclosure is affirmed [in Irigaray], but only insofar as the elements that make up place inhabit and suffuse the universe as a whole, now considered as a gigantic sievelike vessel – which, though entirely enveloped, leaks throughout'.[22] Irigaray's emphasis on permeability derives from her consideration not only of woman-as-place, but also of the role that sexuality plays in our relation to the world. 'There are times', she writes, 'when that relation of places in the sexual act gives rise to a transgression of the envelope, to a porousness, a perception of the other, a fluidity.'[23] Sexual permeability signals an openness to the world, incarnated in a beloved.

When Valentine is forced out of the world, he has only language with which to conjure the absent Silvia. For better or for worse, it is not easy for Valentine to 'feed upon the shadow of perfection' (III, i, 177) in his banishment:

> O thou that dost inhabit in my breast,
> Leave not the mansion so long tenantless,
> Lest, growing ruinous, the building fall
> And leave no memory of what it was.
> Repair me with thy presence, Silvia.
> Thou gentle nymph, cherish thy forlorn swain.
>   (V, iv, 7–12)

Although Valentine identifies Silvia as 'thou that dost inhabit in my breast' (7), she is a curiously absent tenant. Where Silvia's overwhelming presence once permeated Valentine's self and world, her absence now hollows him out. And with a 'mansion so long tenantless' (8) in his breast, Valentine fears that the container itself will begin to collapse. Permeability, once an instrument for conceptualising desire, has become for Valentine a vehicle for conceptualising loss. The boundary between self and world is compromised as much by Silvia's 'fair influence' (III, i, 183) as it is by her absence. Where is Silvia when the walls of the mansion are on the brink of crumbling, 'leav[ing] no memory of what it was' (10)? Where is anyone when there are no boundaries (not even the memory of a boundary) to distinguish one place from another, or from ourselves? Taken to this extreme, permeability gestures toward both the dream and the nightmare of desire: that Silvia is everywhere, if indeed she is anywhere. And if Silvia is everywhere, then where is Valentine?

Before he meets Silvia, Valentine appears to know where he is and where he wants to be. The opening words of the play establish his independence of mind: 'Cease to persuade' (I, i, 1), he commands his protean friend before leaving him to strike out on his own. But Valentine's discovery of Silvia among 'the wonders of the world abroad' (I, i, 6) jeopardises his own place in that world. His servant Speed is the first to notice the difference in him: 'now you are metamorphosed with a mistress, that when I look on you, I can hardly think you my master' (II, i, 29–31). And yet, *contra* Speed, metamorphosis does not fully account for Valentine's particular experience of desire – he is not so much *changed* by Silvia as he is *lost*, cancelled or emptied out by his longing for her. Valentine responds in kind when he laments his banishment in the following act, refusing even to answer to his own name:

> *Pro*: Valentine?
> *Val*: No.
> *Pro*: Who then? His spirit?
> *Val*: Neither.
> *Pro*: What then?
> *Val*: Nothing.
>
> (III, i, 193–8)

Where and what is Valentine? No spirit, no name, not even a thing. The nightmare of desire is that Silvia has so overwhelmed Valentine that even his 'spirit' is banished. And this loss in particular cues our sense that he is spent, that he has been reduced to a state of post-coital depletion. Once, Silvia could replenish or even constitute his essence. If she can still do so now, it takes the paradoxical form of filling him with emotions that empty him out. When Valentine and Proteus volley the words 'No Valentine' four times in five lines (III, i, 210–14), his absence is rendered glaringly, and again paradoxically, present. Hence the metaphor of the ruinous, tenantless mansion of Valentine's breast; barely standing and dismally empty, it exists only to bear the mark of a tenant who no longer lives there. This haunting image of the empty container poses a quiet but palpable threat to any metaphor of desire as openness, receptivity or permeability.

In the following chapters, I investigate erotic metaphors of spatial containment and permeability in Lyly's and Shakespeare's plays. Permeability, which may leave at least some version of our selves intact, is, for Lyly's and Shakespeare's characters, accessed through domains of fluidity, melting, disrobing or, more generally, metamorphosis. Chapter 3 surveys these metaphors in Lyly's *Endymion*, a play in which erotic intimacy is imagined largely as an interior experience. Chapter 4 focuses on Shakespeare's *Antony and Cleopatra*, in which the lovers make worlds of each other. Permeability has the capacity to be a more accommodating host to conceptualisations of desire than full-blown displacement. After all, some of its source domains highlight the generative properties of erotic desire. But because fluidity can lead to dissolution, it can also turn destructive. Feeding and nurturing shade into cannibalism. Sexual penetration becomes violent. In both Lyly's and Shakespeare's plays, metaphors of permeability mark characters who are vulnerable to, hungry for and humbled by their scenes. As Gaston Bachelard writes, 'On the surface of being, that region where being *wants* to be both visible and hidden, the movements of opening and closing are so numerous . . . that we could conclude on the following formula: man is half-open being.'[24]

Notes

1. Carolyn Steber, '9 Differences Between Loving Your Partner and Being in Love with Them, According to Experts'.

2. Kenny Sogunle, 'The Difference Between Falling in Love and Loving Someone'.

3. Kenneth Burke, *A Grammar of Motives*, 7.

4. Jan Purnis, 'Bodies and Selves: Autoscopy, Out-of-Body Experiences, Mind-Wandering and Early Modern Consciousness', 200. Purnis quotes George Lakoff, 'Sorry, I'm Not Myself Today: The Metaphor System for Conceptualizing the Self', 102.

5. Burke, *A Grammar of Motives*, 22.

6. Ibid., 24.

7. See Stanley Wells, 'The Failure of *The Two Gentlemen of Verona*', 161–73. Wells is quoted in Charles A. Hallet, '"Metamorphising" Proteus: Reversal Strategies in *The Two Gentlemen of Verona*', 153. For a discussion of George Eliot's reaction to the play, see Inga-Stina Ewbank, '"Were man but constant, he were perfect": Constancy and Consistency in *The Two Gentlemen of Verona*'.

8. Hallet, '"Metamorphising" Proteus', 172.

9. Ewbank, 'Were man but constant', 103–4.

10. Like 'substance', the word 'essence' presents a paradox that obscures the distinction between scene and agent. Entry four in the *OED* defines 'essence' as '"substance" in the metaphysical sense; the reality *underlying* phenomena; absolute being' (emphasis added). The fifth entry, which cites Valentine's lines, even more explicitly defines 'essence' as a scenic word: 'that by which anything subsists; foundation of being'. See 'essence, n.,' in *The Oxford English Dictionary*, 2nd edn, 1989, *OED Online*, Oxford University Press. Available at: <http://dictionary.oed.com/cgi/entry/50078144> (last accessed 4 October 2009).

11. The *OED* defines 'influence', first, as 'the action or fact of [water] flowing in', and also as an astrological term: 'the supposed flowing or streaming from the stars of an ethereal fluid acting upon the character or destiny of men, and affecting sublunary things generally'. See 'influence, n.,' in *The Oxford English Dictionary*, 2nd edn, 1989, *OED Online*, Oxford University Press. Available at: <http://dictionary.oed.com/cgi/entry/50116443> (last accessed 4 October 2009).

12. The domain of eating is often used to conceptualise sexual activity as a threat to the boundary between self and world. See Claude Rawson, 'I Could Eat You Up: The Life and Adventures of a Metaphor'. For a broader anthropological context for this metaphor, see also Claude Levy-Strauss, *The Raw and the Cooked*.

13. Rawson, 'I Could Eat You Up', 107.

14. See George Lakoff and Mark Johnson, *Philosophy in the Flesh*, 337–90.

15. Zoltán Kövecses, *Metaphor and Emotion*, 26, 29.

16. Lakoff and Johnson, *Philosophy in the Flesh*, 36.

17. Gail Kern Paster, *Humoring the Body*, 6. Paster points to similarities between modern cognitive science and the early modern psycho-physiology of the passions. Both models reject post-Enlightenment mind–body dualism, emphasising instead biological materialism and the embodied mind. See pages 17–21, 25–7. Mary Thomas Crane draws upon Paster's work, as well as Lakoff and Johnson's theories, when she emphasises 'the importance of spatial image schemas of the body as a container, vulnerable to various kinds of penetration and impressionability'. See Crane, *Shakespeare's Brain*, 161.

18. Paster, *Humoring the Body*, 18.

19. Ibid., 19.

20. Luce Irigaray, 'Place, Interval: A Reading of Aristotle, *Physics IV*'.

21. Ibid., 35.

22. Edward Casey, *The Fate of Place: A Philosophical History*, 336.

23. Irigaray, 'Place, Interval', 41.

24. Gaston Bachelard, *The Poetics of Space: The Classic Look at How We Experience Intimate Places*, 222.

CHAPTER 3

'A PETTY WORLD OF MYSELF': INTIMACY AND EROTIC DISTANCE IN *ENDYMION*

At the end of Act II, John Lyly's Endymion is bewitched into an onstage slumber, in which he remains for nearly half of the play. Among the minor plots that unfold around his slumbering body is the comic episode featuring Sir Tophas, the *miles gloriosus* of Lyly's play. Infatuated with a geriatric sorceress, Tophas announces to his page, Epiton, that he is no longer a complete 'noun substantive' (III, iii, 16), but instead has become 'a noun adjective . . . because I cannot stand without another' (III, iii, 17–19). Although Tophas's passionate desire for the old hag is ridiculous, his suggestive declaration of his reliance upon her resembles Valentine's line about depending on Silvia's 'fair influence' to be 'kept alive'. Epiton, who considers himself impervious to love, chides his master's foolish behaviour, calling him 'an amorous ass' (III, iii, 120). He eventually falls out of favour with Tophas but he tells his fellow pages not to worry, for he can be 'complete' (IV, ii, 15) even while he is in disgrace with his master:

> I am an absolute microcosmos, a petty world of myself. My library is my head, for I have no other books but my brains; my wardrobe on my back, for I have no more apparel than

is on my body; my armoury at my fingers' ends, for I use no
other artillery than my nails; my treasure in my purse. *Sic
omnia mecum porto.*

(IV, ii, 40–5)[1]

Epiton describes an agent who carries his scene on his back;
the absolute microcosmos is sealed up, complete and impen-
etrable. He needs nothing and desires no one.

Although this fantasy of self-containment is as unattainable as the moon herself (Epiton promptly sets off to
appease Tophas and mend their relationship), it is a powerful counterpoint to the plight of characters in the play like
Endymion and Eumenides, who 'are in love up to the ears'
(I, iii, 1). To be 'a petty world of myself' is to escape the
vulnerability consequent upon opening oneself to desire.
Bachelard writes of 'half-open' beings; but what does this
mean? Is not even the smallest aperture, the slightest per-
foration, a categorical openness? Is the only way to avoid
the threat of displacement to seal oneself within the chaste
embrace of Aristotelian place? The improbable fantasy that
any of us could be perfectly finished or 'complete' looms
large in a play whose eponymous hero falls hopelessly in
love with the moon, 'whose figure of all is the perfectest'
(III, iv, 165).

Eumenides calls his friend's passionate, if hopeless, desire
for the moon 'monstrous' (I, i, 30): how exactly does one
make love to a giant rock in the sky? Most scholars under-
standably do not take Endymion at his word when he
declares his love; instead, they construe his odd affection in
three more palliative, if less charming, ways. The first variety
of interpretation brings Cynthia down to earth by fastening
on to her incarnation as Endymion's Queen. David Bevington favours this approach when he writes, 'the Cynthia in
Lyly's play is certainly *like* the moon', claiming that Endymion creates 'an elaborate conceit *comparing* his mistress to

the moon'.[2] Most critics share Bevington's view of Cynthia as more mistress than moon, although the second variety of interpretation specifies that the mistress is Elizabeth I. This, in turn, gives rise to allegorical readings – a regular feature of Lyly scholarship – according to which *Endymion* is Lyly's own panegyric to his Queen.[3] A fortunate by-product of both of these interpretive stances is that they happen to circumvent the moon problem.

In the end, we never do comprehend the precise nature of Endymion's beloved. Endymion never makes Bevington's comparison. Instead, he avers plainly that he 'love[s] the moon', praising Cynthia's 'settled course', her 'increasing and decreasing', and her ability to 'waxeth young again' (I, i, 20–1, 40, 42, 59). She is sometimes called Cynthia in the opening scene but at other times she is 'the moon'. In the same breath, Endymion praises her as a 'thing' and 'my mistress' (57). This proliferation of names, each with its own sense, suggests not only ambiguity but also multiplicity and abundance.[4] It cues the presence of the moon (at times waxing, at times waning) in every utterance of Cynthia's name, just as it signals the presence of a female body behind each reference to the moon's celestial one. Still, it is telling that Endymion declares his desire to 'possess the moon' (18) some fifteen lines before Cynthia is properly named. If we follow Endymion's lead, we are forced to grapple with the strange problem that plagues him throughout the play: how *does* a man make love to the moon?

The third and most popular way around this question is to interpret Endymion's love as chaste reverence rather than passionate erotic longing.[5] These readings often emerge from allegorical readings because such devotion to Elizabeth is somewhat at odds with staging intense and all-consuming erotic desire.[6] As Michael Pincombe notes, 'For Lyly, the very creation of the panegyrical figure of Eliza tends to suppress the erotic drama that he was really more interested in and more committed to.'[7] But if we loosen our attachment to allegory and take our cues from Endymion's words, we find that he in no way suppresses the erotic drama. Loving the moon is the height of both eros and drama for Endymion, who specifically rejects the more tepid designations of 'loyalty and reverence' and 'honour' in favour of 'love' and 'pleasure' (V, iv, 165, 172–5). Of course, it is difficult to conceive of any pleasure that one can take in the solitary and isolating experience of loving the moon. The erotics of such a fixation can easily be read as one-sided or masturbatory, but I argue that Endymion finds fulfilment in what, by the end of the play, develops into a shared erotic relation with Cynthia.

Before Endymion and Cynthia achieve anything like mutuality, Lyly's protagonist pines in solitude, as any lover might for an unattainable beloved. In the play's opening scene, Eumenides worries that his friend's overwhelming desire for the moon will cause Endymion to 'deprive himself of the sight of the sun' (I, i, 91–2), and soon enough his fear comes to pass. By Act II, a frustrated Endymion declares that his love for Cynthia has pulled him out of the world in which he sees 'nothing excellent, nothing immortal' (II, i, 48). For Endymion, as for so many of Lyly's protagonists, to fall in love is to withdraw inside himself, dwell in fantasy and speak in soliloquy – hence, choose solitude over sociability. Unlike Shakespeare's Valentine, who pines for his beloved's nearness and 'influence', Lyly's Endymion *requires* a vast distance separating him from the one he loves. Alone on stage, he begs Cynthia, 'Remember my solitary life, almost these seven years. Whom have I entertained but mine own thoughts and thy virtues? What company have I used but contemplation?' (15–18). Endymion bemoans his isolation from the world and yet he spends his solitude contemplating, even celebrating, this quality in Cynthia, 'whose perfection alloweth no companion nor comparison' (28–9). While Cynthia's remoteness elevates her in the night sky, Endymion's reclusive life burdens him with a physical 'heaviness' (II, iii, 23) that 'nail[s him] to the ground' (IV, iii, 12) in a slumber that claims him for nearly half the play.

Endymion's lovelorn slumber is presented as a curse: his sleeping body, immobilised and impervious to the flutter of activity surrounding him, manifests the simultaneously isolating and unravelling experience of consuming (in this case, unrequited) love. His predicament is peculiar and yet it is familiar: people who do not reciprocate love are as distant as the moon. They confirm the boundary between self and world by reminding us of what we cannot have, of what is always outside our grasp. But unrequited love is also conducive to pleasure. Endymion may be said to fall in love with someone outside his grasp, and so to suffer. Or we may say that he *chooses* to love someone he can never have, and that he does this because there is something in it for him. Although Cynthia's indifference torments him, it seduces him as well. For nearly half of his opening speech, Endymion fixates on Cynthia's immunity to outside influences, coveting the moon as a 'thing' (I, i, 57) that affects others but is not affected, 'whose fair face neither the summer's blaze can scorch nor winter's blast chap, nor the numbering of years breed altering of colours' (63–6). Endymion's discourse is, among other things, a fantasy of invulnerability. 'Time cannot touch' (66–7) Cynthia but then neither can Endymion. The very qualities that make her impervious to erotic desire – indeed, to desire of any sort – unleash Endymion's desire in response, making him all the more desperate to move the 'unmovable' (36) moon.

This fantasy of perfect intactness draws from the language around Cynthia, who is 'of all circles, the most absolute' (III, iv, 179). What would Endymion do with such a being if he were ever able to 'possess' her (I, i, 18)? Her very shape, 'a circle of all figures the perfectest' (III, iv, 177), presents not only a geometric ideal but also an ontological one: Gaston Bachelard defines 'roundness' as the purest form of being. It seems impossible to imagine a tangible or sexual connection to such perfection, but an erotic quality emerges when Bachelard describes its allure: 'Everything round', he writes, 'invites a caress.'[8] Endymion, too, conceives of Cynthia's physical shape in distinctly erotic language, imagining her waxing and waning form as 'coming out of thy royal robes where-with thou dazzlest our eyes' (I, i, 74–5). But for Endymion, any form of contact with such perfection dazzles; to behold Cynthia's 'fullness' (69) all the time would be overstimulation. Thus, he spends much of his opening speech praising Cynthia for her ability to pull back, to 'detract from thy perfections' and modestly 'decrease thy gleams' (71, 73) most nights of the month, magnifying the distance between them. With an erotic power so great that her admirers cannot glimpse her without 'conspir[ing] to ravish' her (69), Cynthia's ability to magnify the distance between them protects Endymion from his own overwhelming desires.

For Endymion, indulging in such distance is what he must do in order to conceive of Cynthia's majesty. Stepping back and elevating her may be the only way he can hold all of her in his mind or in his regard. Bachelard writes about the experience of looking at a village from different vantage points. From close up, we cannot conceive of the entire vil-lage – we see it only in small slivers until we pull back far enough to capture the whole. But no matter how much space separates Endymion from Cynthia, he cannot quite possess her in the irenic way that Bachelard imagines: 'Distance dis-perses nothing, but, on the contrary, composes a miniature of a country in which things become reconciled. They then offer themselves for our "possession," while denying the distance that created them. We possess from afar, and how peacefully!'[9] Endymion finds no peace in looking up at the sky. Although he dreams early in the play of 'possess[ing] the moon' (I, i, 18), he either cannot or will not deny the distance that separates them. Instead, he relishes the distance, praising Cynthia for her strangeness above all else, eroticising the very things that stand in the way of his dream.

Such a decisive boundary separating him from Cynthia should crystallise Endymion's sense of self but these boundaries have the opposite effect: they cloud his identity. To defend against this loss, Endymion becomes desperate to prove himself to Cynthia – to demonstrate his love and to assert his mere presence, repeating in soliloquy, 'I am that Endymion . . . that Endymion . . . that Endymion' (II, 1, 37–8, 40, 44). By Act II, his soliloquy takes on the language of self-exposure rather than that of generous praise, becoming a desperate plea for his beloved's attention, a form of enlargement. 'To use a magnifying glass is to pay attention,' writes Bachelard, 'but isn't paying attention already having a magnifying glass? Attention by itself is an enlarging glass.'[10] Endymion's hunger for enlargement – his need to be seen and known by Cynthia – intensifies as he hides from the world. In the opening soliloquy of Act II, Endymion describes his alienated existence as that of a man 'who, divorcing himself from the amiableness of all ladies, the bravery of all courts, the company of all men, hath chosen in a solitary cell to live only by feeding on thy [Cynthia's] favour' (II, i, 44–7). Deeply isolated and self-contained, Endymion none the less 'feed[s]' on the moon – he is not completely alone. Endymion reveals his permeability to Cynthia even from the confines of his 'solitary cell'. He soliloquises but he addresses his words to Cynthia, too. This makes for an intimacy with her that is oddly predicated on the distance between them, both theatrically (he *is* speaking in soliloquy) and spatially (she is present but distant).[11]

At the end of his soliloquy, he reveals his wish that Cynthia will recognise his isolation as evidence of his love: 'Thus mayst thou see every vein, sinew, muscle, and artery of my love, in which there is no flattery nor deceit, error nor art'

(II, i, 48–50). Retreat from the world's gaze is none the less tantamount to utter exposure to the object of desire, to a wish to be stripped barer than naked, stripped of his skin. Lyly could have figured Endymion's exposure as an act of disrobing, shedding clothes rather than flesh, baring his naked body instead of his innards. But he opts for a more disturbing level of exposure: Endymion's desire makes visible that which ought to be hidden from Cynthia's penetrating gaze. The image that Endymion conjures in his desperate attempt to assert his identity does violence to it. Indeed, he aspires to still greater visibility than this. In conversation with Eumenides, he laments that his 'thoughts have no veins, and yet, unless they be let blood, I shall perish' (I, i, 31–2).[12] Swollen with thoughts of desire, Endymion seeks his remedy in another act of exposure, this time of his blood. The restorative powers of bloodletting call to mind the relief of ejaculation, another potential purgation for Endymion's thoughts of love.[13] On the one hand, he imagines a kind of orgasmic release at knifepoint. On the other hand, he would expose himself by peeling back layer after layer until nothing at all is left.

Endymion nearly gets his wish at the end of Act II, when he falls into a slumber so deep that it threatens to obliterate him altogether. Cynthia and Eumenides both refer to Endymion's onstage coma as a 'dead sleep' (III, i, 2; III, iv, 18–19) after decades pass without any change in his condition. Such an all-consuming slumber might seem to offer an escape from vulnerability by pulling Endymion out of the world. But sleep can deepen one's connection to the world, as Garrett Sullivan suggests in his study of vitality in the sixteenth and seventeenth centuries. Sleep was imagined as a way of interacting with one's environment by tapping into the lower faculties – the vegetative and sensitive parts of the Aristotelian tripartite soul. As a state of vegetation, sleep fosters what Sullivan calls a creature's 'compliant relationship to its environment'.[14] Endymion's prostrate body manifests his compliant relationship with Cynthia. In sleep, he yields to a beloved who stands for the world.[15]

The permeability Endymion achieves in sleep signals his vitality. His 'dead sleep' turns out to be quite lively, filled with vivid dreams that are, first, dramatised in dumb show (II, ii) and then narrated by Endymion when he awakens (V, i). Sleep, even a deathly one such as Endymion's, can be an unusually dynamic and creative state of being.[16] In a study of onstage slumber in medieval and Renaissance plays, David Bevington argues that Endymion's prolonged sleep dramatises his inner conflict. Sleep, according to Bevington, can expose a character's defencelessness. 'In several late Elizabethan plays,' he writes, 'sleep is presented not as slothful or inattentive, as in so many medieval dramatizations, but as the innocent rest of those who are about to be victimized.'[17] Right before our eyes, Endymion's onstage slumber dramatises vulnerability, openness and displacement just as profoundly as his metaphors do.

Sleep is a permeable state, but the moments just before and after sleep are especially so. These in-between states often foster 'hypnagogic' experiences, which Andreas Mavromatis defines as 'hallucinatory or quasi-hallucinatory events taking place in the intermediate state between wakefulness and sleep'.[18] One of the most common features of hypnagogia is a heightened state of receptivity and suggestibility. According to Mavromatis, hypnagogic experiences open the subject to both external suggestion (from the experimenter) and internal suggestion (from the subject's own imagination). Endymion's uncharacteristically long sleep and protracted waking render him especially vulnerable to Cynthia, and perhaps more significantly, to his own imaginings of her.[19] If, following Mavromatis, a 'loosening of ego boundaries' or 'egolessness' lies 'at the root of all hypnagogic experiences', then Endymion's precarious grasp on his own identity, before falling asleep in Act

II and then just after waking in Act V, testifies to his loosened ego boundaries, which are conceptualised in terms of dissolution or melting away.[20]

At the end of Act II, Endymion desperately seeks an escape from the inner world that preoccupies him, resolving to 'beguile myself with sleep; and, if no slumber will take hold in my eyes, yet will I embrace the golden thoughts in my head and wish to melt by musing' (II, iii, 4–7). Such sleep may offer Endymion escape but it intensifies his solitude, opening him to the world and removing him from it. His private dreams are exposed to the audience's gaze and later to Cynthia's enquiry. When Endymion recounts his dreams for Cynthia, we discover that the 'golden thoughts' he longed to indulge took a darker turn in sleep. His first dream features 'a lady passing fair but very mischievous'; holding a knife in one hand and a 'looking glass' in the other, she threatens to cut his throat (V, i, 88–90). Although her two attendants try to sway her – one in the direction of cruelty, the other toward mercy – the lady at last curbs her violent impulse upon seeing her reflection in the mirror. The dream elicits a conflicted reaction from Endymion: 'I started in my sleep, feeling my very veins to swell and my sinews to stretch with fear, and such a cold sweat bedewed all my body' (98–101). Sexually aroused at the prospect of capturing the lady's attention, Endymion's swelling body realises the erotic potential of what Bachelard describes as 'a consciousness of enlargement'.[21] The lady's knife, penetrative and castrating, arouses fear and lust in Endymion's sleeping body in equal measure.[22] Act II's 'embrace' is now, in Act V, first threatened by violence and then pre-empted by a nocturnal self-embrace that reaches beyond the dream world of 'golden thoughts' into the physical world in which Endymion's 'sinews . . . stretch' and he then 'bedew[s]' his body.[23]

Endymion's alarming dream (along with his charged reaction to it) becomes the play's own nightmare to sort out.[24]

What can it mean that the Cynthia figure in Endymion's vision carries a knife in one hand and *a looking glass* in the other? Although these two implements may seem like strange bedfellows, the image of a powerful woman wielding the mirror and knife would have been familiar to early modern audiences – and was certainly familiar to Lyly. The lady in Endymion's dream evokes Anatomia, 'the reductive deity of division', who presided over the dissecting room.[25] For Jonathan Sawday, Anatomia is 'a mistress of erotic reduction – a fantasy expression of male surrender – whose chief attribute was the power to divide'.[26] While she dissects with her knife, Anatomia studies the body with a looking glass, exposing and cataloguing its mysterious inner workings. It comes as little surprise that Endymion conjures this deity in his nightmarish fantasy of Cynthia, whom he had implored to 'see every vein, sinew, muscle, and artery of my love' (II, i, 49–50). This crucial episode in Endymion's dream reveals the terrifying fantasies (or are they realities?) that inform his desire to be made visible, knowable and vulnerable to Cynthia's piercing gaze. Vulnerability, from the Latin *vulnerare* (to wound), is recast from an emotional or psychic experience into a physical reality in Endymion's dream.[27]

Of all the dream material that Endymion recounts, this stands out as the only episode that animates his sleeping body. If Endymion's slumber represents a kind of living death, then his dream truly exemplifies the permeability of this state, poised as it is between his real and fantasy worlds, with material effects that extend beyond his imagination. In his dream, Endymion finally gets his wish: at last, the lady sees him. But at what cost? She threatens to see him as meticulously and comprehensively as he wants to be seen – beneath the clothing that covers him and under the flesh that contains him. The lady is not the only one who threatens to scrutinise and dissect him. His dream affords Endymion the opportunity to turn the mirror back on himself and see his desire reflected there, following his need for exposure all the way through to its terrifying and fatal conclusion. When the lady relents, she re-establishes the distance Endymion praised Cynthia for – diminishing her glow and her 'fullness' (I, i, 69). From this new latitude, her gaze permits him to exist. By choosing the mirror over the knife, the lady upholds the emblem of re-established distance; where the knife promises full disclosure, the mirror signifies indirection or mediation. It offers only reflection and representation.[28] As it turns out, the lady's mercy protects Endymion not from her malicious companion who 'provoked her to execute mischief' (V, i, 95), not even from the lady's own violent impulses, but rather from *himself* – from his overwhelming and destructive desire for a level of exposure that is tantamount to self-effacement.

It bears remembering that Endymion is not alone in his desire for self-effacement; his masochistic urge plagues the other lovelorn characters in the play.[29] His best friend Eumenides, who has fallen hopelessly in love with the recalcitrant Semele, apparently desires a similar escape: 'Ah, I faint, I die! Ah, sweet Semele, let me alone, and dissolve by weeping into water!' (III, iv, 79–81). Eumenides's wish, first, to be 'let . . . alone' and then to dissolve by weeping into a well, echoes his friend's desire for solitude and 'to melt by musing'. Although David Bevington glosses Eumenides's line as a wish for his own dissolution ('let me dissolve . . . ') the subject of the verb is unclear. Eumenides could either desire his own dissolution into water, or he could wish that 'sweet Semele' would dissolve as a result of his weeping. This ambiguity reflects – and, moreover, enacts – Eumenides's desire for dissolution; it also brings him dangerously close to Semele, gesturing toward an intimacy unlike any that Endymion can share with Cynthia, one that might render Eumenides indistinguishable from his beloved.

Endymion melts away not only in sleep, but also in the scene of his waking. He is released from the soporific spell that has bound him for decades by a kiss from Cynthia, whose mouth, she proclaims, 'hath been heretofore as untouched as my thoughts' (V, i, 25). He receives her kiss while in a state of heightened permeability – in sleep – and the kiss ushers in a hypnagogic suggestibility that opens Endymion to her influence in ways that equally threaten and confirm his sense of self. Although Cynthia's lips cause Endymion 'to stir' (30), he wakes with a feeble grasp on his own identity. Distraught by his friend's inability (or unwillingness) to speak upon waking, Eumenides asks, 'hath this long sleep taken away thy memory?' (37); and again, 'Hast thou forgotten thyself, Endymion?' (43). Although Endymion is uncertain about his own name (his first words are, 'Endymion? I call to mind such a name' [42]), he recognises Cynthia's name as soon as it is uttered. Only after she names him properly – 'I am Cynthia, and thou Endymion' (52) – does he take possession of himself. A slumber that turned Endymion into an 'absolute microcosmos' now leads him to a disorienting and overwhelming dependence on his beloved to secure his identity, to will him back into existence with her mouth and voice.

Sleep and hypnagogic waking are both destructive (egoless) and generative. Mavromatis writes that creativity is linked to hypnagogia (in his chapter on creativity, he has a section on 'Openness'), citing examples of artists, from Goethe to Keats, who believed that sleep provided them with a creative spark either in dreams or upon waking.[30] The scene of Endymion's waking reveals sleep's destructive and constructive properties. His loss of self creates an opportunity for Cynthia to claim and reconstitute him with her voice. Endymion already anticipated this creativity in an earlier address to Cynthia, when he identified himself as 'that fish – thy fish, Cynthia, in the floor Araris – which at thy waxing is as white as the driven snow and at thy waning as black as deepest darkness' (II, i, 35–7). This tiny fish, utterly responsive to the changes of the moon, evokes the profound intimacy and vast distance between Endymion and Cynthia. It also confirms Endymion's egolessness and his receptivity to Cynthia across the ever-widening space that separates them. In Act V, Cynthia names him, and in Act II, the moon colours 'thy fish' in her image. Endymion's openness to Cynthia correlates with the fish's visibility to the moon, since the fish brightens only when the moon is out. But the moon also is exposed to this fish, which not only has special access to her, but which absorbs her light.

Bachelard discusses the 'intimate immensity' of such a relationship. Endymion's connection to the moon answers to our own private relationship with the immensity of the world:

> One might say that immensity is a philosophical category of daydream. Daydream . . . contemplates grandeur. And this contemplation produces an attitude that is so special, an inner state that is so unlike any other, that the daydream transports the dreamer outside the immediate world to a world that bears the mark of infinity.[31]

Bachelard's daydreamer must be at once removed from the object of contemplation and also vulnerable to the influence of the 'immense' scene that surrounds her or him. To be transported in this manner requires both distance and openness, the coincidence of which defines Endymion's relation to Cynthia's grandeur, especially in his sleep. Accounts of hypnagogia extend the category of contemplation in ways that recall Bachelard's description. Mavromatis defines contemplation as 'an attitude of placing a spatial and/or temporal distance between oneself and objects', and notes that hypnagogia traverses this distance through the experiences of 'fascination' and 'absorption'.[32] The hypnagogic subject's active absorption in 'imaginal activities' results in a kind of reciprocal absorption – what Mavromatis calls 'a *subjectification of the object*', wherein the dreamer 'internalises' the object of fascination.[33] Like the fish who absorbs the light of the moon, the hypnagogic subject absorbs the object of his fascinated attention, even across a vast distance that 'bears the mark of infinity'.

Such absorption in 'imaginal activities' risks displacement but Endymion never loses his place in the world or in the play. Although he comes close to death in his slumber and his dream, his prolonged sleep is what captures Cynthia's attention, making him most visible to her after all. Cynthia's acknowledgement of Endymion's desire grants him Bachelard's 'consciousness of enlargement', the 'feel[ing] that we have been promoted to the dignity of the admiring being'.[34] She pays attention to his attention, united in what Bachelard calls 'an identical expansion'.[35] She secures his fragile identity when she names him, and he comes as close as he will get to possessing her physically when she kisses him. When Endymion awakes to her kiss as an old man, he begs Cynthia to allow him to continue in his solitary 'sweet contemplation' (V, iv, 173). He promises her that he will 'softly call it love' (171–2) only to himself; he will 'name it honour' (173) to anyone who can hear. He longs to continue dreaming of 'impossibilities; with imagination of which I will spend my spirits' (170–1). Bevington glosses 'spend my spirits' as 'expend my breath' but surely Endymion means masturbation and orgasm.[36] What seemed like a condemnation – a life of imagining and daydreaming with no hope of 'possess[ing] the moon' – now sounds like a consummation. Endymion assures Cynthia that this contemplative existence will allow him to 'live of all men the most content, taking more pleasure in my aged thoughts than ever I did in my youthful actions' (174–6). As a reward to Endymion for his constant love, Cynthia restores his youth. Just as the fish absorbs and reflects Cynthia's fullness and colour, now Endymion waxes young again.

Endymion's situation at the end of the play looks remarkably like it did in the very beginning. Although the other characters have paired off in typical comic fashion, Endymion is (again, still) alone with his thoughts. Lyly acknowledges the generic problem of his play: his Prologue notes that 'we present neither comedy, nor tragedy, nor story, nor anything, but that whatsoever heareth may say this: "Why, here is a tale of the Man in the Moon"' (Prologue, 9–12). But what sort of dramatic protagonist ends right where he begins? Not simply a man who falls in love with the moon, Endymion has apparently become a microcosm of the moon. His solitude recalls the moon's singular place in the sky; Cynthia's perfection, according to Endymion, 'alloweth no companion nor comparison' (II, i, 29). But the difference between Endymion's solitude and his youth in Acts I and V is that these qualities have been reconstituted as gifts from and reflections of Cynthia. Endymion finds a way out of his earlier nightmare: like the lady in his dream, he chooses the mirror over the knife. An open container receptive to the erotic scene that surrounds and overtakes him, Endymion has been renamed and remade by Cynthia, in her image.[37] He now *shares* his solitude with her.

Endymion achieves what Valentine cannot sustain during his banishment: an ability to feed upon shadows and find nourishment there. Just as Silvia is both scenic and partial agent to Valentine, so Cynthia is Endymion's consummate scene (the moon is, of course, everyone's scene). Now she inhabits him as well. For Valentine, distance erases even the memory of his beloved but Endymion carries Cynthia's 'unmovable' (I, i, 36) presence with him always; she never leaves the mansion of Endymion's breast. Both Cynthia and Endymion are made immense through such an interaction; by devoting his imagination to Cynthia, Endymion enlarges her in his mind. Although she is perfect in the night sky, Endymion's attention is what completes her where she lives in his imagination. Bachelard sees this mutual expansion depicted in a poem by Rilke, in which the speaker contemplates the immense image of a tree. 'The tree needs you', Bachelard writes, 'to give it your super-abundant images, nurtured in your intimate space ... Then, together, the tree and the dreamer, take their places, grow tall.'[38] Endymion opens himself to Cynthia in the way Bachelard's dreamer brings the infinite grandeur of the world into his consciousness through contemplation.

Bachelard's description of intimate immensity is based on a version of permeability that is both catastrophic and constructive: 'It would seem, then, that it is through their "immensity" that these two kinds of space – the space of intimacy and world space – blend. When human solitude deepens, then the two immensities touch and become identical.'[39] The mutuality that Bachelard describes pertains to Endymion's regenerated inner life, now no longer purely solipsistic or narcissistic. If, as Paster argues, the relation between self and world is reciprocal, it need not be equal or balanced.[40] The asymmetry between Endymion and Cynthia separates them and it allows them to participate together in an imaginative union.

When Cynthia rejuvenates Endymion, she praises his constant affections, commanding him to 'persevere, Endymion, in loving me, and I account more strength in a true heart than in a walled city' (V, iv, 179–80). Although this is a command, Endymion has been primed to receive it as a gift. 'Love me,' he hears her say. Think about me. Take me into your imagination. *I give myself to your imagination.* What she offers him is not possession as Endymion initially conceived of it; rather, by sanctioning his fantasies, Cynthia gives him an imaginative claim on her. He has her permission to make and remake her in his mind, just as she has remade him in fact. Surely this kind of shared authorship is erotic, so to imagine Cynthia is, for Endymion, to be generative and possessive, too. Endymion's bond with Cynthia recasts Levinas's claim that infinity cannot be synthesised or assimilated, perhaps because Endymion is first assimilated *by her*.[41] It is, after all, Endymion's very egolessness that finally secures his purchase on Cynthia. His receptivity inspires Cynthia's receptivity to his 'true heart' in return.

Cynthia's comparison of Endymion's heart to 'a walled city' recalls boundedness and self-sufficiency, the 'absolute microcosmos' of Epiton's imagining. Although I began this chapter by dismissing Epiton's image as the stuff of dreams, I return to it in order to suggest that the fantasy of the absolute microcosmos may be attainable not as an escape from desire, but instead as an indulgence of desire. Endymion's desire for Cynthia seals him off from the rest of the world but it also binds her to him, keeping her within the sturdy walls of his imagination, where he can feed on her shadow. In other words, Epiton's microcosmos is, for Endymion, a *form* of desire. One can love perfection only from a great distance; intimacy with infinity takes place in the imagination, where Endymion can claim Cynthia entirely, where she never loses her glow. She is Other, but she is also his – container and contained, inside and outside, both. Desire for something infinite and immense, for someone perfect and unattainable, can only ever take the form of imaginative pleasure. Lyly's *Endymion* insists that this pleasure is also profoundly erotic.

Notes

1. *Sic omnia mecum porto*: 'Thus I carry all things with me.' The word 'microcosmos' is doubly significant in these lines, since the Tophas and Epiton subplot functions as a kind of microcosm of the main action in *Endymion*.

2. Bevington, 'Introduction', in *Endymion*, 1–72, esp. 16 (emphasis added). Compare Mary Beth Rose's description of *Endymion*: 'The hero of the play conceives an impossible, idealizing love for the Moon, who . . . descend[s] to the action in the form of a chaste and benevolent queen' (*The Expense of Spirit*, 24). Philippa Berry specifies a queen in her account

('the male courtly lover was called upon to imitate his queen'), while the moon functions as a symbol ('the private, emotional and feminine sphere of experience symbolized by the moon') in *Of Chastity and Power: Elizabethan Literature and the Unmarried Queen*, 115.

3. Most scholarship on *Endymion* starts from this allegorical premise. See Michael Pincombe's chapter on self-allusion and panegyric in *Endymion* (*The Plays of John Lyly*, 79–112) for a representative example. Natalia Khomenko notes that *Endymion* was 'presented as a panegyric' ('"Between You and Her No Comparison": Witches, Healers, and Elizabeth I in John Lyly's *Endymion*', 56). Christine M. Neufeld argues that the ambiguity of Cynthia's form is a way of exploring Elizabeth's unique power, which 'lay in the creative potential of her contradictions, not in her concretisation of a stable identity – a condition Lyly seeks to celebrate in Cynthia' ('Lyly's Chimerical Vision: Witchcraft in Endymion', 365).

4. I use the word 'sense' following Gottlob Frege's distinction between a term's sense (its mode of presentation) and its reference (the object it signifies). See 'On Sense and Reference', 37.

5. Historically, critics have been hard on Lyly for this abstract and esoteric treatment of eroticism on the stage. One such example is Mary Beth Rose's account of Lyly's 'view of sexual love as abstract and impersonal, polarized, static, emotionally simple, and morally predictable' (*The Expense of Spirit*, 35). Although scholarship has emerged that challenges this view for other Lyly plays (most notably *Galatea* and *Love's Metamorphoses*), Endymion's desire is typically read as devotion to a queen or neo-Platonic love. C. C. Gannon explains Endymion's contemplation of Cynthia in neo-Platonic terms: 'The Endymion myth symbolizes the virtuous man's yearning for God and God's reciprocal desire to unite souls to him' ('Lyly's *Endimion*: From Myth to Allegory', 224).

6. One notable exception to this tradition is Jacqueline Vanhoutte's essay, 'Age in Lust: Lyly's *Endymion* and the Court of Elizabeth I'. As her title suggests, Vanhoutte sees in Endymion's lust an allegorical figure of the ageing courtier,

particularly relevant to Elizabethan England when the play
was first performed in 1588 (51).

7. Pincombe, *The Plays of John Lyly*, 79.
8. Bachelard, *The Poetics of Space*, 236. The final chapter of
The Poetics of Space, 'The Phenomenology of Roundness',
has the premise '*das Dasein ist rund*, being is round' (232–41,
esp. 234).
9. Ibid., 172.
10. Ibid., 158.
11. Soliloquies have often been charged with creating theatrical
distance and detachment. On this dynamic in Shakespeare,
see Michael Mooney, *Shakespeare's Dramatic Transactions*,
1–22, and Kent Cartwright, *Shakespearean Tragedy and Its
Double: The Rhythms of Audience Response*, 11–20.
12. Images of veins appear in several speeches and convey a
painful and unnatural experience of permeability. At Endymion's waking, he recounts a dream that features a clus-
ter of beetles that suck the blood from an eagle's vein in
order to kill it (V, i, 143–8). Tellus also mentions veins in her
account of her passion for Endymion, which caused her to
feel 'a bursting in almost every vein' (V, iv, 87–8).
13. Humoral physiology links blood and semen through the process of transmutation. Elaine Hobby notes the commonly held
belief that 'special vessels in the men's stones (testicles) turned
blood into semen', in her 'Note on Humoral Theory', in Jane
Sharp, *The Midwives Book, Or the Whole Art of Midwifery
Discovered*, xxxiii. An excess of bodily humours could cause
frenzied erotic desire, which could be relieved by bloodletting
or ejaculation. For the political consequences of such purgation in Shakespeare's *The Rape of Lucrece*, see Catherine
Belling, 'Infectious Rape, Therapeutic Revenge: Bloodletting
and the Health of Rome's Body'.
14. See Garrett A. Sullivan, Jr, *Sleep, Romance and Human
Embodiment: Vitality from Spenser to Milton*, 16.
15. Ibid., 16. If, as Sullivan suggests, the sleeping body 'blurs the
distinctions among man, plant and animal' (1), Endymion's
slumber might close the gap that separates him from Cynthia

by producing a shared connection. With heightened beastly and plantly faculties, Endymion too becomes an ambiguous, indeterminate creature.

16. I am indebted to William Sherman for introducing me to the creative properties of sleep in his paper, 'Revisiting the House of Sleep', presented at the Shakespeare Association of America meeting, Washington, DC, April 2009.

17. See David Bevington, 'Asleep Onstage', 66.

18. Andreas Mavromatis, *Hypnagogia: The Unique State of Consciousness between Wakefulness and Sleep*, 3. Mavromatis notes that Aristotle used the term 'psychagogia' in his *Poetics* to account for the audience's experience of captivation in the theatre.

19. This vulnerability may also extend to the actor who plays the sleeping Endymion; he becomes the object of the audience's gaze without being able to look back.

20. Mavromatis, *Hypnagogia*, 68.

21. Bachelard, *The Poetics of Space*, 184.

22. The erotic aspects of this dream have not been addressed in Lyly scholarship. Bevington interprets the dream as a repudiation of Endymion's 'lusts', which, he argues, 'are not expressly erotic; indeed, we have seen how he turns to Cynthia as a release from his own carnality' (*Endymion*, 23). Eros enters Bevington's analysis of the dream with respect to Tellus rather than Cynthia. In Endymion's dream, he argues, 'The errant protagonist must learn to eschew ... fleshly desire (in the person of Tellus)' (26). Although we hear that Endymion once loved (and perhaps lusted for) Tellus, we never see this in Lyly's play; what we do see is Endymion's expressly erotic infatuation with Cynthia.

23. The early modern association between lust and sleep can be traced to the period's predominating belief in the Aristotelian tripartite soul. Garrett Sullivan notes that both conditions reside in the sensitive, or animal, rather than the rational soul: 'passionate excess and immoderate sleep are states of being over which reason has no restraining influence' (Sullivan, *Sleep, Romance and Human Embodiment*, 17). Sleep was

often understood to be a form of passionate excess in its own right. Although sleep is sometimes imagined as 'a *binding* of the senses', Sullivan points out that it also 'encodes an *overindulgence* of the senses' (18).

24. Although Cynthia promises Endymion that 'Gyptes at our better leisure shall expound' the dream (V, i, 103–4), he never does. Bevington notes that 'the audience is left to interpret for itself' (103–4n).

25. Jonathan Sawday, *The Body Emblazoned: Dissection and the Human Body in Renaissance Culture*, 3. Mark Dooley has noted Lyly's familiarity with anatomy in *Euphues* and in *Love's Metamorphosis*. Of the latter play, Dooley writes, '*Love's Metamorphosis* develops the links between the emerging medical discourse of anatomy and the use of texts to explore or anatomize particular concepts' ('The Healthy Body: Desire and Sustenance in John Lyly's *Love's Metamorphosis*', §2). Dooley compares the character of Famine in *Love's Metamorphosis* with Sawday's Anatomia, since both women present 'a picture of the interior of a body; a picture which is designed to place emphasis on its physical workings in order to better understand its requirements' (§13). In *Love's Metamorphosis*, Famine has 'skin so thin that thou mayest as lively make an anatomy of her body as she were cut with chirurgeons' (qtd in Dooley, §13).

26. Sawday, *The Body Emblazoned*, 184. Anatomia's accoutrements have a rich history in their own right, originating with a monstrous woman who inspired many a nightmare: 'The attributes of *Anatomia* – the knife and the mirror – return us to the Medusa myth, and that structure of reflective glances and reductive instruments associated with the donations of Athene and Hermes to Perseus – the hunter of the Medusa' (183). Freud associates Medusa's head with the terror of castration in his 1922 essay, 'Medusa's Head': 'To decapitate – to castrate. The terror of the Medusa is thus a terror of castration that is linked to the sight of something' (Freud, 'Medusa's Head', 202). This 'terror of castration' is cued by Endymion's horrified response to the lady's knife as it angles toward his outstretched throat.

27. The *OED* lists the Latin *vulnerābilis* (wounding) and *vulnerāre* in the etymology of 'vulnerable'. See 'vulnerable, adj.', in *The Oxford English Dictionary*, 2nd edn, 1989, *OED Online*, Oxford University Press. Available at: <http://www. oed.com/view/Entry/224872> (last accessed 21 June 2014). Within the early modern 'culture of dissection' (Sawday, *The Body Emblazoned*, 3), the physical wound was often conceived in profoundly erotic terms. Sawday cites the episode from Golding's translation of Ovid's *Metamorphoses*, complete with Lylian sinews and veins, in which Apollo flays the satyr Marsyas: 'Nought else he was than one whole wounde. The griesly bloud did spin / From every part, his sinewes lay discovered to the eye, / The quivering veynes without a skin lay beating nakedly' (qtd in Sawday, *The Body Emblazoned*, 186). Sawday describes Marsyas's body as 'caught in a moment of violent homoerotic possession', his entire body made vulnerable and visible as it transforms into a 'whole wounde' (186).

28. The mirror's reflection of an object recalls dissection: Sawday writes, 'It is, perhaps, this very impossibility of gazing within our own bodies which makes the sight of the interior of other bodies so compelling. Denied direct experience of ourselves, we can only explore others in the hope (or the fear) that this other might also be us' (*The Body Emblazoned*, 8).

29. Later in the play, Cynthia curses Tellus, 'who is made all of love' (IV, iii, 131), with a fate similar to Endymion's 'wish to melt by musing' (II, iii, 7): she will be left to 'melt herself in her own looseness' (IV, iii, 131–2).

30. See Mavromatis, *Hypnagogia*, 186–218, for the chapter entitled 'Creativity'.

31. Bachelard, *The Poetics of Space*, 183.

32. Mavromatis, *Hypnagogia*, 70. Mavromatis describes these phenomena in response to Jean-Paul Sartre's accounts of hypnagogia. See Sartre, *The Psychology of Imagination*, 48–51.

33. Mavromatis, *Hypnagogia*, 70.

34. Bachelard, *The Poetics of Space*, 184.

35. Ibid., 202.

36. Bevington, *Endymion*, 170–1n.
37. Cynthia's kiss can be understood as a version of the Ovidian kiss that Claude Rawson singles out for its 'attempted incorporation' (Claude Rawson, 'I Could Eat You Up: The Life and Adventures of a Metaphor', 107). Because Cynthia is divine, such a kiss poses no threat to her life. Taking from the moon does not diminish her glow.
38. Bachelard, *The Poetics of Space*, 200. Bachelard continues, 'Never, in the dream world does a tree appear as a completed being.'
39. Ibid., 203.
40. In his study of Irigarayan place, Edward Casey writes about this kind of reciprocity 'in the capacity of each sex to "receive the self and envelope the self." Between men and women there has to be reciprocal (albeit asymmetrical) transport: '"mutual enveloping in movement"' (328). Quotations in Casey are from Irigaray, 'The Envelope: A Reading of Spinoza, *Ethics*, "Of God"', 93, and 'Place, Interval', 54, respectively.
41. See Chapter 2's discussion of Levinas.

CHAPTER 4

BINDING THE VOID: THE EROTICS OF PLACE IN *ANTONY AND CLEOPATRA*

When Antony leaves for Rome in Act I of Shakespeare's play, Cleopatra is left alone to indulge in a vision of him on his horse. She asks Charmian,

> Where think'st thou he is now? Stands he, or sits he?
> Or does he walk? Or is he on his horse?
> O happy horse, to bear the weight of Antony!
> Do bravely, horse! For wot'st thou whom thou mov'st?
> The demi-Atlas of this earth, the arm
> And burgonet of men. He's speaking now,
> Or murmuring 'Where's my serpent of old Nile?'
> For so he calls me.
>
> (I, v, 18–26)

Two things stand out in Cleopatra's daydream: first, its unmistakable eroticism, and second, its preoccupation with Antony's whereabouts. Its eroticism lies in Cleopatra's desire not simply to observe Antony on his horse but to become the 'happy horse' he mounts, to 'bear the weight of Antony' (20) herself. Of course, much later in the play, Cleopatra must cope with the arduous physical reality of overcoming Antony's weight when she and her women hoist his body into her monument. But here, in Act I, she takes pleasure in her fantasy of Antony's body bearing down on hers and in the reciprocating prospect of supporting his weight from beneath him. If Cleopatra's fantasy is palpably erotic – perhaps sodomitical, or submissive, or bestial, or idolatrous – it is also manifestly placial.

Cleopatra would have it that she can both *be* Antony's place and *place* him: that is, fix him in time and space ('Ah, ha! You're caught!' [II, v, 16], she later dreams). Cleopatra's playfulness competes with her longing; it becomes clear that erotic self-indulgence is in contention with a compulsion to locate her lover. Her 'Where think'st thou he is now?' is just one among many iterations of what we might call interrogative place deixis. At her second entrance, Cleopatra asks, 'Saw you my lord?' and 'Was he not here?' (I, ii, 79). 'Where is he?' (I, iii, 1) are her first words in the following scene, then 'See where he is' (I, iii, 2). Even in her dream, Cleopatra imputes to Antony an answering version of her recurring compulsion: '*Where's* my serpent of old Nile?' (I, v, 25, emphasis added). So compelling is the question of 'where' for Cleopatra that she voices it in her fantasy of her lover's private murmurs.

Of all the murmurings that she could dream into the mouth of her 'demi-Atlas' (22), Cleopatra's 'where' confirms our readiness to charge love with the daunting task of anchoring or placing us in the world. Often conceptualised through spatial schemas, love can create for us a sense of place, but it can also produce a profound anxiety about displacement. We observed this with Valentine in *The Two Gentlemen of Verona*, and Cleopatra, too, appears to suffer from what Edward Casey calls 'place-panic'.[1] At the very start of the play, Cleopatra is already concerned about boundaries. Antony must specify precisely 'how much' (I, i, 14) and then 'how far' (I, i, 16) he loves her. She, in turn, will 'set a bourn how far to be beloved' (I, i, 16). John Gillies identifies Cleopatra's desire for a bourn as part of the classical trope of orbic limits, and he comments that 'this image of limits is also an image of desire'.[2] To impose limits is to define and therefore enable desire.

As we have seen elsewhere, in both Lyly's and Shakespeare's plays, erotic desire threatens the possibility of contained place more often than it confirms it. The language of desire in *Antony and Cleopatra* stubbornly invokes the container schema, only to reveal immediately that its limits are inadequate. Like Endymion's wish for veins to contain but ultimately to purge his thoughts, the boundaries of Antony and Cleopatra's affair seem to exist only to be breached. Permeability is cued at every turn, from the swelling of the Nile (II, vii, 20) to Antony's own body, unable 'to hold this visible shape' (IV, xiv, 14). Even the play's opening image of Antony's 'dotage . . . o'erflow[ing] the measure' (I, i, 1–2) depends upon the container schema and violates its limits. Given Shakespeare's insistent dramatisation of Antony and Cleopatra's affair as boundary-breaking, it is reasonable to ask, *to where* exactly does Antony's dotage overflow? What exists outside place, beyond 'measure'? Would the 'new heaven, new earth' (I, i, 17) of Antony's imagining more effectively contain desire? Or is it uncontainable? Perhaps it is an undifferentiated and unbounded void into which Antony's 'captain's heart . . . hath burst' (I, i, 6, 7), and in which Cleopatra will find herself if she fails to heed Charmian's caution to 'keep yourself within yourself' (II, v, 75). Edward Casey writes that 'the prospect of a strict void, of an utter no-place, is felt to be intolerable. So intolerable, so undermining of personal or collective identity is this prospect, that practices of place-fixing and place-filling are set in motion right away.'[3] It is this daunting prospect of empty space that prompts Cleopatra's frequent enquiries into Antony's whereabouts. If he is somewhere, anywhere, then the 'great gap' (I, v, 5) of his absence can be contained.

In Cleopatra's language of limits and longing for boundaries, I find evidence of the play's larger investment in the erotics of placiality. In this chapter, I explore the erotic implications of bounded place and of limitless space in order to trace the erotics of placing one's lover, both metaphorically and physically, in fantasy and in reality, in *Antony and Cleopatra*. I begin by exploring the erotics of place, as opposed to space. A close examination of the language of containment in Shakespeare's play reveals that the 'bourn' of bounded place obtains its erotic charge from the metaphor of sexual bondage, drawing, as it does, from the formal and temporal features of masochism. When Antony and Cleopatra emplace one another or become each other's place, they typically enfetter and embrace one another. The language of sexual bondage responds to the threat of infinite and empty space that looms just beyond the bounded places in the play. This threat takes on particular significance in light of early modern scientific theories about the existence of a cosmological void. In *Antony and Cleopatra*, the lovers eroticise the void by imposing the sturdy boundaries of place on to vacant space. Binding the void allows them to *present* this vacancy to one another, enabling pleasurable experiences of self-loss and self-forgetting. It is, finally, at Cleopatra's monument in Act V that the erotic dynamics of place and endless space converge, 'find[ing] out' (I, i, 17) for the lovers a 'new heaven, new earth' within its walls.

It is perhaps easiest to conceptualise place (as opposed to space) as erotic, since it often takes on the characteristics of an embrace. Aristotle's *Physics*, a foundational work that connects place to containment, defines 'place' as the inner surface of a tight-fitting container that envelops a being. Edward Casey describes Aristotelian place in cosy terms: 'a material thing fits snugly in its proper place, a place that clings to that thing'.[4] Aristotelian place is disciplinary: it encloses and it binds. The disciplinary bondage of place can be rich and generative, like a boundary in the special signification that Heidegger detects in the ancient Greek conception of *horismos*, 'horizon', itself derived from *horos* (boundary): 'that from which something *begins its presencing*'. For a place is indeed an active source of presencing: within its close embrace, things get located and begin to happen.[5]

But what we find in *Antony and Cleopatra* is that 'close embrace' can take the form of the 'Egyptian fetters' that Antony 'must break / Or lose myself in the dotage' (I, ii, 115–16). On the one hand, there is disability; on the other, the pleasure that Antony anticipates when he commands Cleopatra to 'Chain my armed neck' (IV, viii, 14) after he triumphs in battle. Or the pleasure of embrace and the pain of captivity entwine, like 'a lover's pinch, / Which hurts, *and* is desired' (V, ii, 295–6, emphasis added). For the infinitely various Cleopatra, there is no contradiction here. The erotic appeal of circumscribed place is augmented even as (or because) it closes in on her. The strength of its hold only confirms our place in the world, staving off what Edward Casey refers to as 'the existential predicament of place-bereft individuals . . . depression or terror even at the idea, and still more in the experience, of an empty place'.[6]

The erotics of place are tellingly captured in Enobarbus's account of Cleopatra on her barge, enclosed within the confines of 'her pavilion' (II, ii, 209). Enobarbus frames the Queen in the 'close embrace' of his narrative. The scene overpictures Cleopatra even as she overpictures Venus – her barge 'burned' (II, ii, 202); gold is 'beaten' (II, ii, 202); oars 'stroke' (II, ii, 205) and 'beat' (II, ii, 206) the water; and perfume 'hits the sense' (II, ii, 222). Such aggressive verbs reveal the masochistic charge of Cleopatra's eroticism, which in turn provokes the violent scene that Enobarbus describes. Yet Cleopatra herself is apparently impervious or oblivious to the fierce bondage of her surroundings. She 'set[s] a bourn'

(I, i, 16) by functioning as a limit rather than a boundary. According to Casey, whereas boundaries are imposed from outside, limits are internal properties of the entity inside the frame. In a commentary on Euclid's *Elements of Geometry*, Proclus writes, 'the limits surrender themselves to the things they limit; they establish themselves in them, becoming, as it were, parts of them and being filled with their inferior characters'.[7] It is counterintuitive but eminently logical that infinitely various Cleopatra should be restricted or finite, even a source or seeker of limits. Her bondage is part of a collaborative undertaking; beyond the limit that Cleopatra establishes within herself exists the boundary that corrals her from outside, in both Enobarbus's captivating words and the audience's collective imagination.

Amidst the tumult of beating oars, the surge of lustful water and the flutter of 'divers-colored fans' (II, ii, 213), Cleopatra is exceptionally still. Like an inanimate portrait of Venus, she is a fixed point around which 'pretty dimpled boys' (II, ii, 212) and 'gentlewomen' (II, ii, 216) constellate.[8] Even when we hear that she 'O'erpictur[es] that Venus where we see / The fancy outwork nature' (II, ii, 210–11) – as if Cleopatra's 'own person' (II, ii, 207) breaks through the barge's aesthetic and Enobarbus's narrative frame – we never quite see that 'person' as opposed to the ornate, enclosing scene. Enobarbus imbues her scene (or is it his?) with erotic longing, with masochistic pleasure ('the oars . . . made / The water which they beat to follow faster, / As amorous of their strokes' [II, ii, 204–7]) and with phallic arousal ('the silken tackle / Swell with the touches of those flower-soft hands' [II, ii, 219–20]). What can account for the pleasure that we (along with Enobarbus and his onstage audience) take in this imaginative exercise of placing Cleopatra, if not the pleasures of sexual bondage? In our collective desire for her – our longing to know her, to 'word' (V, ii, 192) her, to 'encloud' her in our 'thick breaths' (V, ii, 212–13), to pin her down and so fix her in space and time – we too occupy this scenic frame, binding Cleopatra in our fantastic embrace. To bind one's lover is to prolong desire for the binder and the bound, drawing out the moments before sexual gratification. The account of Cleopatra on the Cydnus has a similar effect: it removes us from the present scene in Rome and brings us into a state of arrest, engaging but stymieing our desire, inciting but not quite appeasing hunger. This is true not only for the audience but also for Antony and for the crowd that gazes on Cleopatra within the narrative frame. Indeed, everyone who watches her approach is bound up in the same lyrical state of prolonged desire. A collective state of arrest prevails within the theatre. No one is immune. So it is with sexual bondage, which begins with a clearly delineated captor and captive but then sees both participants being absorbed into the experience of suspended desire and deferred gratification.

The slow and deliberate erotic pace of this scene corresponds to the aesthetic and temporal rhythms of masochism. Cleopatra's lyrical approach on the Cydnus forces her audience(s) into the attitudes of waiting and suspense that Gilles Deleuze identifies as 'essential characteristics of masochistic experience'.[9] According to Deleuze,

> This is partly because the masochistic rites of torture and suffering imply actual physical suspension (the hero is hung up, crucified or suspended), but also because the woman torturer freezes into postures that identify her with a statue, a painting or a photograph.[10]

Enobarbus's speech casts Cleopatra in the role of both the captive and the captor: she is enfettered by the 'silken tackle' (II, ii, 219) of Enobarbus's scenic frame, but she is also frozen in the posture of Venus, the woman torturer of Deleuze's description. It is Cleopatra's 'infinite variety' (II, ii, 246) that seems to allow her to occupy both roles

within the masochistic relationship throughout the play.
From Act I, when she repeatedly enquires into Antony's
whereabouts, to Acts IV and V, when she awaits Antony's
(and then death's) arrival in her monument, we are accus-
tomed to seeing Cleopatra in the masochist's posture of
waiting. Waiting is arguably Cleopatra's main action in the
play. Her imaginative engagement with Antony – her ability to conjure him and the pleasure she takes from placing
him with her mind – blossoms in his absence and depends
upon her experience of suspended time.[11] What is unique
about the barge scene, then, is that now she makes *Antony*
wait. She even makes the air around Antony wait for her,
unable as it is to leave him and look on her without making
'a gap in nature' (II, ii, 228). Her erotic power threatens
to undo nature, and yet here it emerges from her captivity.
Being placed so firmly and securely in Enobarbus's account
releases a compensatory mobility for Cleopatra; bondage
affords her erotic freedom, a power over time and space
that she can command from within the scenic frame.

Although Enobarbus can describe Cleopatra's scene in
painstaking detail, 'her own person' (II, ii, 207) is ineffable;
it 'beggared all description' (II, ii, 208). As Jonathan Gil
Harris observes, the Egyptian Queen is glaringly absent from
Enobarbus's account. She is framed by his words but the picture inside is blank:

> her 'cloth of gold' thus encloses what is effectively 'a gap in
> nature'. The speech serves as a rhetorical counterpart of a
> rococo mirror, its extraordinarily ornate and copious frame
> enclosing a subtly camouflaged glass in which Enobarbus's
> Roman listeners glimpse whatever they want to see.[12]

While Harris contends that Cleopatra's absence functions
as a mirror for Roman desire, I believe that her corporeal
absence – which, like her statuesque stillness, is itself a source

of masochistic power – signifies nothing more or less than empty space, a 'gap' – and *not* a mirror – 'in nature' (II, ii, 228). Enobarbus encourages us to entertain this possibility, to take Cleopatra out of the picture but not to replace her, not even with an object of our own imagining (as Harris suggests). What do we imagine, for example, when we hear these words?

> The city cast
> Her people out upon her; and Antony,
> Enthroned i' th' marketplace, did sit alone,
> Whistling to the air; which, but for vacancy,
> Had gone to gaze on Cleopatra too,
> And made a gap in nature.
>
> (II, ii, 223–8)

Enobarbus's description of the city violently displacing her people evokes a deeper and more profound void than just an empty place. Drained of air, the marketplace becomes a vacuum – an active and aggressive negative space that reinforces the threat of the void that dominates a great deal of the play.

For all the bounty, surfeit, fecundity and overflow that we hear about in Act I, Antony and Cleopatra draw frequently from the metaphorical domain of vacancy in those early scenes. The cues are multiple: 'absence' (I, ii, 171), 'oblivion' (I, iii, 90), 'idleness' (I, iii, 93–5), 'vacancy' (I, iv, 26) and 'gap' (I, v, 5). Such gaps – in nature and time – pose a particular threat within the context of early modern scientific and religious thought. Speculations by early modern theologians and scientists gave rise to what Edward Casey has called 'the ascent of infinite space' over localised place in medieval and Renaissance philosophy.[13] The rise of spatiality resulted in part from a list commissioned in 1277 by Pope John XXI of 219 condemnations of doctrines that limited the power of God, including God's ability to make new worlds or move the

present world to a different location. In order to accommodate these new cosmological possibilities, the spatial imagination itself grew more capacious. Edward Grant traces the
intellectual process that gave rise to the new prominence of
voids and vacuums: 'If God moved the world rectilinearly,
it was further assumed not only that a void space would be
left behind but also that the world itself moved into and out
of other empty spaces that lay beyond.'[14] To defend God's
power, then, was to acknowledge at least the *potential* – if
not the real presence – of infinite and endless space.

Not surprisingly, the concept of a void or vacuum has
proved difficult to accept or even to conceive. The existence
of a sheer void – the existence, that is, of empty space with
no fixed referent at all, no boundaries to mark anything –
comes at a high ontological and epistemological cost, and
thus has been hotly contested from antiquity to the present
day.[15] Edward Grant summarises the debate over the void's
existence, its physical features and its philosophical, religious
and scientific implications:

> The void was from the outset, and almost inevitably, sub-
> jected to a double entendre. Was it an unintelligible, total
> privation incapable of existence – a true 'nothing'? Or was
> it a nothing conceived of as a something, a something with
> definite properties that could range from a pure dimen-
> sionless emptiness to a three-dimensional magnitude, and
> even be conceived of as God's infinite and omnipresent
> immensity?[16]

According to Grant, all of these conceptualisations have
existed at one time or another: in fact, many at the same
time. While Aristotle's definition of the void as 'place bereft
of body' depends upon the void's boundedness as a place, the
Stoics imagined a void without bounds, defining the universe
as 'a finite material world surrounded by an infinite extended

void space'.[17] The void was debated on the basis of its dimensionality (can it be measured?), its conceivability (can it be imagined?) and even its location in the cosmos (are vacuums positioned in between bodies within the bounded universe or are they extracosmic, stretching beyond the known horizon?). Historically, the range of responses to these questions has been as broad as the array of questions themselves, and the stakes of the different claims have been high.

We have already seen Antony and Cleopatra invoke multiple definitions of void space throughout the play. They too are exploring dimensions and implications of the void that preoccupied the philosophers and scientists who preceded them. As we might expect, the prospect of an utterly boundless and dimensionless void is so daunting for Shakespeare's characters that it is unimaginable in its purest form. Valentine comes close when he envisions the walls of the empty mansion in his breast crumbling down 'and leav[ing] no memory of what it was' (V, iv, 10). Without the memory of a boundary, he begins to approximate what a pure void might be like – but even here, Valentine *places* this spectacle of bleak spatiality within his breast. More often than not, then, vacuity is conceptualised via metaphors of displacement, specifically the threat of being cast out of a place whose boundary (or memory, at least) persists.

In *Antony and Cleopatra*, displacement is often couched in hypothetical language, marking the void specifically as a threat or a potential. Cleopatra invokes the threat when Antony leaves her in Act I and she pledges to write him every day, 'Or I'll unpeople Egypt' (I, v, 78). Her image of an 'unpeople[d] Egypt' anticipates Enobarbus's account of Cleopatra's strange ability to provoke a city to cast out its entire people. The empty space, the remainder, is perhaps best described by Francesco Patrizi of Cherso: 'When [space] is filled with a body, it is *locus*; without a body, it is a vacuum.'[18] To 'unpeople Egypt' is to evacuate its bodies;

Cleopatra's verb reminds us of the people who once lived there, even as it emphasises the negative space that remains. Her verb is also noteworthy for its disproportionality, for such wholesale depopulation constitutes a displacement that is glaringly incommensurate with the act of writing Antony a letter every day. This imbalance only heightens the void's status *as a threat*; clearly, Cleopatra has no intention of 'unpeopl[ing]' her country, so we are meant to consider the void only in hypothetical terms, as a kind of present absence. She raises the same threat in Act III, when Antony accuses her of being 'coldhearted toward me' (III, xiii, 158). If her assurance in Act I is disproportionate, her response in Act III is outrageously so:

> Ah, dear, if I be so,
> From my cold heart let heaven engender hail,
> And poison it in the source; and the first stone
> Drop in my neck: as it determines, so
> Dissolve my life! The next Caesarion smite!
> Till by degrees the memory of my womb,
> Together with my brave Egyptians all,
> By the discandying of this pelleted storm,
> Lie graveless, till the flies and gnats of Nile
> Have buried them for prey!
>   (III, xiii, 158–67)

Again, Cleopatra paints a picture of utter desolation, of 'graveless' Egyptian sons and daughters subject to a power so great that it banishes bodies from their places with tempestuous violence. Again, her wildly disproportionate response to Antony suggests that this bleak vacancy exists as an idea rather than as a reality. None the less, by conjuring it for Antony (and for herself and for us), Cleopatra insists on its potentiality just beyond her 'bourn'. The intensity, detail and sheer length of her description – ten lines in response to Antony's three-word question – demonstrate the self-indulgence of such imaginings. Like looking out at a threatening storm from the safety of an enclosed shelter, the terror of the void reinforces the necessity and the pleasures of being confined within the 'snug fit' of the place she creates with Antony.

Cleopatra speaks of the void in hypothetical, distanced language; but near the end of the play, Antony experiences this threat viscerally when his identity is at stake. He conceptualises his loss of identity as a self-inflicted banishment from the 'frail case' (IV, xiv, 41) of his body or self – a loss, that is, of place. Donald Freeman has shown that the container schema plays a vital role in Antony's conceptualisations of this loss.[19] From the depths of his sorrow and shame, Antony looks up at the changing shapes of the clouds:

> That which is now a horse, even with a thought
> The rack dislimns and makes it indistinct
> As water is in water.
>
> (IV, xiv, 11)

The horse that once constituted Cleopatra's placial fantasy of Antony now loses its shape in Antony's grief. Although the grammar of the phrase 'water . . . in water' gives the illusion of containment in a place, the image itself – water in water – overtakes the particularity of place, leaving formless space in its wake. Even as Antony experiences his loss of self as banishment from place, he looks out into the cosmos for analogues for this emptiness. Searching beyond the clouds, he laments that

> my good stars that were my former guides
> Have empty left their orbs and shot their fires
> Into th' abysm of hell.
>
> (III, xiii, 145–7)

Antony's scene, no longer an Aristotelian, circumambient enclosure ('Chain my armed neck'), has become abyssal space; the barrenness of 'th' abysm of hell' beneath him rivals the vacant orbs above. His empty orbs speak directly to the early modern interest in cosmic space, in vacuums and in gaps in nature.

Antony's 'good stars' orient him along a vertical axis, with the 'empty' heavens above and 'the abysm of hell' below. According to Francesco Patrizi, the dimension of depth distinguishes the void from previous conceptualisations of space. He emphasises the three-dimensionality of void space, adding depth where Aristotle had accounted for only breadth and length. According to Patrizi, 'the vacuum itself is nothing else than three-dimensional Space'.[20] The addition of depth (*profundum*) invests the concept of vacuity with an evaluative or hierarchal quality – things have higher value as they move up in vertical space and become 'baser' (V, ii, 290) as they move downward. This correlation exemplifies the workings of primary conceptual metaphors: the sensorimotor domain of vertical orientation structures our system of subjective judgement into metaphors such as 'more is up', 'happy is up', 'good is upright' and 'moral weakness is falling'.[21] Antony's experience of the void's verticality, then, highlights the bleakness and sense of gloom of empty space. Depth and verticality shape much of the catastrophic language in *Antony and Cleopatra*. Cleopatra imagines the threat of the void as a downward movement when she envisions 'half my Egypt . . . submerged' (II, v, 94) and when she later yearns to '[s]ink Rome' (III, vii, 15). When she dares to envision her reality of the void – death itself – she does so along the same vertical axis. At Antony's death, she laments that '[t]he crown of the earth doth melt' (IV, xv, 64), whereas Cleopatra rises up, becoming 'fire and air; my other elements / I give to baser life' (V, ii, 289–90). Death is often conceptualised in terms of vertical space because of the associations of heaven and hell with height and depth, respectively; bodies are lowered down into the ground and spirits ascend. Unlike Cleopatra, Antony retreats to the place-setting confinement of bondage when he acknowledges that 'force entangles / Itself with strength' (IV, xiv, 48–9), then imagines his death as a 'seal' (IV, xiv, 49) rather than as a dissolution. This is to seal a document but it is almost as if Antony imagines himself covered in wax. Unlike Cleopatra, who commands the asp to 'untie . . . this knot intrinsicate / Of life' (V, ii, 304–5), Antony longs to be blanketed by death, envisioning it as 'a lover's bed' that he can 'run into' (IV, xiv, 100–1).

Antony's eroticised image of being 'a bridegroom' enveloped '*in* my death' (IV, xiv, 100, emphasis added) is unsurprising in light of the pleasures he takes from bondage in life, especially life with Cleopatra. The place that Cleopatra offers him does not neutralise the threat of the void, but instead contains it and thus permits them both to explore its erotic appeal. Binding the void imposes limits on its length and breadth but preserves its depth, allowing Antony to lose himself within the place Cleopatra makes for him.[22] In *Antony and Cleopatra*, the experience of self-loss is imagined in two ways. The first is a kind of displacement, where people are 'cast . . . out' (II, ii, 223–4) of cities and even out of their bodies, with only an empty frame ('frail case' [IV, xiv, 41]) or 'gap' (I, v, 5) in their wake. Because displacement forces the lovers to contend with the daunting prospect of empty and unbounded space, this experience is rarely imagined as a source for eros. The second type of loss in the play is distinctly erotic, conceptualised as a bounded void. Bounded loss still draws from the features of space – depth, vacuity, verticality – but rather than being cast out, Antony and Cleopatra are lost *within* the place they make for one another. This type of loss depends upon metaphors of verticality (depth is what enables experiences of 'loss within' or being *over*whelmed), but unlike displacement, bounded loss plumbs the erotic potential of depth. Cleopatra explores this potential in her fantasy of being beneath Antony as his horse; there is also her fantasy of drawing him up on her fishing line.

Even at their first meeting, Cleopatra is imagined as a deep but bounded place in which Antony can reside: 'When she first met Mark Antony, she pursed up his heart' (II, ii, 196–7). Somehow, Cleopatra is able to capture and contain Antony's famously swollen heart, itself so big that it 'hath burst / The buckles on his breast' (I, i, 6–8). If to 'purse up' his heart is to envelop it, then here, at least, Cleopatra's erotic power eclipses Antony in an enclosed place wherein his heart can disappear. A still more telling account of her erotic power over Antony's heart emerges from his own fantasy, in Act IV, just after he has defeated Caesar in battle:

> O thou day o' th' world,
> Chain mine armed neck; leap thou, attire and all,
> Through proof of harness to my heart, and there
> Ride on the pants triumphing!
> (IV, viii, 13–16)

Where Antony once lamented Cleopatra's 'strong Egyptian fetters' (I, ii, 115), he now entreats her to 'chain my armed neck' (IV, viii, 15) in celebration. His identity as a soldier and a Roman newly reaffirmed, Antony takes pleasure in placing himself within Cleopatra's chain-like embrace, casting her as the erotic scene around him: 'thou day o' th' world' (IV, viii, 13). The armour around his neck is apparently not binding enough for Antony; his demand that she 'chain' his already 'armed neck' conjures another (apparently pleasurable) heavy restraint. Such an image recalls Antony's instructions to his soldiers from a few lines earlier, to 'clip [hug] your wives' (IV, viii, 8). With their roles as victors secure for the time being, Antony's place-affirming talk of 'clip[ping]' and 'chain[ing]' seems apt.[23]

This time around, Antony – or his heart, at least – is the horse and Cleopatra is the imagined encompassing rider. But what exactly does it mean to 'leap thou, attire and all, / Through proof of harness to my heart, and there / Ride on the pants triumphing' (IV, viii, 14–16)? How does one 'ride on the pants', and why 'attire and all'? Unlike Cleopatra's whimsical dream of being his horse, Antony describes a startling fantasy of a completely clothed Cleopatra riding his naked panting heart as though it were a steed. At the outset, they are both attired (he in harness, she in what?), but in due course, he becomes vulnerable, exposed and stripped down to his beating heart, while she, apparelled (perhaps in Isis's 'habiliments' [III, vi, 17]), mounts what would have to be a grossly oversized heart if it is to bear her weight. This fantasy draws from the placiality of Cleopatra's happy horse but it introduces a degree of vulnerability nowhere present in her daydream. In what is arguably his unique moment of triumph in the play, Antony submits his heart to Cleopatra's enveloping thighs.

Why would Antony choose this particular moment – the afterglow of an identity-affirming, place-fixing, heroic battle – to indulge in a fantasy of submission and envelopment, his heart receding into Cleopatra's embrace? Has this latest conquest offered him enough security and stability to stave off place-panic? Or is there something else about having one's outward identity confirmed that inspires a longing for erotic dissolution? In his 1591 tract, titled *De Vinculis in Genere* (*On Bonding in General*), Giordano Bruno contends that the desire to remain intact comes from the same source as the desire 'to be completely transported into the loved one'.[24] According to Bruno, who writes about intimacy in terms of bonds and bondage, the principal effect of Cupid's bond is a wish to be placed – for lovers to 'remain firm . . . *in* themselves' (emphasis added) – and to be displaced – 'unrestrained, opened up and thrown wide open' – at the same time: 'Thus it happens that the bond by which things wish to be where they are and not to lose what they have also causes them to wish to be everywhere and to have what they do not possess.'[25] For Bruno, the desires to be placed and to be lost are compatible rather than competing. In Antony's fantasy, his heart is not so much *dis*placed as it is *re*placed between Cleopatra's spread legs, coming into contact with the most intimate parts of her body. Each lover creates a place for the other: Antony is the steed beneath Cleopatra and her body sur-rounds Antony's heart. The image of Antony's enveloped heart recalls Bruno's description of the erotic bond, which is strongest when part of the object 'is in the bonding agent, or when the bonding agent controls it by one of its parts'.[26] Cleopatra's body enables a mitigated type of erotic loss for Antony – his heart is exposed (for neither the first nor the last time in the play), but rather than being displaced from his body with no destination, it is relocated between her legs. Antony is only lost in so far as he is given over to her pleasure.[27]

Early in the play, we learn that Cleopatra's body-as-place has inspired pleasurable loss in previous lovers. When she recounts her affair with Gnaeus Pompey, Cleopatra portrays herself as a container in which he would lose himself:

> great Pompey
> Would stand and make his eyes grow in my brow,
> There would he anchor his aspect, and die
> With looking on his life.
>
> (I, v, 31–4)

Cleopatra describes a kind of self-loss that is made possible within a bounded but deep place. Pompey can indulge in the obliterating erotic pleasures of what Jonathan Gil Harris calls 'narcissistic self-contemplation' only after she has given him a locus in which he can 'anchor his aspect'.[28] Cleopatra activates the container schema when she recalls Pompey's eyes growing '*in* my brow'. The loss that she inspires is imag-ined as a disappearance *into* a bounded but deep body that is capacious enough to 'purse up' her Roman lovers' ever-expanding bodily organs, from Antony's 'burst[ing]' heart to Pompey's 'grow[ing]' eyes. Hers is the same body that can bear up and even give birth to idleness itself: 'Tis sweating labor / To *bear* such idleness' (I, iii, 93–4, emphasis added). Pregnant with idleness, her body contains the languor and hollowness it engenders.

Less corporeal but no less coveted is the place Antony provides as a scene for Cleopatra's self-loss. The motives for Cleopatra's urge to forget herself differ from Antony's: where he is able to access the pleasures of bounded loss only after he has confirmed his martial identity, Cleopatra longs for this experience precisely when she perceives that her place in Antony's world is threatened. When Antony leaves her or when her life is at stake – that is, when Cleopatra is faced with the prospect of empty space – she seeks out the anaesthetic pleasures of a bounded place into which she can disappear:

> Courteous lord, one word.
> Sir, you and I must part, but that's not it;
> Sir, you and I have loved, but there's not it:
> That you know well. Something it is I would –
> O, my oblivion is a very Antony,
> And I am all forgotten.
> (I, iii, 86–91)

Although it sounds as if she is saying that she has forgotten what she was about to say, it is apparently *herself* that she cannot remember or be mindful of. '*I* am all forgotten', she announces, and yet she names her oblivion '*a very* Antony'. Such particularity reflects her need to impose limits on the void of oblivion. To remake her oblivion in the shape of Antony – to make, as it were, a place out of empty space – is to forget herself *in* her lover rather than in the endlessness of oblivion. It is not difficult to see the appeal of binding the void, of shaping it as one's home or one's lover. The erotic pleasures of bondage and discipline – the pleasures of setting and reinforcing limits – paradoxically liberate Cleopatra, enabling her experience of self-loss. Bondage slows time and restricts even the vastness of 'oblivion' within its confines. In effect, binding the void is what allows Cleopatra to *inhabit* it. From within its 'bourn', she can forget herself by 'sleep[ing] out this great gap of time / My Antony is away' (I, v, 5–6). To call Antony's absence a 'gap' is to settle it within boundaries, to postulate a starting and an ending point.

Of course, the play's most extraordinary contained setting is the monument, its final scene of bounded loss for both Antony and Cleopatra. The monument's sturdy walls (Plutarch describes 'gates that were very thick and strong, and surely barred'), along with its height and depth, figure this setting as the ultimate circumscribed void, a scene of both forgetting and remembering, a place for death and a space for poetic birth.[29] Although theatre historians debate the location and appearance of the monument (did Cleopatra appear in the gallery above the platform stage or was a free-stranding structure brought on to the stage?), it seems clear that its height and boundedness were among its prominent features.[30] One particularly rich dramaturgical source for this monument is the *locus* of the early modern stage (also known as the *domus* or *sedes*), which Robert Weimann describes as an enclosed, illusionistic playing space separated from the audience, often by a raised scaffold.[31] Unlike the generalised, undifferentiated *platea*, which is level with the audience, the upstage *locus* is a delimited and identifiable place such as a home or palace. In *Antony and Cleopatra*, the monument is *locus*-like in its specificity, its distinctiveness and, of course, its placiality. Raised up high, the seat of a queen (*sedes*) and wife (*domus*), the monument provides the bourn that Cleopatra desires and it offers Antony a 'visible shape' (IV, xiv, 14) at last. For Cleopatra, the monument is more hospitable than death 'on Nilus' mud', where she would lie 'stark nak'd' while 'water flies / Blow me into abhorring!' (V, ii, 58–60). Moreover, the monument's secure walls will save her from loathsome 'sweet dependency' (V, ii, 26) on Caesar. For Antony, the monument provides a refuge from the empty 'abysm of hell' (III, xiii, 147) that Stanley Cavell has described

as the retreat of the world.[32] When Cleopatra hoists Antony up
to her, she provides him with a place in which to die, in which
to bind the void.

Over the course of the play's final scenes, the monument
gains enormous psychic and representational force. Death-
bed and marriage bed, grave and throne ('put on my crown'
[V, ii, 280]), prison and fortress ('I am safe' [IV, xv, 27]),
the monument has multiple spatial, placial and erotic meanings. It is where Cleopatra experiences 'immortal longings'
(V, ii, 281) and her ever-foolish wishes (IV, xv, 38); it is built
to withstand the relentless pressure of Roman temporality;
and ultimately, it must become the 'new heaven, new earth'
(I, i, 17) of which the lovers dream and for which they die.
But before Cleopatra reconceives of the monument as an
intimate erotic place in which to 'quicken' (IV, xv, 40) her
'husband' (V, ii, 287), she must first cope with its stubborn
materiality, and with the way it initially keeps eros *out* rather
than encloses it within.

Whatever was the size of the monument, Cleopatra's language suggests that she takes solace from the fact that it binds
and restricts her. Caesar may implore her to 'make not your
thoughts your prisons' (V, ii, 186) but Cleopatra sees herself
as a voluntary captive. Her sense of confinement is most evident when twice in two lines she says she 'dare[s] not' (IV, xv,
22, 23) leave the monument's compass to kiss Antony. But to
take refuge in the monument's cold embrace is also, masoch-
istically, to defer erotic consummation. For Antony's part,
eros is not so much deferred as it is denied when he first
approaches Cleopatra's monument. If, as I have been suggesting, placiality is the primary source for eros in *Antony
and Cleopatra*, and if the monument represents the play's
most contained and defined place, then Antony's struggle to
enter its bounds reflects his inability to access the erotics of
bounded loss. Although there is little doubt that Antony has
experienced a sense of loss when he arrives there, this loss

is felt as a displacement rather than a loss *within* a place, which can evoke pleasurable self-forgetting. His heart, once imagined as an erotic organ that Cleopatra could ride, now occasions his displacement. He imagines himself dying, not from a broken heart but when his strong and intact heart is displaced from the container of his body:

> O, cleave, my sides!
> Heart, once be stronger than thy continent,
> Crack thy frail case.
>
> (IV, xiv, 39–41)

Here it is not his heart that is responsible for his displacement so much as it is his weight and the daunting height of the monument up to which he is heaved. The dimension of depth enables pleasurable self-loss but, initially, the monument's verticality is what keeps Antony from reuniting with Cleopatra and thus stands in the way of his pleasure.[33]

The lovers' struggle to overcome the monument's height recasts Cleopatra's fantasy of drawing Antony up with her 'bended hook' (II, v, 12) in an entirely different register. Now, the best on offer is to hoist his bloodied, dying body clumsily up into her monument. This awkward, even comic, staging of Antony's suspended body bound in ropes and chains spectacularly travesties the play's earlier ecstatic images of sexual bondage. However we imagine the performance of the play's stage direction, '*They heave Antony aloft to Cleopatra*' (IV, xv, 38), it is likely that some type of apparatus would have been necessary to bind Antony and then hoist his body up to Cleopatra's level.[34] Have the 'silken tackle' from Enobarbus's account of Cleopatra's barge rematerialised at her monument, now less erotic and even more functional? Certainly, Antony's heart, now panting simply to keep him alive, is no longer a horse or chariot that she can mount. Theodore Leinwand writes that Antony's wounded body in this scene is utterly impassive, indifferent to meaning or any signification at all – 'more lump than human, more brute than affect-laden'.[35] Oblivious to the monument's verticality and to its layers of meaning and significance, Antony's impassive body is more closely associated with horizontal breadth than with vertical depth. And at his death, Cleopatra imagines Antony along the same horizontal axis:

> The crown o' th' earth doth *melt* . . .
> O, *withered* is the garland of the war;
> The soldier's pole is *fallen*. Young boys and girls
> Are *level* now with men.
> (IV, xv, 64–7; emphasis added)

This gives the lie to Cleopatra's fantasy of an erect and towering Antony who 'stands . . . or walk[s]' (I, v, 18–19) at her bidding. His collapse ratifies her rueful acknowledgement that 'wishers were ever fools' (IV, xv, 38).

Cleopatra's assertion in Act V that her 'desolation does begin to make / A better life' (V, ii, 1–2) marks a shift in the monument's significance, particularly in its ability to host Cleopatra's final and ultimate experience of bounded loss. The monument's physical characteristics – its boundedness and specificity – enable Cleopatra to lose herself within the expansive scene she dreams for Antony. The association of the early modern *locus* with the *domus*, or domestic sphere, illuminates the monument's placial significance to the couple. Cleopatra offers herself as Antony's wife ('Husband, I come' [V, ii, 287]), making for him a home and marriage bed within the monument. 'The invention of marriage', writes Cavell, '*is* the (is Cleopatra's, whoever that is) response to Antony's abandonment; it is a return of the world through the gift of herself, by becoming, presenting herself as, whatever constitutes the world.'[36] According to Cavell, Cleopatra produces her own theatre in this act of emplacement: 'the return of the world after its abandonment of Antony (the "solution" to the skeptical state) has required the theatricalization of the world. It has to be *presented* to him.'[37] In order to present the world, Cleopatra must reframe its borders (make a new heaven and earth) and make a present of it as a bounded place, a discrete entity that can be given and received. And yet there is something perversely selfish in Cleopatra's gift to Antony, since she ends the play without him, alone as the giver and the recipient of the world she dreams and presents for him. Placing Antony is another act of erotic self-indulgence, marking out a final space in which she can pleasurably lose herself.[38]

This type of pleasurable bounded loss is most poignantly evident in Cleopatra's dream of Antony, an image that draws from metaphors of both place and space. She begins with an image of Antony as container: inside the confines of his face 'stuck / A sun and moon' (V, ii, 80–1). Rather than imagining a scene that contains him, like Enobarbus's earlier speech about her, Cleopatra remakes Antony himself as the cosmos – his body forms every placial boundary she envisions. As her integrating anti-blazon progresses, building him vertically from top to bottom, her images become more capacious.[39] And yet each scene she creates in her dream is bound by his flesh, his limbs, his voice, even his 'livery' (V, ii, 91). Antony's 'legs bestrid[ing] the ocean' (V, ii, 83) call to mind Antony's earlier fantasy of Cleopatra straddling his panting heart. Here, his legs form an oversized (and, again, eroticised) frame, binding the vast space of the ocean. Antony's enormous limbs seem to defy gravity; the indifferent mass of flesh she struggled to lift is transubstantiated. The immensity of Antony's body compels Cleopatra to broaden her ever-widening imaginative scope and yet it also acts as a limit – each time his limbs stretch outward, they punctuate and cap the scene she dreams for him ('his reared arm / *Crested* the world' [V, ii, 83–4; emphasis added]). The pleasures she takes from placing Antony are doubled because her imagination binds an Antony who, in turn, binds the world.[40] As Cleopatra reinvests Antony's body with erotic and affective significance piece by piece, she finally arrives at Antony's 'delights', which 'were dolphinlike, they showed his back / Above the element they lived in' (V, ii, 89–91). 'Above' his 'element' and 'past the size of dreaming' (V, ii, 98), Antony at last belies her lament that 'wishers were ever fools' (IV, xv, 38), and reveals the capacity of Cleopatra's imagination to bind and place even the most colossal of men.

Cleopatra's dream ushers in a final scene of bounded loss in the play – her suicide by the asp, a death she envisions as 'a lover's pinch, / Which hurts, and is desired' (V, ii, 295–6). To imagine 'the stroke of death' as a 'lover's pinch' (V, ii, 295) is, once again, to conceive of suicide shaped by a masochistic erotics of bondage. Early in this final scene, Cleopatra imagines her death in the monument as a placial limit, a 'thing that ends all other deeds, / Which shackles accidents and bolts up change' (V, ii, 5–6). Her conceptualisation of death draws from the monument's physical features – its boundedness and rigidity – which she ultimately takes on herself: 'My resolution's *placed* . . . I am *marble-constant*' (V, ii, 239 and 241, emphasis added). Images of bondage saturate Cleopatra's language during her final moments of the play – she invokes the bonds of marriage ('Husband'), of orgasmic reunion ('I come') and even of maternity ('see my baby at my breast, / That sucks the nurse asleep'). Within this context, the visual spectacle of asps slithering on her body recalls either her barge's 'silken tackle' or her own 'strong toil of grace'. Cleopatra's language suggests that death's firm 'pinch' and painful sting can lead to pleasurable self-loss. She implores the asp to 'be angry' (V, ii, 306), but the pain of its 'sharp teeth' (V, ii, 304) gives way to the soothing mildness of self-loss, 'as sweet as balm, as soft as air, as gentle – ' (V, ii, 312). Only after Cleopatra's place-affirming dream of Antony from within the monument's bourn, and only with her destination in the afterlife resolutely fixed ('Methinks I hear / Antony call' [V, ii, 284]), does Cleopatra imagine her life unravelling, the bonds loosening at last, imploring the asp 'this knot intrinsicate / Of life at once untie' (V, ii, 304–5).

Does Cleopatra 'return' the world to Antony, as Cavell suggests, or does she create a 'new heaven, new earth' (I, i, 17) for them to dwell in? What world could they inhabit if he keeps growing 'by reaping' (V, ii, 89)? The erotics of the place she imagines derive from the final scene she occupies – the monument's boundedness, much like Antony's place-affirming battle with Caesar in IV, viii, inspires Cleopatra's erotic dissolution and self-loss at the end of the play. The generative properties of the monument recall Giordano Bruno's account of infinite space, which is endless because it is always potentially filled. Bruno, along with Nicholas of Cusa and others, wrestled with the powerful and puzzling claim that the universe has its centre 'everywhere' (*ubique*) and its circumference 'nowhere' (*nullibi*).[41] Bruno expands on this claim by flipping the two terms, considering the possibility both 'that the centre of the universe is everywhere and the circumference is nowhere' *and* 'that the circumference is everywhere, but the centre is nowhere'.[42] He imagines a universe in which we are always on the edge of things, creating new centres of perspectival viewing from each new position we inhabit on the periphery. Centre and circumference collide, according to Casey: 'the freedom of reaching out from successive centers is thereby counterpoised with the inhibition of being hemmed in by a series of circumferences'.[43] Every time we stretch out, we extend the circumference to accommodate our reach, a process that is infinitely repeatable and thereby leads to a conceptualisation of infinite space.

Bruno's notion of space pertains to Antony and Cleopatra's experiences of bounded loss because although it is infinite and endless, it still has 'circumference . . . everywhere'. Like Cleopatra's dream of Antony, Bruno's cosmic vision is infinite without being vacuous.[44] The erotics of circumference are best captured in Cleopatra's expansive image of Antony's 'delights' as 'dolphinlike' (V, ii, 89 and 90). She dreams of an Antony whose pleasures extend beyond the reach of his scene – 'above the element he lived in' – but who contains his own limit, creating a new placial boundary out of his capacity for erotic pleasure. The very image of Antony's dolphinlike back emerging from the water, its curvature and upward reach, calls to mind Bruno's sprawling but steady circumference. That Cleopatra summons this image to describe Antony's capacity for *sexual pleasure* in particular reveals the play's investment in the erotics of binding, even (and perhaps most importantly) in Cleopatra's famously immense dream. Her capacious imagination is itself bounded by metaphors that bind and then present the immensity of infinite space – to Antony, to herself and to us.

Notes

1. Casey defines place-panic as the fear of being without a place, and consequently lost in the void of space. See Edward Casey, *The Fate of Place*, 6).

2. John Gillies, *Shakespeare and the Geography of Difference*, 68.

3. Casey, *The Fate of Place*, 6.

4. Ibid., 58.

5. Ibid., 63. Casey quotes Martin Heidegger from 'Building Dwelling Thinking', in *Poetry, Language, Thought*, 154.

6. Casey, *The Fate of Place*, 6.

7. Proclus, *A Commentary on the First Book of Euclid's Elements*, 71, qtd in Casey, *The Fate of Place*, 63.

8. A fixed point is Casey's primary example of a limit, as opposed to a boundary, because it is self-enclosed, self-contained and isolated. Yet Casey also asks, 'isn't a point something that is *always* surrounded – indeed, *totally* surrounded in the space in which it is placed and thus as fully ensconced in its own surrounder as any sensible body?' (*The Fate of Place*, 60).

9. Gilles Deleuze, *Masochism: Coldness and Cruelty*, 71. Cleopatra and Antony both conceive of pleasure according

to this slowed lyrical rhythm. The opening scene of the play features an Antony who feels pleasure as a kind of prolonging of time: 'There's not a minute of our lives should *stretch /* Without some pleasure now' (I, i, 46–7, emphasis added). Time bends to pleasure in the masochistic aesthetic Deleuze describes, and both lovers are subject to this suspense at various points in the play.

10. Ibid., 33. Deleuze's depiction of the woman torturer is based on his study of Leopold von Sacher-Masoch's 1870 novel, *Venus in Furs*. See Deleuze, *Masochism*, 47–80.

11. Deleuze writes, 'Pure waiting divides naturally into two currents, the first representing what is awaited, something essentially tardy, always late and always postponed, the second representing something expected and on which depends the speeding up of the awaited object. It is inevitable that such a form, such a rhythmic division of time into two streams, should be "filled" by the particular combination of pleasure and pain. For at the same time as pain fulfills what is expected, it becomes possible for pleasure to fulfill what is awaited' (*Masochism*, 71).

12. Jonathan Gil Harris, '"Narcissus in thy Face": Roman Desire and the Difference It Fakes in *Antony and Cleopatra*', 418.

13. See Casey, *The Fate of Place*, Chapter 5, 'The Ascent of Infinite Space: Medieval and Renaissance Speculations' (103–29).

14. Edward Grant, *Much Ado About Nothing: Theories of Space and Vacuum from the Middle Ages to the Scientific Revolution*, 109.

15. Frank Kermode discusses the fear of space ('Nature abhors a vacuum') in his introductory essay to a special issue of *The Journal of Medieval and Early Modern Studies* on space and place in early modern English theatre. See Kermode, 'Experiencing the Place and Space of Early Modern Theater', 6.

16. Grant, *Much Ado About Nothing*, 3.

17. Ibid., 199. Grant notes the historical tendency of scholastics to reject the existence of three-dimensional void space and the tendency of non-scholastics to accept it. Aristotle's definition of the void is found in the *Physics* IV.1.208b25–6.

18. From Francesco Patrizi, *Nova de Universis Philosophia* (1587): 'Qua plenum corpore est, esse locum. Qua vero sine corpore est, esse vacuum' (Benjamin Brickman, '*On Physical Space: Francesco Patrizi*', 231). Patrizi's definition of the void relies on spatial and placial properties: it is vacuous, a quality of infinite space, but it is also a three-dimensional container, an image we associate more with place.

19. Whereas Freeman emphasises the role of the container schema in structuring Antony's sense of Roman, masculine and military identity, I focus on its capacity to generate the erotic experiences of both lovers. See Donald C. Freeman, '"The rack dislimns": Schema and Metaphorical Pattern in *Antony and Cleopatra*', 457.

20. 'This vacuum, like *locus*, must have three common dimensions – length, width, and depth' (Patrizi qtd in Casey, *The Fate of Place*, 126, and Grant, *Much Ado About Nothing*, 386).

21. George Lakoff and Mark Johnson elaborate on the cognitive structure of basic philosophical ideas – and of morality in particular – in Chapter 14 of *Philosophy in the Flesh* (290–334).

22. The notion of a 'bindable' void draws from the Stoics' definition: 'Void space was thus conceived as a three-dimensional receptacle for the finite cosmos' (Grant, *Much Ado About Nothing*, 107).

23. In this speech, Antony also explores pleasures of permeability reminiscent of Endymion's metaphors in Chapter 3. The tidy image of Antony's soldiers 'clip[ping]' their wives is followed by the messier, more disturbing language of congealing wounds; Antony no sooner talks of embrace than he instructs soldiers to let their loved ones 'kiss / The honored gashes whole' (IV, viii, 10–11). Does this mean that the kisses will repair the gashes, making the broken flesh 'whole' again, or does Antony imagine the wives covering the gashes with their 'whole' mouths, just as Cleopatra later hopes to 'quicken' the wounded Antony 'with kissing' (IV, xv, 40)? Whatever erotic content we find in Antony's

image, the pleasures he describes arise from the metaphorical domain of permeability: tears mingling with blood, lips pressed against gashes.

24. Giordano Bruno, *Cause, Principle, and Unity, and Essays on Magic*, 171.
25. Ibid., 171.
26. Ibid., 157.
27. Antony's reputation for 'bounty' suggests that he is familiar with giving in order to gain (see IV, vi, 32 and V, ii, 88–9).
28. Harris, '"Narcissus in thy Face"', 421.
29. See Thomas North's translation of Plutarch's *The Life of Marcus Antonius* (1579), cited in Michael Neill's edition of *Antony and Cleopatra*, 356. In Plutarch, the monument is depicted as a kind of fortress, where Cleopatra 'locked the doors unto her, and shut all the springs of the locks with great bolts' (cited in Neill, *Antony and Cleopatra*, 354).
30. Theodore Leinwand provides a brief summary of the monument's staging history in 'The Shakespearean Perverse'.
31. Weimann contends that actors in medieval and Renaissance drama made use of two playing spaces on the stage: the upstage *locus* and the downstage *platea*. Audiences in Elizabethan London would have been familiar with a divided playing space, which is traditionally defined by the specificity, or placiality, of stage locations. (See Weimann, *Shakespeare and the Popular Tradition in the Theater: Studies in the Social Dimension of Dramatic Form and Function*.)
32. Stanley Cavell, *Disowning Knowledge in Seven Plays of Shakespeare*, 28.
33. The domain of verticality now cues a specific and serious threat for Cleopatra too, one that is utterly devoid of eros. Antony first alerts her to the possibility that Caesar will 'hoist thee up to the shouting plebeians' (IV, xii, 34), and she reverts to this image twice from within the monument: 'Shall they hoist me up' (V, ii, 55); 'Mechanic slaves . . . shall / Uplift us to the view' (V, ii, 210–12). The shame that Caesar plans to inflict on her will be experienced along the same vertical axis that once spelled pleasure.

34. The types of apparatus vary. Theodore Leinwand refers to David Garrick's production, in which 'Cleopatra, and her Women, throw out certain Tackle' (see Richard Madelaine, *Antony and Cleopatra*). Other possibilities include chains, ropes, pulleys and strips of fabric. North's translation of Plutarch's *The Life of Marcus Antonius* mentions 'certain chains and ropes, in the which Antonius was trussed' (qtd in Leinwand, 'The Shakespearean Perverse', 119–20).

35. Ibid., 126. Leinwand draws upon Gilles Deleuze's account of perverse structure to describe the superficiality of Antony's body in IV, xv. According to Deleuze, perversion is defined as 'the autonomy of the surface, independent of, and against depth and height' (Gilles Deleuze, *The Logic of Sense*, 132).

36. Cavell, *Disowning Knowledge*, 28. Cavell describes Antony's sceptical crisis in spatial terms: 'The recession of the world is this play's interpretation of what I have called the truth of skepticism, that the human habitation of the world is not assured in what philosophy calls knowledge' (25).

37. Ibid., 31.

38. In his essay on Freudian transference and love in *Antony and Cleopatra*, David Hillman notes that Cleopatra 'manages her loss' of Antony throughout the play by repeatedly conjuring him in various forms (fish, reel and so on). See Hillman, '"If it be love indeed": Transference, Love, and *Anthony and Cleopatra*', 318.

39. Lisa S. Starks writes of Cleopatra's anti-blazon, 'the degeneration of Antony is followed by his regeneration as a Colossus through Cleopatra's poetic imagination, making the severed flesh whole again through the word' (Starks, 'Immortal Longings: The Erotics of Death in *Antony and Cleopatra*', 249). This image of a woman rebuilding a man piece by piece recalls Isis's reassembly of Osiris.

40. Jean-Paul Sartre writes of the lover: 'I must be the one whose function is to make trees and water exist, to make cities and fields and other men exist, in order to give them to the Other who arranges them into a world . . . In one sense if I am to be loved, I am the object through whose procuration the world

will exist for the Other; in another sense I am the world, I am the ground-as-object on which the world detaches itself. Thus I am reassured' (Jean-Paul Sartre, *Being and Nothingness: An Essay on Phenomenological Ontology*, 369).

41. This complex and famous assertion has been put to various uses, including as a cornerstone for a kind of early modern phenomenology: if there is no stable centre of the universe (such as the earth or the sun), then everywhere is a possible centre, depending on the perspective from which the universe is being perceived. This idea led Nicholas of Cusa to establish a relativistic approach to cosmology ('the perception of the universe is relative to the place of the observer' [Casey, *The Fate of Place*, 117]). For a play such as *Antony and Cleopatra*, which features a torrent of perspectival shifts during the first four acts, the idea of a constantly shifting centre is particularly relevant. Janet Adelman has suggested that the 'movement of perspectives, rather than the revelations of a psychodrama or the certainties of a morality . . . is most characteristic of *Antony and Cleopatra*' (Janet Adelman, *The Common Liar: An Essay on Antony and Cleopatra*, 30).

42. Bruno, *Cause, Principle, and Unity*, 89.

43. Casey, *The Fate of Place*, 123.

44. 'Infinite space', Bruno writes, 'is endowed with infinite quality' (qtd in Casey, *The Fate of Place*, 121). The 'infinite quality' of Bruno's space stands in opposition to the emptiness that leaves Antony 'unqualitied with very shame' (III, xi, 44). See Giordano Bruno, *On the Infinite Universe and Worlds* (1584), in *Giordano Bruno: His Life and Thought*, 258.

PART III

CREATIVITY

EROTIC SUBJECT, OBJECT, INSTRUMENT

Love is work.
Love is active.
Love requires cooperation.
Love requires a discipline.
Love is an aesthetic experience.
Love involves creativity.
Love creates a reality.

These are a handful of the entailments of 'Love is a Collaborative Work of Art', a representative example of what George Lakoff and Mark Johnson call 'new metaphor'. Unlike everyday metaphors, new metaphors exist 'outside our conventional conceptual system, metaphors that are imaginative and creative. Such metaphors are capable of giving us a new understanding of our experience.'[1] The world-making capacities of new metaphor are especially resonant in 'Love is a Collaborative Work of Art', which conceptualises love as artfully creating a reality. From the list of metaphorical entailments above, we can see that this new metaphor builds upon more conventional metaphors that I have explored, particularly in Part I, where the domains of stillness and motion shape eros as a dynamic action, a process of becoming. In Part III, I analyse aesthetic features of this creative process, in which making love also remakes Lyly's and Shakespeare's lovers.[2]

Eros's creative and metamorphic power on Lyly's and Shakespeare's stages has been central to the arguments of the preceding chapters of this book. In *Galatea* and *Endymion*, we have seen Lyly's lovestruck characters undergo radical changes, from gender transformation to age reversal. It is no surprise, then, that Lyly entitles one of his plays *Love's Metamorphoses*. Shakespeare, too, dramatises the power of eros to 'translate' the likes of Helena (I, i, 191) and Bottom (III, I, 114). On Shakespeare's stage, erotic identities both dissolve (Angelo's self-fracturing, Antony's self-loss) and regenerate (Cleopatra's crocodile, Antony's 'dolphinlike' delights). Each new metaphor produces a slightly different Angelo or Antony or Galatea or Cynthia, such that characters themselves become labours of love, projections of desires (sometimes their own, sometimes those of a beloved). Lyly's and Shakespeare's lovers are, in short, collaborative works of art. But what exactly is the relationship between making love and making lovers? Can we separate the lovers from the erotic relations that they make together? How do we distinguish lovers who are bound up in their 'collaborative work of art'?

John Lyly embeds such questions in the grammatical structure his characters use to ask them. In true Lylian fashion, he presents this problem obliquely, in the form of a Latin joke. Near the start of Act II of *Campaspe*, Diogenes tells his servant, '*non egeo tui vel te*' (II, i, 44). Preserving the Latin grammar, his line translates as 'I have no need of you, nor do I need you.' Repeating himself with a difference, Diogenes reminds us that the language of need is itself needy; as it reaches from subject to object, it blurs the distinction between them. The joke itself derives from William Lilly's *Grammar*, where it models verbs that can take objects in both the genitive and the accusative cases.[3]

The subject ('I') and the object ('you') are grammatically linked in a part-to-whole relationship (genitive), and yet they are also marked as two separate entities (accusative). Diogenes's *egere* ('to need') belongs to a special class of Latin verbs of 'filling' or 'lacking'. When *egere* takes an object in the genitive case, it indicates incompleteness or a missing part. Thus Diogenes's haughty attempt to declare his independence from his servant loses some of its steam.

Lyly's more profound grammar lesson in *Campaspe* teaches us about the intrinsic interdependence of erotic subjects and objects. Diogenes's locution, 'I have no need of you', is contradicted by its own grammar because the part-to-whole relationship reveals that 'you' possess 'me'. That Latin verbs of needing and wanting take objects in the genitive case is a testament to these objects' power over subjects. But, at the same time that the genitive highlights the shared *genus* of subject and object ('I' am 'of you'), the accusative indicates a break between them. Even at the most basic level of grammar, need both undermines and sharpens the separateness and integrity of the desiring subject and desired object. The object of need is thus part of the self *and* part of the world. What happens, then, when we conceptualise love as a collaborative work of art – as a new, and therefore separate, creation? When love is something we make, it too shares our *genus*. But when eros is a work of *art* in particular, rather than a natural or organic product of a relationship, its separateness is perhaps even more pronounced. An object in the world, a product of mutual erotic skill and artistry, love as a collaborative work of art invites a third term, which often proves to be a mediating noun – a filter, a buffer, an artistic instrument – between ourselves and our beloveds.

Kenneth Burke comments on this instrument in his section on Agency in *A Grammar of Motives*. He cites an anecdote from Victor Lenzen's *Procedures of Empirical*

Science to illustrate the fluid relationship of subject, object, and instrument:

> If one taps an object with a stick held firmly in the hand, 'the stick is an apparatus that may be viewed as part of the observer'. (Note the term 'part of,' which here gives us merger.) But if the stick is held loosely, the stick itself becomes the perceived object, 'and the partition is between stick and hand'. (The stick here is 'apart from' the observer.)[4]

When I hold it tightly, the stick is a part of my body; as a prosthesis, it becomes an instrument that enables my engagement with objects in the world. When I hold it loosely, the stick is a part of that outside world. A slack grip allows me to *feel* its apartness from my body: I sense it *in* my hand, its temperature, its weight and its firmness. But the moment I tighten my grip in order to do something with the stick (that is, to use it on an object, to push aside a curtain, to nudge a horse), it becomes a part of me again. A slight difference in my grip radically changes the stick's ontology. The capacity of the instrument to shift back and forth, and my own power to bring about that shift by subtly changing my deportment, confirm the instrument's instability and mutability.

Between subject and object, then, Burke places an instrument, the means by which we affect, or engage with, the world. What does Burke's example tell us about the role of an instrument in an erotic subject / object relation? We might imagine an erotic instrument to be merely the means by which a desiring subject pursues a beloved object, such as an instrument of seduction or courtship (say, flowers or gifts). Considered in this narrow way, the instrument is categorically distinct from the subject and the object. It is incidental to the experience of desire because of its separateness, and because it is a means of *pursuit* rather than part and parcel of desiring itself. Gifts or flowers are deployed as a way of obtaining a beloved, not a means of desiring her. Burke's anecdote, by contrast, emphasises the instrument's categorical connection, its potential fusion, with the desiring subject who deploys it. The prosthetic stick in Burke's example functions as an intimate part of the desiring subject; in an erotic relationship, it closes the gap that separates would-be lovers and can itself be said to be responsible for their relation, their relatedness. Such an erotic instrument might take the form of a shared language (verbal, gestural, physical), a shared set of rituals (lovemaking, bondage or submission) or a shared imaginary (mutual fantasies, beliefs or even lies). Such instruments are not left behind; rather, absorbed into the relationship, they enable it. They become a medium both shared by and coextensive with the desiring subject and object. Instrumentality, then, becomes the very *way* in which we access and express not only our own erotic capacities but those of our lovers.

The erotic relation adds a layer of complexity to Burke's instrument because, unlike the example of a stick opening a curtain, the object of erotic desire is no mere inanimate thing – our desires are directed at other desiring subjects. A vital part of a dynamic relation, an erotic instrument necessarily partakes of its vitality. To consider instrumentality, then, is to consider the ways in which desire itself is a creative act – we *make* desire just as we say we make love. Take, for example, the erotic instrument of a shared fantasy: anything but a static object, it is what lovers craft, reshape and refine as their very means of desiring. Such fantasies both create desire and prove themselves to be the evolving creative products of desire. As is the case with a shared language, a mutual fantasy makes the lovers, just as it is made by them: 'Therefore I lie with her and she with me / And in our faults by lies we flattered be' (Shakespeare, Sonnet CXXXVIII, 13–14).

On Shakespeare's stage, mutual erotic fantasy is perhaps most dynamically realised in the collaborative work of art that is Cesario. An erotic subject, object and instrument,

Twelfth Night's Cesario is a labour of Viola's love, a living monument to her brother and a 'smiling . . . monument' (II, iv, 115, 114) for Orsino. But others collaborate in the making of Cesario as he becomes a projection of Olivia's and Orsino's (and perhaps the audience's) collective artistries. Cesario is thus a creature of desire – creature in the sense that Julia Reinhard Lupton sketches in her description of 'Creature Caliban':

> Derived from the future-active participle of the Latin verb *creare* ('to create'), *creature* indicates a made or fashioned thing but with the sense of continued or potential process, action, or emergence built into the future thrust of its active verbal form . . . The *creatura* is a thing always in the process of undergoing creation; the creature is actively passive or, better, *passionate*, perpetually becoming created.[5]

Cesario is described as a creature once, at the very end of the play: 'An apple cleft in twain is not more twin / Than these two creatures' (V, i, 218–19). That Antonio uses this word at the moment of Cesario's revelation reminds us of his identity as 'a made or fashioned thing', a work of collaborative art laid bare in the play's protracted final scene. But, following Lupton, Cesario is an ongoing process rather than a finished product. Cesario keeps becoming Cesario through his continued exchanges with Orsino and Olivia – dialogues that are always charged with erotic intensity. His process of becoming extends even through the play's conclusion, when, ending with a 'future thrust', Orsino beckons 'Cesario' – not Viola – to 'come' (V, i, 378), in his final speech of the play.

Cesario is a process and a product, or object, of love but he is also an erotic subject. Valerie Traub's assertion that 'it is as the object of another woman's desire that Cesario finds her own erotic voice' testifies to the reciprocal, mutually creative relationship between the subject and object of desire.[6] Fashioned in part by Olivia's desire – her erotic overtures provoke

Cesario's 'I am the man' (II, ii, 25), an assertion of his very existence – Cesario speaks ever more forcefully as a desiring subject. David Schalkwyk notes that *Twelfth Night* 'makes possible a *split* subjectivity in the shape of a single body represented and perceived in two aspects at once: young man and young woman, friend and lover, *philia* and *eros*'.[7] Viola and Cesario both live inside 'a single body' in Schalkwyk's account, as two subjects that represent different aspects of love. This image of Viola and Cesario as two alternating subjects in one shape resonates with Maurice Merleau-Ponty's discussion of the 'double sensations' within the body. Merleau-Ponty's example is of mutual touching, in which the left hand touches the right, which can feel itself being touched. Neither an inert object nor an active subject, the right hand can at any point become the hand that touches. Merleau-Ponty makes the important clarification that 'the two hands are never in the simultaneous relationship of touched and touching to each other'. He elaborates,

> When I press my two hands together, it is not a matter of two sensations felt together as one perceives two objects placed side by side, but of an ambiguous set-up in which both hands can alternate the roles of 'touching' and 'being touched'. What was meant by 'double sensations' is that, in passing from one role to the other, I can identify the hand touched as the one which will in a moment be touching.[8]

Perhaps, like Merleau-Ponty's touching hands, Viola / Cesario is ever alternating, passing imperceptibly from one role to the other, never a coherent whole. But this rhythm is what gives Cesario his erotic power and makes him a dynamic process, both a subject and object, creator and creature of desire. Like two hands pressed together, and like the hand that grips the stick in Burke's account, the shift from touching to touched – from 'a part' to 'apart' – can transpire countless times in a single instant.

Can we name with confidence the speaker of, 'What I am, and what I would, are as secret as maidenhead' (I, v, 207–8), or the one who would 'make the babbling gossip of the air / Cry out "Olivia"' (262–3)? Is this Viola or is it Cesario? Every edition tells us that it is Viola, but more than one undergraduate student in my classroom has contested that speech prefix (indeed, one student found it downright offensive). Perhaps this is an instance of two hands pressed together, in which it takes only an act of will or imagination to pass from one role to the other. But as Cesario begins to edge out Viola – as he 'sing[s] . . . loud' (I, v, 260) in a voice that arguably drowns out 'drownèd Viola' (V, i, 236) – he takes on still another role, that of the erotic instrument. In many ways, Cesario appears to exist solely as an instrument of desire. His main function in the play, after all, is as a proxy, an instrument of Orsino's desire for Olivia. He is also the means by which Viola enacts her desire for Sebastian, and by which she expresses, and perhaps realises, her desires for Orsino. And Cesario has been seen as an instrument for Viola's own seduction of Olivia – a 'conduit', as Goran Stanivukovic writes, 'through which both a woman's praise of another woman is conveyed and the absent male lover's desire for a distant lady is transmitted'.[9] In this way, Cesario is 'a part of' Viola; in Burke's example, Cesario is the prosthesis that enables Viola to engage with the world. Theatrically, he is a part Viola plays, and he speaks a 'part' (I, v, 172) Orsino writes.[10] Thus Cesario is a metamorphosed Viola and he is apart from her, a mutual fantasy, the 'dream' (II, ii, 26) of many collaborators.

It is Cesario's erotic instrumentality – his part-and-apartness – that generates some of the most artful language of the play.[11] In Christine Varnado's account of erotic instrumentality and the 'pleasures of getting used' in *Philaster*, she argues that 'erotic energy lodges in the instrument's stylistic "art"'.[12] Such erotic energy is powerful enough to awaken both Olivia and Viola from grief and death as Cesario ventures 'out of my part' (I, v, 172) and seduces Olivia in his own language. It may be that Orsino lives somewhere in Cesario's poetry, either as commissioner of his text or as beneficiary of Viola's affections. And it may be that Viola's unrequited longings are the ones that produce Cesario's desire to 'Hallo your name to the reverberate hills' (I, v, 261). It may also be that Olivia's desires inspire and provoke Cesario's poetry, drawing out his erotic skill with 'How does he love me?' (243) and the even more provocative 'Why, what would you?' (256). Cesario's apartness as an instrument need not alienate or insulate him from other desiring subjects. A part of them and apart from them, his artful voice emerges, quite improvisation-ally, from the collaborative desires he makes possible as their instrument.

In Part III, I explore the role of the erotic instrument as a medium of mutual creation and lovemaking. As in the exam-ple of Cesario's artful voice, such instruments exercise cre-ative power over the lovers who find themselves transformed by a collaborative process. When they undergo or initiate such processes, Lyly's and Shakespeare's characters release a capacity inside themselves and one another that amounts to a virtuosity, a sense of divinity, even. My account of the erot-ics of making stands in opposition to traditional accounts of the sonneteer or artist who narcissistically falls in love with his own creative work. I reveal a surprisingly anti-narcissistic process that constantly reminds us that to need, *egere*, is to make ourselves 'a part of', *tui*, a process that reminds us that we cannot, and do not, go it alone. The other gives himself to the creator's brush, pen, voice or imagination and, as would a muse, releases a complementary artistic skill. For the char-acters in Shakespeare's *Twelfth Night*, as for Lyly's Apelles, the instrument is *a part* of the object. Apelles falls in love not quite with himself as he has known himself but with that newly discovered part of himself that is enabled by, inflamed by, even created by the act of erotic desiring.

This section considers the erotic instruments in Lyly's *Campaspe* and Shakespeare's *Taming of the Shrew*. In both plays, the process of erotic creation begins when lovers activate a dormant artistic capacity in one other. The process of painting instrumentalises Apelles's erotic relation with Campaspe, and the process of storytelling (making fiction, twisting language, telling lies) instrumentalises Petruchio's erotic interactions with Kate. Campaspe and Kate are shaped by these creative processes but they become co-creators as well, Campaspe as a model who willingly submits to the artistic process and Kate as an interlocutor whose words verify the pair's mutual lies. As long as the lovers continue to create together, their erotic relationships flourish, exceeding the sum of their parts. Painting and storytelling – the instruments that they employ – are absorbed into their relationships, shaping their interactions according to particular artistic features (pigment and canvas, verb tense and mood), and more generally, by defining eros as a dynamic and creative process. In time, however, a finished product – a completed portrait or a fully realised story now untethered to the lovers' imaginations – emerges. No longer their intimate instrument, no longer *a part of* their shared imaginary, this finished product becomes an object in its own right, an object defined, first and foremost, by its *apartness*, its remove from the lovers and from the processes of creation. Once Alexander, as patron and king, acquires Campaspe's portrait, and once Kate and Petruchio's fictional language is turned into propaganda for marital propriety, the 'supernal effects' (*Campaspe* I, iii, 32) of erotic creation dull and diminish. The best the lovers can do is try to defer this autumnal, melancholic outcome. The energy given over to dilating the creative process testifies to the allure of its transformative power over the lovers – its ability to awaken and elevate their creative capacities – and so to the significance of instrumentality in erotic relations.

Notes

1. See George Lakoff and Mark Johnson, *Metaphors We Live By*, 139–40. The full list of entailments is almost a page long, ranging from 'Love Demands Sacrifice' to 'Love Cannot be Achieved by Formula' and 'Love Requires Funding'.

2. In *Thinking Sex with the Early Moderns*, Valerie Traub traces the history of the phrase 'to make love', which originates in the early modern period: 'Our common phrase "to make love" was used as early as 1567 to mean "to pay amorous attention; to court, woo," but apparently did not allude to engaging in sexual *acts* until 1929' (147).

3. Most Latin verbs take an object in the accusative case, whereas the genitive case is typically used to pair nouns together in a possessive relationship, often translated into English by using the preposition 'of'. Most likely, the sentence invokes the partitive use of the genitive case, in which the genitive marks a part-to-whole relationship (for example, *pars civitatis*, 'part of the state'). For other instances of this type of genitive, see Bridgette L. M. Bauer, 'The Definite Article in Indo-European: Emergence of a New Grammatical Category?'

4. Kenneth Burke, *A Grammar of Motives*, 415.

5. Julia Reinhard Lupton, 'Creature Caliban', 1.

6. Traub, *The Renaissance of Lesbianism in Early Modern England*, 57.

7. David Schalkwyk, *Shakespeare, Love and Language*, 59.

8. Maurice Merleau-Ponty, *Phenomenology of Perception*, 93.

9. Goran Stanivukovic, '"Two lips, indifferent red": Queer Styles in *Twelfth Night*', 167–8.

10. Although Orsino remarks on the resemblance of Cesario's 'small pipe' (I, iv, 32) to 'a woman's part' (34), Cesario's 'pipe' and 'part' almost certainly allude to male genitalia as well. Cesario is thus also 'a part of' Viola in this sense. The prosthetic stick in Burke's example has phallic power, too.

11. A number of scholars have remarked on the erotic power of Cesario's verbal wit. See Stephen Greenblatt's 'Fiction and Friction', in *Shakespearean Negotiations: The Circulation of Social Energy in Renaissance England* (esp. 89–93), and

Valerie Traub's *Renaissance of Lesbianism*: 'As a surrogate for the Duke, Cesario speaks some of the most beautiful love lyrics in the play' (56).

12. Christine Varnado, 'Getting Used, and Liking It: Erotic Instrumentality in *Philaster*', 26, 52. Although Varnado distinguishes *Philaster* as a more mutual and genuinely three-way erotic relationship than the tense and conflicted love triangle in *Twelfth Night*, her discussion of Bellario's artifice can illuminate Cesario's identity as an artful erotic instrument.

CHAPTER 5

'LOVE'S USE' IN *CAMPASPE*

As in Lyly's *Galatea*, the eroticism in *Campaspe* builds through oblique language that enables lovers to 'Tell all the truth but tell it slant,' as Emily Dickinson writes. Apelles and Campaspe fall in love almost instantly, and yet they 'dazzle gradually', spending their scenes with a paintbrush and canvas lodged firmly between them, not to mention all the words that fill the gaps that remain.[1] What is Lyly showing us about the nature of erotic experience (Apelles's and Campaspe's in particular) on a divided stage such as this? To begin, he dramatises what we already know: that erotic experience comprises much more than just physical contact. Lyly confirms this by scrutinising the roles that instruments – easel and canvas, pigments and words – play in Apelles's and Campaspe's erotic relation. While anything that stands between two lovers may be an obstacle to the fulfilment of their erotic desire, it may also prove an instrument of desire. An object placed between two bodies in some kind of dynamic relation invariably increases the friction between them. It creates drag – it obstructs – but it also generates heat, a potential source of erotic pleasure. As Lyly demonstrates, such friction is felt within imaginative, linguistic and conceptual realms, not just in the physical world. A goodly portion of the play consists of Apelles and

Campaspe employing artistic and linguistic media that both bring them into relation and keep them apart. The portrait of Campaspe that Apelles paints is more than the sign of their erotic relationship – it is its medium. That which stands between them provides the means by which they love one another, by which they reorder their own world and the world outside them, imbuing both with the creativity, richness and nuance that characterise Lyly's own art no less than Apelles's.

The opening scene between Apelles and Campaspe occurs in and around the painter's workshop, a setting that visually binds their dialogue together with the act of artistic creation.[2] It is perhaps this backdrop that prompts the lovers to recognise each other's creative capacities almost instantly. As early as their first exchange, Apelles and Campaspe acknowledge their individual artistic talents and ambitions, but perhaps more importantly, their first few lines together establish the artful medium that will distinguish all of their dialogues. Theirs is a language of ambiguity and nuance that subtly grafts the lovers' artistic sensibilities on to their erotic relationship.[3] In their dialogue, they reveal that each is wise to the other's artistry; each is attentive to the instruments, or in Campaspe's words, the 'device[s]' (III, i, 16), that the other employs.[4] In this scene of flirtation, their language is highly crafted and stylised in its form, equivocal and sprawling in its meaning, careful and measured in its delivery. Indeed, Apelles and Campaspe *talk art* even as they talk artfully – their flirtation consists of talk about each other's artfulness. In a few short lines, Campaspe and Apelles establish art as their erotic medium. Together they arrive at and deploy a metaphor – 'Desiring is Creating' – which will enable their erotic relationship throughout the play.

Apelles begins by confessing his doubt that there could possibly 'be any colour so fresh that may shadow a countenance so fair' (III, i, 1–2). This sounds like the familiar conceit about 'fair[ness]' that exceeds the capacities of pigment, brush and canvas. Still, there is something odd about 'fresh', the adjective that Apelles chooses to describe the quality that his paint lacks. What is a 'fresh' colour or 'fresh' paint? Is it new, or is it vigorous and lively (as the *OED* would have it)?[5] Apparently, it is Campaspe's *aliveness*, not only her beauty, that Apelles sets out to capture. He is in the line of Zeuxis (to whom Apelles's servant alludes), who could paint such life-like grapes that 'birds . . . have been fatted by [them] in win-ter' (I, ii, 67–8). Of course, Campaspe is not a painted grape. And Apelles's interest in his subject's 'fresh[ness]' is no less erotic than it is artistic. His opening lines make the tight con-nection between art and eros that characterise his subsequent interactions with the lady. Apelles's painting also differs from Zeuxis's in terms of the type of artistic skill it requires. Where Zeuxis strives to make something artful out of something rela-tively plain – a mere grape – Apelles's task is to bring out the 'fresh' quality that already resides within Campaspe. He illu-minates his subject in paint, suffusing her with a vital glow that captures the luminosity that radiates from within her. His talent and his desire later 'maketh [her] ears to glow with thoughts' (IV, ii, 4). According to E. H. Gombrich, the histori-cal Apelles was famous for the luminosity of his paintings, and for using a thin line of white paint to create the three-dimen-sional effect whereby an object appears to glow and protrude outwards.[6] This technique, which Gombrich calls 'the line of Apelles', enables Apelles both to honour his subject's form and to enhance it with an extraordinary lustre.

If Apelles elevates his model, making her into art by prizing her 'fresh[ness]' above his own artistic capacities, Campaspe reciprocates by diminishing herself. She responds to Apelles's opening lines by referring to her own features as ill formed: 'a hard favour, which maketh you to despair of my face' (III, i, 6–7). In order to be remade by Apelles, Campaspe fashions herself as 'hard' and unattractive (later she worries that her 'disordered countenance' will result in a 'deformed counterfeit' [III, iv, 71–2]) so that Apelles can build her back up and elevate her through the artistic process. Such self-fashioning is an artistic talent in its own right. Although Campaspe herself is not a painter, she adopts an active role in the creative process as Apelles's model. Wendy Steiner's recent study of the model's role in the artistic process characterises 'her' creative power as a particular type of virtuosity: 'The model, in short, can play every role in aesthetic communication. She is a polyfunctional virtuoso.'[7] What roles are available to Campaspe as she sits for Apelles's portrait? As a participant in the artistic experience, Campaspe interprets the artwork and the significance of the creative process itself. As the sitter for the portrait, she contributes artful, stylised and subtle poses, and thus takes on the role of co-author of the work. By degrading her own physical features, Campaspe makes it possible for Apelles to reshape and illuminate her in paint.[8] She artfully diminishes herself and he augments her with his art – they reciprocally, if asymmetrically, contribute to a shared process of artistic creation.[9]

Even before Campaspe exposes her virtuosity at what we might call self-deprecation, she reveals another skill that distinguishes her role in the artistic and erotic process: she interprets the lovers' interactions by employing a language that bridges art and eros. While Apelles is busy crafting her portrait, Campaspe is deftly crafting the 'Desiring is Artistic Creation' metaphor that will ignite and sustain their erotic experience together. She begins quite simply and subtly by using euphuism, Lyly's signature prose style of symmetries and antitheses, to compare Apelles's painting and his flirting: 'Sir, I had thought you had been commanded to paint with your hand, not to gloze with your tongue' (III, i, 3–4). To paint and to 'gloze' are both artful techniques, but Campaspe uses the former verb to describe portrait making and the latter to describe seduction. Placing these techniques side by side bridges the gap between them, drawing attention to their shared connotations (one can 'gloze' with a paintbrush, too), grafting the features of art-making on to their experience of lovemaking.[10] Such a metaphor recasts desire as something *made* rather than something felt, something that depends upon each lover's skill. Hence they fall in love with each other's virtuosity. It is Apelles's 'device' of flattery that Campaspe finds seductive. Her metaphor also activates an erotic relation that privileges ornament over plainness, and complexity over artlessness, indicating her tacit recognition that the first technique in each of these antitheses stands the best chance of producing the friction responsible for their shared erotic pleasure.

Campaspe exposes Apelles's artfulness, but she employs similar techniques of her own and he is quick to detect them. According to Apelles, Campaspe's lament about her 'hard favour' is a display of her skill at diminishing herself, even though she 'know[s her] own perfection' (III, i, 10). He identifies her technique as an affected modesty in which 'you seem to dispraise that which most men commend' (III, i, 10–11). Apelles's art of 'gloz[ing]' and Campaspe's art of 'seem[ing]' are their highly self-conscious instruments of lovemaking. He identifies the seductive quality of her art: its affected modesty 'draw[s men] by that mean into an admiration, where feeding themselves, they fall into an ecstasy' (III, i, 11–13). Connecting her art to eros (acknowledging its erotic power), Apelles merely reinforces the relationship Campaspe has already established between artistic and erotic creation. Apelles's recognition of her artistry should inoculate him: that is, it should set him apart from the men who fall into 'admiration' and 'ecstasy' in response to Campaspe's affected modesty. But Apelles still falls in love with her. Or he falls in love with her artfulness, with the *seeming* in her seeming modesty, the process of her artistry rather than its product.[11]

In the remainder of their opening dialogue, the couple plays on various meanings of the word 'colour' – whether hue, paint, blushing, artifice, rhetoric or complexion – culminating with Campaspe's teasing assertion that Apelles is 'so long used to colours you can do nothing but colour' (III, i, 16–17). This claim patently reinforces the connection between art and eros that has been steadily building to this point. Apelles's 'colours' are, of course, his paints, but now Campaspe insinuates that his art of 'colour[ing]' is a seductive 'device' that she can 'withstand' (16). And yet, she falls in love with him. Like Apelles, her ability to detect artfulness allows her to withstand its effects, even as she falls in love with the virtuosity that inspires them. The lovers' instrumentality is itself erotic but their erotic relation also requires the *exposure* of this instrumentality. Instrumentality becomes erotic when its 'how' is laid bare; seeing each other's devices or instruments reminds the lovers that they are engaged in an evolving process. The counterintuitive goal of such exposure is not to disarm one's lover, nor to strip her of her devices, but rather to batten on those devices. He lies with her and she with him. Such is their lovemaking.

At the same time that Apelles and Campaspe collaborate on her portrait, they craft a language that transforms artistic into erotic gestures, gestures that have the power to transform the lovers themselves. Often, it is Campaspe who initiates this process, such as when she taps into a shared language, according to which 'colours' can mean painting, talking and still more than this. Apelles's response to the lady's play on 'colour' adds yet another layer of meaning: 'Indeed the colours I see, I fear will alter the colour I have' (18–19). Using the same word to describe the object ('the colours I see' in Campaspe's complexion), the instrument ('any colour so fresh' – that is, paint) and now himself as the subject confirms the overlap among subject, object and instrument of desire. Artistic process transforms the lady from mere 'earthly mettle' (II, ii, 81) to paint and it can also 'alter' the painter's own 'colour'. But what sort of alteration does Apelles imagine here? Hunter writes that the line can be read as a premonition that Apelles will turn pale or blush, but blushing is more apt since Apelles uses the verb 'alter' rather than 'lose'.[12] Apelles fears that his own flesh is susceptible to change; if it reddens with desire – if, that is, Campaspe's beauty stirs his blood so that it rises to the surface – his flesh, like Campaspe's, will be made legible, acquiring its own 'fresh[ness]' through the artistic process. Through the inter-animating experiences of painting and desiring, Apelles and Campaspe remake themselves.

Apelles's excellence in the erotic relation is to illuminate and elevate the potential of Campaspe's artistry. For her part, Campaspe's self-deprecating postures paradoxically augment her artistry as their erotic interaction progresses. With each detail Apelles adds to the portrait, Campaspe becomes more adept at refining their metaphor: he saturates the portrait with 'colours' and she saturates their words, gestures, ideas and images with erotic meaning. In this way, she is truly being *made* – not only as an erotic object, but also as an erotic subject – with each stroke of Apelles's brush, shaped in the same way he sketches the contours of her face and form.[13] Hence it is not only Campaspe's language but also her role in their erotic relationship that becomes more artful, rich and stylised. In her later scenes with Apelles, Campaspe taps into the full measure of her 'polyfunctional virtuos[ity]' as a model, subtly shifting her postures from receptive to interpretive, from creative to responsive. Such postures carry more than artistic significance – each reveals Campaspe adopting new erotic attitudes that broaden and elevate her experience of desire.

This breadth is evident in their second scene together, when Apelles and Campaspe explore new ways to fashion themselves as artists and artificers. Campaspe's opening line reflects her responsive role as the model in their creative collaboration. She tends not to initiate conversation but to respond to what Apelles says, and she directs her erotic responses into portrait making, collapsing artistic process into erotic posturing:

> *Apelles.* I shall never draw your eyes well, because they blind mine.
> *Campaspe.* Why then, paint me without eyes, for I am blind.
>
> (III, iii, 1–2)

Campaspe's eyes have blinded Apelles; but what is the source of her purported blindness? Hunter remarks that 'It is not clear what Campaspe means by this.'[14] She apparently absorbs and reflects his sensory experience in her own body, which now functions as a portrait of *Apelles*, or at least, of Apelles's erotic experience, registered here as blindness. Again, the roles of subject, object and instrument are conflated in their erotic relation, and again, Campaspe directs Apelles to capture this relation on the canvas when she implores him to 'paint me without eyes'. Campaspe's virtuosity as a model has been to convert self-deprecation into art. Now she turns an even more destructive force – mutual- and self-blinding – into an aspect of creation.[15]

In the rest of this scene, Campaspe assumes the role of aesthetic and erotic interpreter, reflecting Apelles's art back to him as she does in their opening exchange, and continuing to develop the relationship between art and eros that the lovers have initiated together. Campaspe's power to make art by interpretation is not hers alone; the theatre audience shares in this erotic and creative potential as interpreters of Lyly's play. The play's prologue invites the audience to use their imaginations to co-create the visual experience of *Campaspe*: 'Whatsoever we present we wish it may be thought the dancing of Agrippa his shadows, who in the

moment they were seen were of any shape one could conceive' (The Prologue at the Court 13–15). Chloe Porter has
recently identified similarities between the 'discourses of
making' in the prologues in *Campaspe* and in Shakespeare's
Henry V. Of *Campaspe*'s prologue, Porter writes, 'the royal
audience is encouraged to engage with the play as a representation of unfixed meaning which may be reshaped
according to individual spectator perspective'.[16] In a play
that dramatises the erotics of creating art from the multiple
perspectives of the painter, the model and the interpreter,
the theatre audience is presented with a unique opportunity
to participate in the lovers' collaborative process, sharing in
the erotics of making throughout the play.

Campaspe's role as interpreter and critic becomes more
pronounced as Apelles points out classical scenes depicted
in portraits in his studio, nearly all of which feature Jupiter
ravishing an unsuspecting woman (Leda, Alcmena, Danaë,
Europa), and Campaspe sustains the couple's reciprocal
mode of speech. Their dialogue follows the call and response
pattern of their slant rhyme couplet about blindness; now,
however, each time that Apelles introduces an erotic episode from a painting, Campaspe proffers commentary.
Rather than address the quality of the artwork, Campaspe
consistently refers to the episode of ravishment itself, mor-
alising on the impropriety of the gods. Once again, they
instrumentalise art in the service of seduction; the paintings
become Campaspe's means of flirtation. Nor does it escape
our notice that, as was the case with Apelles in the previous
scene, so here it is Jupiter who changes shape. The artifi-
cer who ravishes is himself ravished, palpably 'alter[ed]' by
erotic desire.

Of course, whereas Jupiter hides his artifice from the objects
of his desire, Apelles and Campaspe display their artifice to
one another. They even anatomise it. Campaspe queries the
broader implications of each scene, asking Apelles if 'all gods

[were] like Jupiter' (III, iii, 24), and wondering about love and lust as they pertain to 'men on earth' (III, iii, 26). Then they not quite chiastically generalise about falsity:

> Campaspe: Were women never so fair, men would be false.
> Apelles: Were women never so false, men would be fond.
> (III, iii, 30–1)

Such generalisations about human falseness seem to degrade their own erotic medium. But the lovers' earlier acknowledgement of their own artifice distinguishes them from the men and women to whom they refer. This is not to say that they are somehow more genuine than the others, only that they are *better* at artifice and undeceived by its effects.

Campaspe's virtuosity lies in her ability to guide their artistic process subtly, playing the various roles of art object, interpreter and artist all at once. At the end of their dialogue, she figures herself as an art object by representing herself once again in terms of lack, this time in response to Apelles's question, 'But were you never in love?' (III, iii, 45). Campaspe replies that she has never been in love 'nor love in me' (III, iii, 46). Again, the lady portrays herself as diminished. On the one hand, Campaspe presents Apelles with a freshness and vitality that he struggles to capture; on the other hand, with no love '*in*' her, she is vacant inside, resembling a piece of art more than a person. Steiner shrewdly describes the

> life model [who] typically constructs herself as an image, however much the artist may feel he is the one posing her and determining what aspects of her will be represented. Many models . . . fashion themselves as the image to be rendered.[17]

Campaspe is both that which is interpreted and that which interprets. She is void of love so that Apelles can fill her and she hollows herself in a gesture of shared artistic (and erotic) making. Apelles responds by praising Campaspe's aptitude, her capacity to experience love: 'It is not possible that a face so fair and a wit so sharp, both without comparison, should not be apt to love' (III, iii, 51–2). 'Apt to love' tells us that she is predisposed or inclined both to love (as subject) and to be loved (as object).[18] Her agency – as co-creator, as artist in her own right – derives from her beauty and wit.

Campaspe's wit sharpens as the play goes on; soon her verbal artistry outpaces the famed painter's skill. Even as she confesses her mistrust of men who do not 'speak as they think' (IV, ii, 34), she employs artful and equivocal language. It is Apelles, not Campaspe, who breaks off from their measured and stylised mode of dialogue to ask his beloved plainly to 'give me leave to ask you a question' (IV, ii, 38–9) and then proceeds to enquire, simply and directly, 'Whom do you love best in the world?' (IV, ii, 42). Carefully, subtly and with distinctive art, Campaspe replies, 'He that made me last in the world' (IV, ii, 43). Her response confers upon Apelles the creative power of the artist, but Campaspe's reply also laconically, even gnomically, connects their artistic process to their erotic relation. By answering Apelles's question about love with a statement about art, she reconfirms her role alongside his in the erotic and artistic enterprise they have undertaken together. Of greater ontological import is her contention that it is not her portrait but rather *she herself* who has been 'made' by Apelles. Campaspe imagines things differently from Roland Barthes, who 'experience[s] a micro version of death' when photographed, at which time he becomes a 'subject who feels he is becoming an object'.[19] For her part, Campaspe asserts that her portraiture gestures toward the kind of afterlife that Harry Berger describes in his response to Barthes: 'what happens after . . . is that sitters begin to rouse themselves, to shake off this death, and to help painters represent them as living subjects by seeming to either try for, or to resist, the effect of objectivity'.[20]

Giving herself up to the 'effect of objectivity', Campaspe participates not in her death but her rebirth. She has enabled 'he that made me last in the world'.

Campaspe speaks this pointed but poignant line in their penultimate scene together. The metaphor they have created is finally equipped to bear this rich and powerful expression of erotic longing and belonging. Campaspe's language is still artful and stylised, but rather than employing euphuistic, parallel structure to connect art and eros in a sentence all of her own, she puts *Apelles's* line to this use. Campaspe's assertion gestures toward climax, a consummation of their scenes of verbal chafing – what Stephen Greenblatt identifies as a 'system of foreplay' in Shakespeare's comedies.[21] Utterly receptive to his 'Whom do you love best in the world?', Campaspe's 'he that made me last in the world' typifies the artful balance we have come to expect of their language. But, in this instance, Campaspe tenderly, if not quite undemonstratively, completes his line. She employs both the form and content of his line only to replace his 'love' with her 'making'. Her acknowledgement of her love and of her own made-ness are – for this moment, at least – inseparable. To love Apelles is to have been remade by him, but only she can confirm this and only by way of a metaphor that credits instrumentality (mutual making) in their relationship. It turns out that they are both and equally lovers and makers.

Apelles continues to reflect on the transformative power of his and Campaspe's artistic process, even after it has ended. Alone with the finished portrait, he employs and extends the metaphor that Campaspe developed. Apelles identifies the act of painting as the instrument of his desire for Campaspe in the opening lines of his soliloquy: 'Has thou *by drawing* her beauty brought to pass that thou canst scarce draw thine own breath?' (III, v, 14–15, emphasis added). Like the word 'colour' in the couple's earlier dialogue, 'drawing' and 'draw' here blur the distinction between the lovers.[22] Weaving the language of art into the experience of desire, polysemy and metaphor enable the lovers to access eros through art. And the balance and measure of Lyly's euphuistic structure, as in Apelles's next line, further bridges the gap between art and eros: 'by so much more hast thou increased thy care by how much more thou has showed thy cunning' (III, v, 16–17). So Apelles's 'increased . . . care' stems not just from Campaspe's beauty but from his own 'cunning', too. She has contributed her 'apt[ness]' and he meets it with his 'cunning'; their erotic relation depends on both. Moreover, Apelles's acknowledgement of his skill (his cunning) once again reminds us that not just art, but eros is something made, something responsive to aptitude. Apelles's emphasis on his own cunning may, at first, suggest that he is more interested in himself, attracted more to his own artistic skill and to his process of artistic creation, than he is attracted to the object of his desire, to Campaspe. If this is so, then why has he not fallen in love with the Venus he has been painting, or with any of his other portraits for that matter? Apelles may give us something of an answer when he tells us that he '*showed* [his] cunning' (17). While cunning is inherent, painting Campaspe, and apparently only Campaspe, has rendered it visible: visible to Apelles and visible to Campaspe, too. At the core of their erotic relation is their mutual exposure of their cunning and artfulness. This is what keeps Apelles's erotic desire from aligning with the familiar narrative of the narcissistic artist who falls in love with his own skill. Yes, his cunning has been shown in the portrait, but once it is revealed to Campaspe, she sees, matches and inspires his creative potential with her own. Her self-deprecation, her freshness and colour, her beauty and wit, her aptness to love, her discovery of a language that binds artistic to erotic creation, all of these gifts activate and release Apelles's 'cunning', thereby distinguishing this act of artistic reproduction from any other.

But what happens once the painting is complete? What happens, that is, when the product succeeds the process? No longer *a part of* the lovers' erotic relation, the finished painting stands *apart from* the lovers. Like the stick in Burke's anecdote, the lovers' loosened grip on the instrument turns it into an object; whereas the process of painting bridged the gap between the lovers, the completed painting becomes an obstacle between them. Apelles begins to explore the stakes of this shift when he compares himself to Pygmalion, another artist who fell in love with his creation. Of course, what makes Apelles different from Pygmalion (as Hunter points out in his gloss) is that Pygmalion did not work from a model.[23] Hunter writes that Apelles's reference to Pygmalion is a flawed comparison: 'The analogy with Pygmalion is defective unless we suppose that Apelles, despairing of the living Campaspe because she belongs to Alexander, wishes to have his painting turned into a second Campaspe.'[24] If Hunter is correct, then Apelles's flawed comparison reveals that the object of his desire is no longer just Campaspe; he now longs for the creative process itself, a once mutual but now solitary act.

The completion of the portrait, then, poses a double threat to Apelles and Campaspe's erotic relation – it enforces Apelles's solitude, since his model is no longer present, *and* it signals stasis, the end of the creative process.[25] By comparing himself to Pygmalion, Apelles reminds us of what happens to fantasies and rituals that grow static – they risk becoming artefacts rather than instruments of erotic desire. He desires Pygmalion's ability to animate a lifeless work of art because he wants to resuscitate the erotic instrument that has enabled his love for Campaspe. But in his determination to continue creating Campaspe, now that she is no longer present to do the same for him, Apelles is prepared to sidestep the shared artistic process that has instrumentalised their erotic experience. It is fitting, then, that Apelles begins to test the limits of his creative power in soliloquy, a solitary speech act. His longing to animate Campaspe's portrait reveals Apelles's desire for an artistic capacity beyond his means, and in his solitude, he also stretches the bounds of the language that the lovers have forged together. At this point, the generative power of the lovers' shared metaphor of painting gives way to a language of sculpture that turns out to be destructive; now Apelles, not Campaspe, undergoes a loss of self.

Apelles contrasts his situation and Pygmalion's, not, as one might expect, in terms of the differing objects of their desires, but instead in terms of means – he contrasts his own artistic medium of painting with Pygmalion's choice of sculpture. Apelles wonders if painting is 'so far inferior to carving, or dost thou, Venus, more delight to be hewed with chisels than shadowed with colours?' (III, v, 24–6). Although sculpture is the medium that produces a live woman for Pygmalion, Apelles reminds us here that it is ultimately a destructive art. The sculptor hews and chisels; the painter applies pigment to canvas. Curiously, once Apelles introduces the example of carving, it recurs again and again in his soliloquy. This shift from adding 'shadows' to chipping away at 'substance' illustrates the predicament that Apelles faces now that his painting is finished. The metaphorical entailments of sculpturing answer best to the destructive turn that Apelles's desire takes when he tries to use the portrait as an instrument of divine conjuration, disturbing the balance of the heretofore shared artistic process by seeking to create Campaspe all by himself.

Apelles's turn to sculpture corresponds with a shift in the sensory domains that he uses to conceptualise his interactions with Campaspe. A painter, Apelles begins by considering their interactions in terms of vision. Apelles gazes on his model in order to paint her and, of course, he gazes on her beauty – 'the colours I see' (III, i, 18) – in admiration and desire. But as his soliloquy goes on, he begins to think in terms of tactile erotic activity: optics ('behold' [III, v, 18]) give way to haptics ('kiss . . . and burn' [III, v, 19]). The historical Apelles is cited in Pliny and Vasari as an exemplar of artistic and erotic decorum, largely because the artistic medium of paint keeps him within the safe zone of 'behold[ing]' rather than caressing. Recently, Victor Stoichita has contrasted Apelles with Pygmalion, the sculptor who transgresses the bounds of art:

> [Apelles] creates a fairly sharp distinction between the erotic attraction of the model and the phantasm with which the painting is imbued – which is why Vasari tacitly accepts it . . . In the context of the *paragone*, pictorial creation and the two-dimensional projection of desire do not prevent the artist from making a distinction between his model and his phantasm-representation, whereas sculptural creation, three-dimensional and palpable, is an invitation to confuse the limits and, hence, to transgress.[26]

For Lyly's Apelles, the shift from optic to haptic language signifies his departure from conventionality and correctness; he transgresses the limits of his art when he conjures substance from shadows and caresses from 'colours'.[27]

Apelles's desire to bring Campaspe to life by animating her portrait reflects the early modern belief in the power of eros to conjure an image of a beloved's soul, known as a phantasm. According to the early modern psychology of erotic desire, a separate conceptual apparatus mediates between the sensory and non-sensory realms.[28] This apparatus belongs to a third ontological category that can translate between the corporeal and the incorporeal worlds, and it is composed of the same spirit (*pneuma*) that comprises the stars. In order to mediate between body and soul, the spirit translates sensory images into 'phantasms', pneumatic images that can be understood by the soul. Ioan Couliano has argued that this third category is fundamental to the early modern psychology of eros, in which desire is defined as 'the pursuit of a phantasm' rather than the pursuit of a love object who exists apart from the desiring subject.[29] Apelles's desire to animate the portrait reveals that Campaspe's phantasm has replaced Campaspe as the object of his creative enterprise.

Perhaps it is his unnatural creative ambitions that prompt Apelles to compare his love for Campaspe to a series of seemingly unnatural attractions: 'Thou mayst swim against the stream with the crab, and feed against the wind with the deer, and peck against the steel with the cockatrice' (III, v, 39–41). The parallel structure suggests that Apelles's comparisons are all fundamentally alike; but the final example in his series is nothing of the sort. While the crab and deer movements resist the natural order prevalent in their respective habitats, the cockatrice's pecking is more closely aligned with art than with nature, and it is decidedly violent. Of course, the cockatrice – a deadly combination of cock and serpent – is itself an artifice. Hunter notes that Alexander was said to have killed a cockatrice by placing a mirror ('steel') before it, prompting it to 'peck against' its own image and ultimately die from its own reflected lethal gaze. The mirror produces a new image and, at the same time, causes the demise of the cockatrice. Unlike what transpires when Venus is hewn, it is now Apelles – the artist rather than the model – who risks destruction in the course of artistic creation that, once again, collapses the distance between the artist and his object.[30] In his earlier premonition that Campaspe 'will alter the colour I have' (III, i, 18–19), Apelles hints at this destruction. The change that both lovers undergo necessarily entails a kind of self-loss, but now that Campaspe is gone, 'alter[ation]' gives way to destruction.

It is fitting that Apelles compares the cockatrice's self-destructive behaviour – its assault on a reflected image and its sculptural mode of attack – with his own just when he begins to pursue Campaspe's phantasm. As it happens, early modern writings about the erotic phantasm also employ the metaphor of sculpture. In his empirical philosophy, Marsilio Ficino conceptualises the phantasm as being carved or engraved on the lover's soul: 'the lover carves [*sculpit*] into his soul the model of the beloved' and the phantasm takes up a residence there, monopolising it and ultimately exiling the lover from his own soul.[31] Couliano describes the consequences of this erotic transaction as dire: 'the subject, bereft of his soul, is no longer a subject: the phantasmic vampire has devoured it internally'.[32] Ideally, the beloved will undergo the same process, making room for the lover's phantasm within her soul so that the subject and object effectively switch places, each continuing to exist within the other's soul. However, in reality, one can never be sure that the beloved will accept one's phantasm, making the experience of erotic desire inherently risky. Like the process of artistic creation, creating a phantasm of the beloved requires the lover to hazard his own subjectivity. And as with the artistic process, it is the loss or lack of mutuality (in the case of phantasmic creation, it is the lack of reciprocal exchange) that poses the greatest threat to the desiring subject.

With his subjectivity at stake, it is unsurprising that Apelles's desires turn inward. His transformation, from artist to lover and finally to conjurer or magician, correlates with a comparable shift in the nature of the objects he plans to paint. Now that he has finished the portraits of Campaspe and Venus, Apelles discloses the artistic achievements that await him:

> Blush, Venus, for I am ashamed to end thee. Now must I paint things unpossible for mine art but agreeable with my affections: deep and hollow sighs, sad and melancholy thoughts, wounds and slaughters of conceits, a life posting to death, a death galloping from life, a wavering constancy, an unsettled resolution, and what not, Apelles? And what but, Apelles?
>
> (III, v, 49–56)

To paint sighs, thoughts, conceits, life, death, constancy and resolution will require Apelles to engage in an activity aligned more with magical conjuration than with artistic invention. Apelles ascribes to his art a Pygmalion-like generative and life-giving power; to paint 'life' itself is to *bring to life*. Moreover, painting 'things unpossible for mine art but agreeable with my affections' marks a decisive shift in the nature of the painting's subject matter. Heretofore, his portraits have depicted objects of desire: a striking goddess and a captive woman. Apelles's new, self-imposed mandate to paint sighs, conceits and thoughts suggests that the sighs and thoughts that Campaspe has drawn out of him have themselves become the objects of his affections. Absent Campaspe, Apelles feels compelled to paint the markers of her absence, redirecting his erotic and creative attentions toward his own longing. Thus Apelles begins to desire his own conceits and thoughts – things that typically constitute the *means* by which a person desires – and so to fall in love with the 'how' of his own erotic desire. That Apelles has begun to desire himself is unsurprising in light of the self-loss he risks in his pursuit of Campaspe's phantasm. What Campaspe once elicited from him, he will now formalise in paint.

Apelles's list of new painting subjects concludes with a puzzling pair of questions that reflect this inward turn: 'and what not, Apelles? And what but, Apelles?' In his first question, the painter acknowledges the staggeringly vast scope of subjects he will need to cover if he is to paint things 'agreeable with my affections'. And yet, his second question distils the range of possibilities to a single subject: himself. The comma after 'but' is Hunter's emendation. He explains that he has 'altered the punctuation and the sense from Q1's "what but *Apelles*". I take the meaning to be, "And what but sighs, thoughts, conceits etc. will I be able to depict?"'[33] This is plausible but the Quarto punctuation is much more suggestive. When Apelles asks himself the question, 'and what but

Apelles?', his shift from painting women to painting thoughts takes another sharp turn: the final object of his erotic desire is himself. Apelles is not so much dismissing his desire for Campaspe as he is acknowledging the effects of their artistic process on his sense of self. His role as Campaspe's maker has 'alter[ed]' Apelles to such an extent that he, too, has been remade by the artistic process. To create Campaspe (or to create sighs, conceits, life, resolution) is to recreate himself: 'what but Apelles?' His desire for Campaspe has become a longing for the version of himself that she unlocks when she inspires him to create. His lines about painting 'unpossible things' and about eventually painting himself reveal Apelles's desire not only to become more intimate with the artistry Campaspe has aroused in him, but also to recover the part of himself that he hazards when he tries to conjure the lady's soul by way of her portrait. If, as it turns out, Apelles is never quite able to use the portrait for this purpose, then it must be because his artwork is the result of a collaborative process that resists independent instrumentalisation like Pygmalion's. That the painter spends the remainder of the play searching for a means – in prayer, in sculpture, in song – by which to conjure Campaspe is evidence of the importance of such creative instruments to their erotic relation. Yet all of Apelles's attempts result in weak substitutions for what he achieves when he collaborates with Campaspe.

The importance of mutuality is especially evident when Apelles finally succeeds in summoning Campaspe's phantasm in the song he sings at the end of his soliloquy. He conjures her simply by imagining her, by animating her in his mind. But the phantasm he creates is almost a negative image of Campaspe herself and thus proves to be a poor replacement for the lady. Apelles's song is about a game of cards between Cupid and Campaspe, in which Cupid stakes everything he has and loses it all to the lady. At the beginning of the song, Cupid wagers his familiar accoutrements ('his quiver, bow

and arrows' [III, v, 73]), but once he loses these, the stakes
become more severe:

> then down he throws
> The coral of his lip; the rose
> Growing on's cheek (but none knows how),
> With these the crystal of his brow,
> And then the dimple of his chin;
> All these did my Campaspe win
> At last he set her both his eyes;
> She won, and Cupid blind did rise.
> (III, v, 75–82)

Minus his coral lip and his blushing cheeks, Cupid is effectively de-blazoned and un-painted. This Campaspe really
does have the power to 'alter ... colour' (III, i, 18) – but
where the lady once summoned blushes, her phantasm now
suppresses them. Couliano writes, 'When Eros is at work,
the phantasm of the loved object leads its own existence, all
the more disquieting because it exerts a kind of vampirism
on the subject's other phantasms and thoughts.'[34] The imagery in Apelles's song suggests that Campaspe's phantasm
poses this vampiric threat; she is literally appalling. Effectively
preying on Love, Campaspe's phantasm now decimates the
erotic relation that the lady had been so instrumental in
co-creating with Apelles.

Although Apelles's song conjures a woman who wields
considerable power over Eros, that is where the similarities
end between the phantasm and lady with whom he has fallen
in love. The phantasm exerts a much more destructive power
as it creates, a power signalled by the language of carving.
Once Cupid is deprived of his 'coral' cheek and 'rose' lip, his
face is subjected to carving and chiselling. Cupid keeps raising the stakes, wagering his brow, then the dimple on his chin
and finally his eyes, but he loses it all to Campaspe's winning
hand. Having initially risked only his 'freshness' and vitality,

Cupid now suffers a loss of his identifying facial features. And yet, as is the case with the other examples of destruction in Apelles's soliloquy, the scene between Campaspe and Cupid proves generative as well. Campaspe's phantasm effectively *makes* Cupid what he is best known for by taking from him, until, at last, 'Cupid *blind* did rise' (III, v, 82). In conjuring Campaspe's phantasm, then, Apelles reimagines the lady's creative power, but with a difference that extends beyond the artistic medium of paint versus sculpture. Whereas the lady's virtuosity lies in her ability to diminish herself artfully, the phantasm diminishes Love itself. She remains perfectly intact in the course of her interaction with Eros; Apelles imagines her chipping away at Cupid instead of risking any loss of her own.

Apelles's soliloquy dramatises his attempt to recover what is unrecoverable – a once-collaborative creative process that enabled the painter's erotic relation with Campaspe. The completed portrait simply cannot do the work of remaking the lady, nor can Apelles's 'cunning'; thus the portrait and his cunning both become objects of his erotic desire in the hope that they can lead him back to the lady. Even Apelles's apparent success in creating Campaspe in song is overshadowed by the phantasm's profound differences from the woman. The sum total of these differences – in their creative power and artistic medium, in their skill and even their temperament – results in the most profound distinction of all: the phantasm lacks Campaspe's 'apt[ness] to love'. The phantasm, although triumphant over Cupid, is manifestly unresponsive to the process of erotic creation. Where Campaspe suffered blindness in response to Apelles's wounded eyes, the phantasm is impassive and invulnerable; in his song, Apelles sees her as an agent of Love's blindness rather than its victim. Although the phantasm's aggression could signal her active engagement in the gambling match, in truth she does very little in the song other than play her cards well. If anyone is doing anything, it is Cupid: the subject of Apelles's song, Cupid, independently and seemingly without prompting, hazards various aspects of his character. But even the erotic quality of the card game quickly dissipates. In the opening lines of the song we learn that the game is being played 'for kisses' (III, v, 72) but these stakes are never mentioned again. And blindness, which had been evidence of the erotic love between Apelles and Campaspe, is seemingly sapped of its erotic significance in the newly risen blind Cupid. Unlike kisses given or received, Cupid's blindness is hardly a prize, since the phantasm does not stand to gain anything from it. The phantasm's erotic detachment reveals the limits of Apelles's creative power now that the lady herself is absent. Presumably, Apelles could have imagined any version of his beloved in his song – a yielding Campaspe, a receptive Campaspe, a kissing Campaspe – but the indifferent woman he conjures suggests that the phantasm has taken on a life of its own. As Victor Stoichita observes, 'the "life" of a masterpiece – already implies, albeit still implicitly – . . . the death of the model'.[35] The qualitative difference between Campaspe and her phantasm suggests that the lady suffers a kind of death as Apelles turns his attentions to recreating her in his solitude.

It makes sense, then, that Apelles is in no rush to move beyond the bounds of his art, that he wants to prolong his time painting Campaspe until Alexander at last demands the finished product. As Peter Sloterdijk notes, portrait art is itself 'a protracting procedure that emphasises or draws out individuality'.[36] For Apelles, who is unable to tolerate the prospect of ending their artistic and erotic interaction, the only way forward is to extend it by adding blemishes to the portrait. This may be a subtle act of homage to Campaspe, whose own intention it was to desecrate herself artfully, to create what she calls a 'disordered countenance' (III, iv, 71) conducive to a 'deformed' painting (III, iv, 72).

But Apelles's deformations also reveal the importance of process over product in an erotic relation. That a great painter,
famed for his ability to create unparalleled works of art, is
willing to damage his portrait in order to prolong the artistic
process testifies to the dangers of imagining any artistic or
erotic relationship as perfect or complete. The lovers' mutual
creativity depends on imperfect and incomplete portraiture.
It is this that makes Campaspe's skill at diminishment so vital
to their relation; her affected modesty stimulates the creativity, betterment and art that alone are the instruments of their
lovemaking.

When Campaspe returns to Apelles's studio for a final
time, their artistic metaphor takes on its deepest erotic significance. Their need to co-create is nowhere more pronounced.
When he puts the final touches to the portrait at the end of
Act IV, Apelles tells Campaspe that he has 'almost made an
end'. Her poignant response is that 'You told me, Apelles,
you would never end' (IV, iv, 1–2). Their barely veiled language works as it often does in plays that feature forbidden
love; the painting (both the activity and the resulting portrait) communicates their illicit feelings. Campaspe's recourse
to the metaphor they have crafted once again instrumentalises the process of painting, making it a linguistic prosthetic
for the things they are unable to say. And like her earlier
rejoinder ('he that made me last in the world'), her gentle
yet wistful reproach again completes Apelles's line. Once
again, Campaspe imbues his words with the balance and
symmetry that have constituted their erotic medium, binding
together painting and loving as coincident experiences that
'never end'. But Lyly subtly demonstrates that Campaspe's
line *is* an ending – it is her response to and her completion of
Apelles's opening words. And this scene is, likewise, an ending. Apelles may have it in mind to prolong the process by
entering into an endless loop of blemishing and then retouch-
ing the portrait. But his aspiration to conjure substance from

shadows now far exceeds anything he set out to accomplish with Campaspe as his co-creator.

The simultaneously futile and transgressive nature of Apelles's ambition comes out in his dialogue with Campaspe as they prepare to part from one another at the end of Act IV. When she asks him what he will do if Alexander forbids him to see her, Apelles replies that he will 'gaze continually on thy picture' (IV, iv, 10). But not for long. In his next line Apelles explains that 'the sweet thoughts, the sure hopes, thy protested faith, will cause me to embrace thy shadow continually in mine arms, of the which by strong imagination I will make a substance' (IV, iv, 12–15).[37] Apelles's preposition 'by' cues the idea of agency but now the instrument of desire is neither his artistic skill nor his cunning – it has become Apelles's desire itself, his 'strong imagination'. Having divested the art of 'shadowing' of its erotic instrumentality, Apelles reimagines the shadow-portrait, animated by the strength of his own desire, as the means by which he can conjure the lady's substance. Even though Campaspe stands right beside him, Apelles dreams of summoning her phantasm via the portrait. His erotic attentions are now directed at the portrait, 'the thing that is likest you' (IV, ii, 47), in Apelles's words. Eros was once the *telos* of their artistic interaction, but now Apelles imagines an erotic embrace that will create Campaspe out of her 'shadow'.

In order to explain Apelles's fixation on the portrait, the King's counsellor, Hephestion, recounts to Alexander the traditional story of the artist's narcissistic desire: 'commonly we see it incident in artificers to be enamoured of their own works . . . poor souls, they kiss the colours with their lips, with which before they were loath to taint their fingers' (V, iv, 15–16 and 22–4). Upon observing Apelles's 'perplexed' (V, iv, 12) looks and his inability to concentrate, Alexander has begun to suspect that 'the painter is in love' (V, iv, 14), presumably with a live person. But apparently Hephestion

sees no difference (or he pretends that there is no difference) between Apelles's love for Campaspe and his desire for
her shadow.[38] Alexander picks up on this pretence when he
devises a love test to 'find it out' (V, iv, 25), 'it' being Apelles's
desire for the substance or the shadow: 'Page, go speedily for
Apelles. Will him to come hither, and when you see us ear-
nestly in talk, suddenly cry out, "Apelles's shop is on fire!"'
(V, iv, 25–7). Later in the scene, Apelles's reaction to the cha-
rade apparently gives him away as a lover: 'Ay me, if the
picture of Campaspe be burnt I am undone!' (V, iv, 92–3).
Of all the love tests Alexander could devise, why would he
choose this particular scenario to expose Apelles's desire for
Campaspe? Why not dissemble endangering the lady herself
instead of her portrait? It seems that Alexander either views
Apelles's attitude toward the painting as symptomatic of the
painter's feelings for Campaspe, or that, like Hephestion, the
King sees no difference between the lady and the 'shadow'
at all.

Apelles's simultaneously dispiriting and decorous response
to Alexander is to insist that he is in love with his painting
rather than the lady who inspired it:

> Not love her. But your Majesty knows that painters in their
> last works are said to excel themselves, and in this I have
> so much pleased myself that the shadow as much delighteth
> me, being an artificer, as the substance doth others that are
> amorous.

> (V, iv, 99–103)

Of course, the king is unconvinced, and Lyly cleverly awards
him the play's final painting metaphor when he expresses his
doubt. 'You lay your colours grossly' (V, iv, 104), he tells
Apelles, with a pun on yet another meaning of 'colours', as
rhetorical flourishes. It would appear that Alexander completely rejects the play's conviction that artifice can serve
as the instrument of erotic experience. In commonsensical

Alexander's mind, art and eros are fundamentally different. The most that he will concede is that Apelles has used the former to hide the latter.

When Alexander resolves to join Apelles and Campaspe together in love at the end of the play, he employs the straightforward and unadorned language we have come to expect from him, informing the lady, 'Campaspe, here is news: Apelles is in love with you' (V, iv, 115–16). This plain speech is bracing, if for no other reason than that neither Apelles nor Campaspe has made any such artless declaration. Alexander has no choice but assertively (and comically) to prompt the conspicuously tongue-tied lovers: 'Apelles, take Campaspe. Why move ye not? Campaspe, take Apelles. Will it not be?' (V, iv, 131–2). The lovers do eventually acquiesce (admitting their feelings in uncharacteristically simple language: 'Pardon, my lord, I love Apelles' [V, iv, 135]) but their reticence cannot be explained by their fear of inciting Alexander's anger. He has repeatedly consented to the match, not to mention encouraged the pair to profess their feelings forthrightly. Evidently, it is the lovers themselves who stand in the way of a happy union at the end of the play. Absent the language of painting as the medium through which to conceptualise and communicate their desire, they are stymied. Without their secret language, the lovers hardly have any language at all.

What the lovers do have is Alexander's plain speech, a language that portends not just the loss of artistry and not just silence, but more ominously, the extinction of eros. Because Apelles and Campaspe's erotic relation is something they have made, it is necessarily artificial. When the lovers replace their own stylised mode of speech with Alexander's plain style, they loosen their grip on the erotic relation they have crafted together. Plainness, for them, is tantamount to dullness; as Cleopatra says, 'there is nothing left remarkable' (IV, xv, 68). Once the lovers stop artfully

210]   *Conceiving Desire in Lyly and Shakespeare*

making their erotic relation, they begin, artlessly, to break it. Because eros is always in process for them, there can be no middle ground, no stasis. Hence even the ending of the play – with its fusion of union and reticence – indicates a desire, on Lyly's part no less than the lovers', to prolong the creative process.

This correlation between the lovers' creative process and Lyly's own dramatic art reminds us that Apelles and Campaspe inherit their self-conscious artifice from Lyly. All of what I have been arguing about the erotic instrument – its dual capacity to bring lovers into relation and to keep them apart; its self-conscious artificiality and made-ness; its responsiveness to process and attenuation upon consummation; its dependence on mutuality – is true of Lyly's dramatic language.[39] In particular, the features of the erotic instrument are hallmarks of Lyly's euphuistic and antithetical prose style.[40] Traditionally, euphuism is defined as an ornamental verbal pattern distinguished by its symmetries and antitheses, especially *isocolon* (clauses of the same length), *parison* (clauses with corresponding grammatical structures) and *paramoion* (words with similar sounds, such as alliteration).[41] Euphuistic balance, antithesis and doubling make Lyly's language an especially apt instrument in its own right: these are the media through which we encounter Apelles and Campaspe's erotic experience, and art-making is the medium through which they access eros. The linguistic density and abundance typical of Lyly's style contribute to the rhythms of deferral and delay that are so vital to Apelles and Campaspe's relation. The tendency of euphuism and antithesis to draw us 'progressively further from an inevitable goal' and 'frustrate the drive of the narrative towards finality and closure' reflects the pace of Apelles and Campaspe's erotic experience, which can flourish only for as long as the lovers can protract their artistic process.[42]

Perhaps more telling than its resistance to closure is euphuism's capacity to bring distinct conceptual and experiential domains into relation with one another. Antitheses are euphuistic stock in trade but Lyly also has penchant for conjoining *un*related concepts or ideas.[43] Leah Scragg writes that the balance, symmetry and ornamental features of euphuism often 'yok[e] disparate areas of experience'.[44] It is unsurprising, then, that euphuism becomes an instrument of Campaspe's own creative and interpretive process throughout the play, from her use of polysemic language ('colours', 'draw') to the symmetries she finds between Apelles's flattering words and his artful brushstrokes. Jonas Barish argues that Lyly uses the 'more general logicality' of euphuism 'to express the composite nature of experience'.[45] To Barish's final phrase, I would add the word 'erotic': for Apelles and Campaspe, euphuism formalises *a composite experience of eros* that artfully draws on the artist's pigment *and* words, on the model's gestures *and* judgements. This 'composite nature' is especially evident in the deployment of instruments as a means of accessing eros; the artistic instruments that stand between Lyly's erotic subject and object are also what bring them together. Euphuism and instrumentality both illuminate symmetries *and* preserve basic divisions between subject and object. The result is a heterogeneous 'composite' erotic experience; euphuistic terms are always held apart by the structure of the sentence, brought together only to be placed on parallel tracks. Such tension and drag is, of course, a prominent feature of instrumentality itself – the greater the adornment, the greater the friction. This is the tension that is constitutive of the erotic process that Lyly dramatises – it is what Apelles longs to preserve in his attempts to blemish and correct the painting, to keep it lodged firmly between himself and his beloved. A play like *Campaspe*, in which eros is so self-consciously artful and highly wrought, reveals the unique capacity of Lyly's dramatic style to act as an erotic instrument in its own right.

Beyond Lyly's own creative project, what can the domain of artistic creation tell us about the properties of erotic desire? Although painting serves many practical purposes in Lyly's play – it is Apelles's profession, the reason he meets Campaspe in the first place, and the activity that accompanies all of their other interactions – it also serves a conceptual purpose. It provides the lovers with more than a vocabulary; it affords them a structure, a conceptual system, which gives their experience of erotic desire its shape, its medium and its meaning. The roles, relationships and entailments of the domain of artistic invention – artist and model, pigment and paintbrush, 'aptness' and 'cunning', gazing and posing, 'gloz[ing]' and 'seem[ing]', representation and reflection – highlight the creative features of the erotic experience. The lovers *make* their desire together by means of the metaphor. And metaphor in turn sustains their erotic experience, just as much as the act of painting, as much as the lovers' newly discovered 'cunning' or 'apt[ness]'. Deprived of their metaphor in the final scene of the play, they have no means of knowing or experiencing desire. Artistic creation is the only way that they can access eros, which is why Apelles clings so desperately to the creative medium in Campaspe's absence. But his problematic attempts at conjuring Campaspe's phantasm, by way of the song or the portrait, reveal the importance of collaboration in making an erotic relation that remains vital and 'fresh' (III, i, 1). No sooner do the lovers relinquish their shared metaphor of artistic process than they forfeit eros itself.

Notes

1. Emily Dickinson, 'Tell all the truth but tell it slant –', 792.
2. G. K. Hunter notes that in the couple's first scene together, 'there is some likelihood that the *Entry* involves a *Discovery*.

The opening dialogue suggests that we first see Apelles actually engaged in painting Campaspe' (*Campaspe*, 86).

3. The linguistic component of this type of erotic relation is the subject of Chapter 6, which focuses on Shakespeare's *Taming of the Shrew*.

4. The word 'device' itself incorporates the ideas of desire and instrumentality. According to the *OED*, its complex etymology results from the mingling of two Old French and Middle English words, *devis* and *devise*. Entry 3a defines 'device' as 'will, pleasure, inclination, fancy, desire'. See 'device, *n*.', in *The Oxford English Dictionary*, 2nd edn, 1989, *OED Online*, Oxford University Press. Available at: <http://dictionary.oed. com/view/Entry/51464> (last accessed 1 June 2012).

5. See 'fresh, *adj.1*' (esp. entry 10), in *The Oxford English Dictionary*, 2nd edn, 1989, *OED Online*, Oxford University Press. Available at: <http://www.oed.com/view/Entry/74535> (last accessed 1 June 2011). Apelles will later compare Campaspe with Venus and note that the lady's countenance is 'somewhat fresher' (III, v, 47) than that of the goddess.

6. See E. H. Gombrich, *The Heritage of Apelles: Studies in the Art of the Renaissance*, 4–15. Gombrich cites an anecdote from Pliny's *Natural History*, in which Apelles competes with the famous painter Protogenes, each drawing a thinner line than the other on a panel. Gombrich interprets their competition as a parable of the invention of three-dimensional lustre in classical art: 'Apelles returning would have bisected [Protogenes's line] by an even thinner line that suggested gleam or splendour, and to this nothing could be added now without spoiling the appearance of the line, which would have begun to stand out from the panel as if by magic' (15).

7. See Wendy Steiner, *The Real Real Thing: The Model in the Mirror of Art*, 27.

8. Evelyn Tribble has shown that 'enskilment' and virtuosity of the boy actor operate in similar ways: 'staged ineptitude and meta-theatricality is used as an ironic means of making skill visible and of drawing attention to the

normally hidden skills of stage presence, wit, aptness, and quickness' (Tribble, 'Pretty and Apt: Boy Actors, Skill, and Embodiment', 633).

9. The metaphor 'Love is a Collaborative Work of Art' brings 'the active side of love . . . into the foreground through the notion of work', write George Lakoff and Mark Johnson. 'This requires the masking of certain aspects of love that are viewed passively. In fact, the emotional aspects of love are almost never viewed as being under the lovers' active control in our conventional conceptual system' (*Metaphors We Live By*, 141).

10. 'Gloze / gloss' also refers to the artistic activity of adding glaze or sheen. See 'gloss, *v.2*', in *The Oxford English Dictionary*, 2nd edn, 1989, *OED Online*, Oxford University Press. Available at: <http://www.oed.com/view/Entry/79133?> (last accessed 1 June 2012). Campaspe deploys a similar technique when she admonishes Apelles in the following scene: 'If you begin to tip your tongue with cunning, I pray dip your pencil in colours' (III, v, 53–4). Here, the parallel arrangement of her euphuistic line binds Apelles's artistic instruments (his pencil dipped in colours) together with his erotic instruments (his tongue tipped in cunning).

11. By contrast, Alexander is quite taken with what he perceives to be Campaspe's 'curst yielding modesty' (III, iv, 142), which suggests that the King resembles the other men to whom Apelles refers in this dialogue.

12. Hunter favours pallor over blushing in his gloss of Apelles's line: 'The beautiful colour of your complexion will, I fear, so affect me that I will turn pale (or blush)' (*Campaspe*, 87).

13. When Alexander asks Apelles, 'Where do you first begin, when you draw any picture?' (III, iv, 81–2), Apelles replies that he starts with the outer contours ('the proportion of the face, in just compass' [83]) and adds subtle details and adornments only after establishing this initial shape.

14. 'It is not clear what Campaspe means by this, unless it is "I too am blinded by love"; but such a remark would seem insufficiently modest for Campaspe. David Bevington suggests

an oblique reference to the traditional blindness of Cupid' (*Campaspe*, 91).

15. Campaspe later confesses her desire to be diminished even further, to be rendered invisible in paint: 'would you could so now shadow me that I might not be perceived of any' (III, iii, 5–6).

16. Chloe Porter, 'Idolatry, Iconoclasm, and Visual Experience in Works by Shakespeare and Lyly', 2.

17. Steiner, *The Real Real Thing*, 22.

18. For 'apt', *OED* 2.b and 4.c read 'fit, prepared, ready' and 'customarily disposed, given, inclined, prone', respectively. (See *The Oxford English Dictionary*, 2nd edn, 1989, *OED Online*, Oxford University Press. Available at: <http://www.oed.com/view/Entry/9969> [last accessed 1 June 2011].) If love is something one can be 'apt to', then it is as much a skill or talent as it is an emotion or state of mind. To align love with aptitude is to emphasise the 'how' of desire. Apelles's gift of painting, his ability to create Campaspe in pigment, makes him 'apt to love' as well.

19. Qtd in part in Harry Berger, Jr, *Fictions of the Pose: Rembrandt Against the Italian Renaissance*, 226. See Roland Barthes, *Camera Lucida: Reflections on Photography*, 13–14.

20. Berger, *Fictions of the Pose*, 226.

21. Stephen Greenblatt, *Shakespearean Negotiations: The Circulation of Social Energy in Renaissance England*, 89. I would emend Greenblatt's formulation, at least in this case; for Campaspe and Apelles, chafing is less foreplay than it is the event itself.

22. The polysemy of 'draw' also suggests that Campaspe's gain is Apelles's loss: breathing life into her image obstructs the painter's own ability to breathe. Once again, the metaphor uncovers the imbricated artistic processes of creation and depletion, of elevation and diminishment, which constitute Apelles and Campaspe's erotic relation.

23. Victor Stoichita notes that Pygmalion's story differs from other narratives of artists whose works came to life. Pygmalion's statue constitutes a simulacrum rather than an image copied from nature: 'Pygmalion's statue is the fruit of his imagination

and of his "art," and the woman whom the gods gave him for a spouse is a strange creature, an artifact endowed with a soul and a body, but nevertheless a fantasy. A simulacrum, precisely.' See Victor I. Stoichita, *The Pygmalion Effect: From Ovid to Hitchcock*, 3.

24. Hunter, *Campaspe*, 102.
25. In the scene just before Apelles delivers his soliloquy, the painter insists that he will 'never finish' (III, iv, 93) the portrait because Campaspe's beauty exceeds the bounds of art.
26. Stoichita, *The Pygmalion Effect*, 56.
27. In his final soliloquy of the play, Apelles comments on his shift from visual to tactile erotic activity, admitting that he has betrayed his own art in his desire for the lady: 'O Campaspe, I have painted thee in my heart—painted? nay, contrary to mine art, imprinted; and that in such deep characters that nothing can raze it out unless it rub thy heart out' (V, ii, 16–19).
28. This psychology, largely Aristotelian, attempts to bridge the division between body and soul that was decisive for Plato. The apparatus that Aristotle identifies in *De Anima* has conceptual and linguistic properties.
29. See Ioan P. Couliano, *Eros and Magic in the Renaissance*, 38–9. Couliano repeatedly notes that the object of desire is the phantasm, rather than the beloved herself: 'the love object plays a secondary role in the process of establishing the phantasm: it is only a pretext, not a real presence . . . We do not love *another* object, a stranger to ourselves . . . We are enamored of an unconscious image' (31).
30. Apelles conceptualises the pain of his desire through the language of carving, specifically as a penetrating wound and canker. The symptoms of his 'affections' include 'deep and hollow sighs', as well as 'wounds and slaughters of conceits' (III, v, 51–3).
31. 'Amans amati suo figuram sculpit in animo' (Marsilio Ficino, *Amore*, II, 8, qtd in Couliano, *Eros and Magic*, 31).
32. Ibid., 31.
33. Hunter, *Campaspe*, 104.

34. Couliano, *Eros and Magic*, 31.

35. Stoichita, *The Pygmalion Effect*, 65.

36. Peter Sloterdijk, *Bubbles: Spheres I*, 163.

37. Hunter suggests that 'Apelles seems to have in mind the Pygmalion story' (*Campaspe*, 116). The relationship between Apelles and Pygmalion here is doubly significant: not only does Apelles yearn to bring his artwork to life, but also he refers here to the medium of sculpture ('substance') over painting ('shadow'). 'Substance' is subject to kisses and 'embrace[s]'; shadows are not.

38. Hephestion is the mouthpiece for conventional (and often misogynistic) beliefs about love; it is no surprise that he is the character who most readily refers to the narcissistic, auto-erotic activity of 'painters . . . playing with their own conceits' (V, iv, 19).

39. Michael Pincombe has suggested a likeness between Apelles's portrait and Lyly's own art: 'Lyly, I think, uses the device of the defaced portrait as an emblem of the way he felt his own art might be deformed by the pressures of writing in a political context such as that of the court, in which, as his own play shows, one had to be very careful what one said or wrote.' See Pincombe, *The Plays of John Lyly*, 46.

40. Jonas Barish claims that *Campaspe*'s 'weak and inconclusive ending' is a result of Lyly's 'peculiar . . . logical style', endemic to the playwright's euphuistic prose. According to Barish, 'the force that has disjoined character or analyzed feeling to create dramatic tension can do little to fuse or recombine them'. See Jonas A. Barish, 'The Prose Style of John Lyly', 34.

41. Barish ('Prose Style', 14–15) cites traditional definitions of euphuism in Morris William Croll and Henry Clemons's edition of *Euphues: The Anatomy of Wit* and *Euphues and His England* (London, 1916).

42. Leah Scragg's edition of *Euphues: The Anatomy of Wit* and *Euphues and His England*, 5.

43. Such odd and unrelated pairings have often unsettled readers and scholars of Lyly's work. Carter Daniel's Introduction to his 1988 edition of Lyly's plays cites various indictments

of the 'preposterous', 'strained' and 'unnatural' quality of his euphuistic pairings. Daniel finds in Lyly's euphuistic language evidence of the playwright's 'comic spirit'. See Carter Daniel's Introduction to *The Plays of John Lyly*, 12–13.

44. Scragg, *Euphues*, 19.
45. Barish, 'Prose Style', 27.

CHAPTER 6

'YOU LIE, IN FAITH': MAKING MARRIAGE IN *THE TAMING OF THE SHREW*

In this final chapter, I turn to the instrumental role of language itself as a medium of erotic experience. The 'Desiring is Creating' metaphor in *The Taming of the Shrew* depends upon the creative power of words, rather than an artist's pigments or a model's gestures, as erotic instruments. The subject of language is by no means new to this section's analysis of creativity; we already have seen Campaspe's euphuism and polysemy weave the lovers' artistic and erotic experiences together. But, unlike the instruments of Lyly's lovers, Kate and Petruchio's art is itself an art of language; they creatively recruit words, stories and lies to make a marriage together. Words themselves *act* in *The Taming of the Shrew* – for Petruchio and Kate, they *create* – and this dynamic quality makes their language something more than solely instrumental. As Kenneth Burke explains,

> Those who begin with the stress upon *tools* proceed to define language itself as a species of tool. But though instrumentality is an important aspect of language, we could not properly treat it as the *essence* of language. To define language simply as a species of tool would be like defining metals merely as a species of tools. Or like defining sticks and

> stones simply as primitive weapons. Edward Sapir's view
> of language as 'a collective means of expression' points in
> a more appropriate direction ... Language is a species of
> action, symbolic action – and its nature is such that it can
> be used as a tool.[1]

The 'Desiring is Creating' metaphor dramatises the dynamic
quality of words: erotic language creates and is thus 'a spe-
cies of action'. For Kate and Petruchio specifically, their
marriage making project requires them to create a private
world through language. Their language becomes as self-
consciously artificial as the synthetic world they build, not
only in its often elaborate and even hyperbolic style, but
also in its content – Petruchio and Kate's words are artfully
styled, but they also are false in their substance, belying the
truth of the real world.

Early on in *The Taming of the Shrew*, it becomes clear
that Petruchio is a liar of the highest order. Even before he
gets down to the business of taming Kate by fabricating flaws
with the meat at their dining table, his words have more
swagger than substance. Bombarding Baptista with a slew
of metaphors before he even meets Kate, Petruchio begins
the process of creating his and Kate's relationship through
words:

> I am as peremptory as she proud-minded,
> And where two raging fires meet together
> They do consume the thing that feeds their fury.
> (II, i, 132–4)

In due course, those 'two raging fires' quickly become
Kate's 'little fire' (135) striving against his 'extreme gusts'
(136), then *Kate's* 'winds' (141) blowing against Petruchio's
'mountains' (141). The pace and fluidity of his metaphors
reflect Petruchio's talent for telling stories, and in particular,
for lying. He creates and emends, only to revise his relation

to Kate again by means of conflicting metaphors, figures that, when taken together, can in no way represent a single truth. Each of his successive metaphors fashions an alternate world – in the first world, the lovers meet as one fire and so move together; in the second, he moves more forcefully than she; and in the third, he does not move at all ('She moves me not' [I, ii, 71]). Such figuration either dispenses with truth – certainly, no one of his metaphors *has* to be true – or it confirms that the only truth that matters is the truth of Petruchio's linguistic virtuosity, his talent for *making* truths. Like Campaspe and Apelles, Petruchio traffics in self-advertising artifice, in a style that aims for flourishes over plainness, fulsomeness over brevity.

It comes as no surprise, then, that Petruchio aims to woo Kate with lies, describing her not as she really is but as he would have her be. His goal is presumably to warrant the truth *of* his assertions – 'thou art pleasant, gamesome, passing courteous' (II, i, 236) – *by* assertion.[2] And yet, there is something decidedly off about Petruchio's plan. To begin with, there is some question as to whether he actually desires these qualities in a wife. When he hears about Kate's wild behaviour with Hortensio – the 'impatient devilish spirit' (II, i, 152) with which 'she struck me on the head' (II, i, 154) – Petruchio responds with an eagerness to meet her:

Now, by the world, it is a lusty wench.
I love her ten times more than e'er I did.
O how I long to have some chat with her!
(II, i, 161–3)

Although Petruchio's words have already been exposed as overinflated and equivocal (his 'ten times' greater 'love' for a woman he still has not actually met is dubious), his excitement is palpable.[3] Petruchio has already declared his desire to gaze upon Kate, 'to make mine eye the witness / Of that report which I so oft have heard' (II, i, 52–3). Here, however, he reveals that his interest lies in her conversation: her 'chat' is what he 'long[s]' for. Then, too, it is the 'lusty' quality that he finds in her aggressive and rebellious behaviour and speech that attracts him. While early modern English 'lusty' connoted sexual desire or fervour, it also spoke to liveliness and vigour.[4] Petruchio's 'long[ing]' for Kate's vigour – sexual or otherwise – calls into question his so-called desire for 'peace . . . and quiet life' (V, ii, 112) in marriage. '[Q]uiet[ness]' apparently makes for as tepid and lacklustre an erotic relation in Shakespeare as in Lyly. Like Apelles, who is first attracted to the 'fresh' quality in Campaspe, Petruchio's response to Kate's liveliness is to employ it in the service of a mutual and erotic end. To 'chat' with her will be to put her vigour *to use* alongside his own.

Still, none of this explains why Petruchio woos with false descriptions. What does he hope to accomplish by blatantly lying to Kate about how she is behaving? Does he really believe that his praise of her 'mildness' (II, i, 192) will magically induce her to retract her claws and become mild? Corinne S. Abate has argued that Petruchio's 'tactics of positive reinforcement' create an affective bond with his future wife. But since Petruchio hatches his plan with the expectation that Kate will display no such 'positive' behaviours to reinforce, Abate's assessment is probably too generous.[5] The most prominent feature of Petruchio's seduction scheme is the gap between his words and Kate's actions: by deliberately mislabelling her behaviour, Petruchio conspicuously introduces the element of artifice into his relation with Kate. Describing Kate in language that stands in such stark contrast to her actions loosens the connection between Petruchio's words and the world they putatively reflect. The result is that his assertions create the possibility of a different world – one that, for all that it is a lie, none the less can conjure a privately and mutually constituted truth. Or it can do this if Kate confirms his untruths. Petruchio may believe that he must 'tame' Kate if he is to secure her confirmation, but Shakespeare reveals that only their mutual erotic and affective experiences enable them to inhabit the shared reality that becomes their marriage. Love and marriage are creative acts for Petruchio and Kate – they *make* marriage just as we say we make love. Their lies are inseminating; from them germinates an intimate, erotic, shared and ever so private imaginary in which 'men and women are alone' (II, i, 313). To inhabit such a world requires of them a mutually constitutive faith in their lies.

Petruchio's storytelling power is tested as early as the couple's first encounter, when he realises that his plan to bring about a series of truths by lying is more difficult to execute than he imagines. Although he intends to woo Kate by responding to her language ('Say that she rail . . .' [II, i, 171]), it is Petruchio who speaks first, Petruchio who speaks eleven of the first thirteen lines of their exchange. Once their lines begin to split more evenly, he struggles to maintain his fictions. When he calls her 'young and light' (II, i, 206) and Kate twists his words in reply, Petruchio veers away from his script and betrays his frustrations: 'Should be? should – buzz!' (II, i, 209). Rather than praise Kate for those qualities he would have her embody, he proves unable to sustain a lie and instead responds to her actual behaviour: 'Come, come, you wasp, i'faith you are too angry' (II, i, 212) and 'you must not look so sour' (II, i, 232). Apparently, Petruchio's fictions only take him so far; Kate's anger and sourness get the best of him, provoking an equally angry and sour response on his part. When she strikes him, he cannot bring himself to praise her gentle touch and instead threatens her with violence in kind: 'I swear I'll cuff you if you strike again' (224). Petruchio's threat sounds more like 'two raging fires' than a stoic mountain impervious to Kate's breeze. If we listen closely, we can hear that his lies fail to make truths precisely when she unsettles him emotionally: language fails him when Kate incites an anger in him that matches her own. When speech acts give way to affective experience, Petruchio and Kate, undoubtedly much to their dismay, find themselves *feeling* together.

A number of scholars have commented on Kate and Petruchio's shared dispositions and linguistic patterns, and such similarities set the tone for a marriage based on mutuality.[6] The likenesses between Petruchio and Kate's temperaments are anything but subtle; at various turns, any number of characters will refer to the pair's mutual 'mad[ness]' (III, ii, 180) and 'shrew[ishness]' ('he is more shrew than she', says Curtis in IV, i, 76). All of this comports with Petruchio's image of 'two raging fires' (II, i, 132). But this metaphor reveals more than mere similarity between the lovers; in it, they become undifferentiated, merging, when they 'meet together', into a single force of nature.[7] Moreover, the rage in 'raging' points to the way their commonalities constellate around affect, around madness, shrewishness, choler and passion. Despite the imbalance of power between them, Petruchio's metaphor suggests that they will eventually share their feelings. But this will take time: before they meet, Petruchio's and Kate's dispositions and qualities are similar but still *separate*. Yes, she and he are both mad, just not mad together.

But when Petruchio threatens to 'cuff' (II, ii, 224) Kate after she strikes him, they are mad together. In that instant, however brief, they feel the same thing at the same time. Their shared affective experience apparently comes from the erotic heat that has built during the pair's verbal sparring match. Petruchio's words cannot make Kate into an obedient wife but it turns out that they can bring about a change in the couple's world. His language makes their scene erotic by imposing on their interactions a crude sexuality that is sometimes merely misogynistic ('Women are made to bear' [II, i, 203]) but which, at other times, might engender erotic activity itself ('come sit on me' [II, i, 201]).

Of course, the imperative force of Petruchio's command is nugatory, since Kate intends neither to 'bear' nor to 'sit on' him. But Petruchio's sexual jokes and provocations carry erotic force, which builds to his refusal to leave Kate 'with my tongue in your tail' (II, i, 221). This statement falls in line with their volley of double entendres and puns but now Petruchio asserts that they are engaged in an erotic activity in the present tense. Rewriting their conversation as analingus, Petruchio would have it that Kate's mouth is a 'tail' that he is penetrating with his tongue. Unlike a command or solicitation ('come sit on me') that Kate can refuse, Petruchio's description insists that something sexually explicit is happening *now*. No, he cannot enforce the physical act that he describes but neither is he quite lying. His tongue is, after all, in her 'tale' if not her 'tail'; hence his language has the curious effect of making their exchange erotic merely by *asserting* that it is. The proof is that Kate now strikes him and so arouses his anger. It is the erotic charge of Petruchio's *language* that prompts their shared affective experience of anger. When he insists that an erotic act is happening in the present tense, that it is an aural effect of their verbal exchange, Petruchio reconceptualises everything the pair has been doing together. The imaginative power of his suggestion is enough to elicit a physical response from Kate, and enough, too, to create the possibility of a private world whose erotic charge can alter the real world they inhabit.

The invention of a separate and private world that lies at the heart of Petruchio's marriage-making project reflects the period's changing ideas about the role of privacy and domesticity in marriage. Although the category of privacy was itself unstable in early modern England – and very much so with regard to domestic life and marriage – there is a growing body of evidence that suggests that privacy was beginning to emerge as a condition or an aspiration of marriage.[8] Petruchio participates in this imaginative project when he uses suggestion and fabrication to conjure a private domestic scene. Since he cannot change the public world with words – calling Kate 'tame' will not tame her – he sets out to create a private world that validates his words.[9] He begins this project in his initial dialogue with Kate but the lies he tells her father at the end of the scene arguably constitute his most important tactic. Petruchio insists that Kate is infatuated with him in private but that they have 'bargained 'twixt us twain, being alone, / That she shall still be curst in company' (II, i, 305–6). '[B]eing alone' itself calls into being a distinction between the couple's private and public behaviour. For Petruchio, this is the very work of marriage – the fabrication of a domestic scene or home, along with a private language suited to it. For all that it is utterly false, the private life that he describes has become a possibility simply because he speaks it into existence. Moreover, the bargain that he says that he and Kate have struck is not only a fiction in itself; it is also a bargain *about* fiction making. The two of them are said to have agreed to act one way 'being alone' and another way 'in company'. He goes on to praise Kate's loving kisses and oaths, boasting how

> 'Tis a world to see
> How tame, when men and women are alone,
> A meacock wretch can make the curstest shrew.
> (II, i, 312–14).

Stephen Orgel glosses Petruchio's 'world' as 'worth a world' but the phrase ''Tis a world' also stipulates a private realm in which 'men and women are alone' (313). Petruchio has begun to create a modern marriage by making a new world, mysterious and unknowable from the outside, inaccessible to anyone but himself and Kate.

When the couple leave Padua, then, they bring with them this imagined private world, with as many erotic and affective possibilities as there are words to name them. To cohabit with him the intimate space that he describes to Baptista, Petruchio interpolates a Kate who covers him with 'kiss on kiss' (309), bestowing caresses and embraces, vows and protests in abundance. Taken together with the sodomitical kisses he insinuates into their earlier exchange, the erotic potential of this imagined world is vast, if not yet mutual. It is *Kate's* kisses (of whatever sort) that Petruchio dwells on in his descriptions, not his own. When the couple finally do arrive at Petruchio's country house in Act IV, he suddenly has to contend with the very real affective experience that the marriage he has made out of lies entails. All at once, he launches a sleep and food deprivation programme: to keep Kate awake, he plans to 'fling' (IV, i, 191) the bed sheets and pillows; 'if she chance to nod I'll rail and brawl / And with the clamor keep her still awake' (IV, i, 196–7). In the 1980 BBC film, John Cleese's dishevelled Petruchio struggles to keep his eyes open during this speech, following up 'if she chance to nod' with a huge, gaping yawn of his own.[10] Cleese's performance reminds us that all of this midnight railing and brawling deprives Petruchio of sleep, too; although his taming strategies are cruel, he suffers alongside his wife.[11] Earlier, at the dinner table, he declares, 'this night we'll fast *in company*' (IV, i, 167, emphasis added). Petruchio easily could have tormented Kate by gorging on mutton while she looks on with longing but he decides to abstain. His reason: the overcooked mutton

> engenders choler, planteth anger,
> And better 'twere that both of us did fast,
> Since of ourselves, ourselves are choleric.
> (IV, i, 162–4)

Rather than emphasise their differences in order to establish dominion over Kate, Petruchio focuses on their similar temperaments and creates a shared experience of hunger for the couple's first night together. In the couple's mutual

experience of deprivation, Corinne S. Abate finds evidence
for Petruchio's creation of a private sphere:

> While Petruchio will not allow Katherine to sit down and
> eat, he denies himself a meal as well, thus continuing to
> subject them both to the same conditions, an act of denial
> which by extension continues his work of constructing a
> private space of their own.[12]

I have been referring to their shared private space but every
production of the play reminds us that Petruchio and Kate
are never quite alone at his country house. In fact, the
only scene in the play in which just the two of them are on
stage together takes place before they are married, in II, i,
when Petruchio first broaches the possibility of a private
world. The country house provides no such privacy – at
least, not if we define privacy in terms of physical isolation
or solitude. When Petruchio denies Kate food and sleep,
he does so with Grumio's and Hortensio's help. Even the
couple's sleepless nights are subject to his servants' scrutiny. That Curtis delivers a report on Petruchio's 'sermon
of continency to her' (IV, i, 173) testifies to the publicity
of the pair's 'bridal chamber' (IV, i, 168).[13] Curtis's report
also suggests that, among Petruchio's other deprivations, he
denies Kate the sexual satisfactions of married life. And of
course, this privation extends to Petruchio as well. Without
food, Kate will want. Without sleep, Kate will want. And
as long as Petruchio stays up all night and shuns food all
day alongside his new wife, he too will want.[14] In the not so
private space of the country house, the newlyweds achieve a
kind of intimacy by way of this privately shared experience –
they *both* go without food, sleep and sex, even among the
servants, friends and peddlers who surround them. For now,
however, Petruchio can accomplish only so much: deprivation does not enable him to create a wife but he can use it

to create desire – a set of mutual desires that he alone has the power to enforce.

Coercion and aggression do, then, play important roles in Petruchio's private world scenario; however, it would be unwise to underestimate the creative efficacy of the couple's pre-eminent shared affective state – their giddiness. Giddiness is the lubricant that loosens Petruchio and Kate's ties to the public world around them. Petruchio tells us that his goal is to 'curb her mad and headstrong humor' (IV, i, 199), presumably by weakening Kate's defences. That two of the surest ways to *incur* madness are starvation and sleep deprivation becomes clear when Kate later complains that she is 'giddy for lack of sleep' (IV, iii, 9). Kate apparently enters into an alternative reality within their quasi-private space. Here, she 'sits as one new-risen from a dream' (IV, i, 175). Having severed their ties to reality, the couple begins to inhabit the private world that Petruchio imagined for his married life with Kate. John C. Bean describes Kate's bewilderment as being

> immersed in chaos, in that irrational world where we lose our bearings and our old sense of truth, and [where] she is challenged to respond as Christopher Sly does in the Induction by yielding to the confusion, abandoning her old identity in favor of a new one.[15]

If, as I am suggesting, such a world is accessible only through *mutually* felt experience, then Petruchio must be giddy as well. And so it is that the widow at the wedding feast comments, in response to a quip from Petruchio, that 'He that is giddy thinks the world turns round' (V, ii, 20). By releasing them from the entailments of the real world, mutual giddiness helps Kate and Petruchio to turn the world on its head. In topsy-turvydom, they may inhabit the private world that Petruchio's lies have unleashed.

Although the couple officially weds in Act III of the play, the final scene of Act IV stages their alternate marriage ceremony in their 'world turn[ed] round'. Vows are made and tested, blessings are bestowed, and now their lies become the truths of their shared imaginary. On Kate and Petruchio's journey back to Padua, this new world is revealed to be colourful and poetic, not to mention creatively and erotically charged. The lovers' fictions, which acknowledge the realities before them, also engender a private scene with realities of its own. At last, they make for one another a marriage that is both publicly recognised and privately meaningful, imagined and real. By distinguishing their truths from those of the outside world, they discover a new way to inhabit that world.

The exchange between Kate and Petruchio as they make their way back to Padua is straightforward enough: Petruchio makes assertions about the outside world that are blatant lies (first that the moon is out when the sun plainly shines, and second that an old man they pass on the road is actually a young maiden), and Kate slowly begins to understand that she must affirm his assertions in spite of what she knows to be true of the actual world. While this much is inarguable, it fails to acknowledge the telling poetic flourishes that Kate and Petruchio can add only and precisely because they have agreed to their own truth conditions. Take, for example, Petruchio's description of the scene: 'Good Lord, how bright and goodly shines the moon!' (IV, v, 2). Kate counters that it is the middle of the day and the sun is shining – 'The moon? The sun. It is not moonlight now' (IV, v, 3). Both lovers make a present-tense assertion but Petruchio tells an unvarnished lie and Kate the plain truth. Plain, too, because where Petruchio embellishes (his moon shines 'bright and goodly' [IV, v, 2]), Kate sticks to the plain facts. It takes time for her to recognise that he is soliciting her, first, to grant his counterfactual premise, then to savour his embellishment of it. It is important that he signal this – a signal he sends by means of his fictions, by employing artful language rather than commanding her to do so – but it is equally crucial that she come to understand for herself that in their world that 'turns round', what matters most is the truthfulness of his *description* of a moon that is nowhere to be seen.

This dialogue launches Kate and Petruchio into a volley of speech acts – assertions and declarations, vows and oaths – that culminates in a shared poetic that instrumentalises their erotic relation. Much of the friction between Kate and Petruchio up to this point has resulted from the conflict between false speech and observable truths – that is, between saying and knowing. Petruchio's project has been to align Kate's speeches with the truths he would have them reflect. But here, when verbs of saying and of knowing abrade one another, the friction creates an erotic spark between the lovers. Petruchio's lesson to Kate turns linguistic when he tells her, 'I say it is the moon that shines so bright' (IV, v, 4). This is less about whether or not the moon is in the sky than that Petruchio *says* it is. As we have come to expect, Petruchio is not interested in what is real, only in what is spoken. For Kate, however, the truth of the real world does matter – 'My tongue will tell the anger of my heart / Or else my heart, concealing it, will break' (IV, iii, 77–8) – it being the only thing she still can claim for herself. Insisting, '*I know* it is the sun that shines so bright' (IV, v, 5, emphasis added), she mirrors the structure of his line, but she substitutes knowing for saying, thereby writing her truth of the sun over his lie of the moon. To bring her into what he has envisioned as their private world, Petruchio must sever Kate's ties to the truth of the public scene by securing her 'faith' (II, i, 186) in his fictions.

Kate's reluctant affirmations of Petruchio's lies constitute her renewed wedding vow in the topsy-turvy world they have created. After their initial round of stipulations about the sun and the moon, their verbs shift from the indicative to the subjunctive mood, broadening to include the future tense alongside the present. Such are the qualities of verbs in the marriage ceremony, in which couples make plans and promises. Even Petruchio's oath, 'by my mother's son, and that's myself' (IV, v, 6), calls to mind the wedding ceremony's confirmation of lineage and its deference to the authority of a higher power. Here, Petruchio as author and deity creates a present and a future reality with his '*It shall be* moon' (IV, v, 7). Kate mirrors his language – another feature of the wedding ceremony – in a reply that also features the subjunctive mood and that culminates in a promise:

> be it moon or sun or what you please.
> An if you please to call it a rush candle,
> Henceforth I *vow* it shall be so for me.
>   (13–15, emphasis added)

Carefully conjoining saying and being, Kate weaves the couple's fictions together with the private realities they create: whatever Petruchio '*call[s]* it . . . it shall *be* so for me'. Co-opting Petruchio's earlier declaration of 'it shall be' but adding the ever-crucial 'for me', Kate comes closest to a marriage vow in this line. She promises her husband a future in which reality, 'for me', can stand apart from that of the observable world.

Taken together, Kate's renewed vow, the couple's mutual giddiness and the fictions that instrumentalise their private world all offer the lovers some creative latitude in their experiences together. When they meet Vincentio in the street, Petruchio's insistence that the old man is actually a 'fresh . . . gentlewoman' (IV, v, 29) is as effusive and rich as ever. In his familiar style, Petruchio waxes poetic about the rosy cheeks, bright eyes and 'heavenly face' (32) of the 'fair lovely maid' (33). Much less expected is Kate's *still more* effusive response, as fanciful and silly as Petruchio's characteristic bombast but with marked variations on his established theme. Petruchio focuses solely on the 'maid's' beauty, which comports with his focus on the couple's earlier conversation about the sun and the moon – Petruchio is mostly interested in making observations (typically false ones) and having Kate confirm them as true. But Petruchio's lies merely build a scene; Kate's fictions *animate* that scene by imbuing it with plot and setting, invigorating its matter with action. She assigns the old man a place in the world and a reason for being, addressing him as a 'Young budding virgin' (36). The old man becomes a marriageable maiden, not only a pretty face, but a character with a story that Kate protracts when she asks, 'Whither away, or where is thy abode?' (37). Gathering steam, Kate next draws a web of relationships around their newly minted virgin, asking after the maiden's parents and 'the man whom favorable stars / Allots thee for his lovely bedfellow' (39–40). In a few short lines, Kate has given Petruchio's pretty young creation kin, social status and an erotic role as well.[16] Kate may be mocking Petruchio's typically elaborate, if empty, words but she has manifestly freed herself (or been freed) from the constraints of the world around her, a world she has found largely unpleasant and unsatisfying up until this point. No longer consigned or resigned to 'tell the anger of my heart' (IV, iii, 77), Kate now produces new affective states, by turns playful and imaginative, and bound only to Petruchio's fancy. As John C. Bean puts it, 'Kate is tamed not by Petruchio's whip but by the discovery of her own imagination' in this scene.[17]

Corrected by Petruchio as to the proper identity of the old man, Kate continues to exercise her new-found mastery of an artful language that animates the world that Petruchio creates. Laurie E. Maguire notes 'the hyperbole of Kate's responses to Petruchio and the imaginative freedom of her addresses to Vincentio'.[18] Like Petruchio's fire and wind metaphors in

Act II, Kate's hyperbole calls attention to the artificiality of the lovers' creative medium. Their ornate lies recall the ornate language of Lyly's painter and model – artifice is all four lovers' lovemaking medium.[19] Once Kate and Petruchio agree on the presence of the moon in the sky or the young girl in the street, they have access to 'bright' (IV, v, 2) gleams and rosy 'fresh' (IV, v, 36) beauty. Their hard-won 'faith' (II, i, 186) in their mutual lies enables them to inhabit these fictions, and in so doing, they call to mind Curtis's line from earlier in Act IV, when Grumio hits him rather than tell him a story: 'This is to feel a tale, not to hear a tale' (IV, i, 56). To 'feel' a tale is to occupy an affective and embodied fiction, turning empty lies into meaningful realities. Kate enacts this shift when she tells Vincentio that she mistakenly addressed him as a young maiden because her eyes 'have been so bedazzled by the sun / That everything I look on seemeth green' (45–6). By cleverly referring back to the couple's initial debate about the presence of the sun in the sky, Kate makes their words meaningful, once again animating the world that Petruchio has created for them by instrumentalising the sun, putting it to *use*.[20] And although Petruchio and Kate have quibbled over what is true and what is false, they end up reconfirming everything that is actually true of the scene around them. By the scene's end, they have agreed that the sun shines above them and that the traveller is indeed an old man. What has been achieved at the end of the scene is a mutual understanding, a promise given, received and tested, which cues the birth of a creative medium for marriage-making that Kate has already begun to explore and refine.

Kate and Petruchio's private world aligns much more effortlessly with the sun's beams and the man's age than it does with the social world that awaits them at Bianca's wedding feast, where *un*easy alignment is painfully evident in Kate's final speech. Kate no longer mirrors and answers Petruchio's lines. In her final speech of the play, Kate must go it alone. In fact, much of what she says appears to be self-authored: Petruchio has not complained to Kate of his 'painful labor both by sea and land' (V, ii, 155), nor has he made mention of her 'soft and weak and smooth' body (V, ii, 171) as a reason for his supremacy. But like the sun's beams and the man's advanced age, Kate's words *do* align with real-world narratives. Is her fulsome declaration of a wife's sub-mission another poetic flourish, a mere difference in degree from her 'mad mistaking' (IV, v, 48) of the old man's wrinkles as the blush of a young virgin's cheek?[21]

What is missing at the end of her forty-four uninterrupted lines of reproach is *Petruchio's* confirmation, *his* poetic flour-ishes that might animate or invigorate the story she has told. He calls her 'a wench' (V, ii, 186), demands a kiss and gloats about winning his bet – but there are no metaphors, puns or assertions, however truthful, to corroborate the world she presents. All the details (of which there are many) are sup-plied by Kate, rather than co-authored by the pair. This is not to say that Petruchio explicitly disagrees with Kate's speech, but to suggest that his silence makes it impossible to assess his faith in the matrimonial story she tells. What we are able to assess is the marked difference in temperature between the marriage she describes now and the one she enters into in Act IV. Although Kate scolds the other women at the table for their 'frosts' (V, ii, 145), the picture she paints of ideal mar-riage has little warmth to it. The only mention of warmth or heat is in Kate's description of the wife who 'liest warm at home, secure and safe' (V, ii, 157) while her husband is out toiling in the world. There is little heat between the couple, certainly none of the sparks that Kate and Petruchio gener-ated in their first encounter, not even the warmth of the sun's beams that they just conjured together.

In its remoteness and its polish, its separateness and its totality, Kate's final speech resembles Apelles's finished por-trait – it stands at a distance from the lovers. When Kate and Petruchio's words are no longer instrumental to their marriage-making, they lose their 'fresh' quality, their vigour, their friction and so their heat. Perhaps this is why so many productions add their own flourishes to the speech: physical cues from either of the lovers, knowing winks or smiles, sounds or gestures of encouragement from Petruchio.[22] Any of these choices speaks to a desire for mutuality, and an acknowledgement that such artful flourishes are the erotic instruments that enable Petruchio and Kate's private understanding. Only when Kate and Petruchio's words are placed in *relation* do the lovers generate friction and heat. A shivering Grumio reminds the audience at the start of Act IV that there is something in the *making* of heat that is itself warming: 'But I with blowing the fire shall warm myself' (IV, i, 8–9). Grumio draws our attention to the means and ends of instrumentality; in his account, the kind of heat that comes from blowing the fire is distinct from the heat produced by the fire itself. The former, the heat of labour and creating, is what sustains Lyly's and Shakespeare's lovers, but only while they make their erotic relations together.

Notes

1. Kenneth Burke, *Language as Symbolic Action: Essays on Life, Literature, and Method*, 15.
2. According to the conventions of speech act theory, developed by J. L. Austin and John R. Searle, Petruchio intends to speak with declarative illocutionary force – that is, his words are meant to bring about a change in the world by asserting that change. See John R. Searle and Daniel Vanderveken, *Foundations of Illocutionary Logic*. See also J. L. Austin, *How to Do Things with Words*.
3. Laurie E. Maguire observes Petruchio's desire to preserve Kate's wildness when he declares his plan to 'curb' – but *not* to break – her 'headstrong humor' (IV, i, 199). Maguire refers

to Coppélia Kahn's identification of 'the most cherished male fantasy of all – that the woman remain *untamed*' (Kahn, *Man's Estate: Masculine Identity in Shakespeare*, 117). See Laurie E. Maguire, '"Household Kates": Chez Petruchio, Percy, and Plantagenet'.

4. See 'lusty, *adj.*', in *The Oxford English Dictionary*, 2nd edn, 1989, *OED Online*, Oxford University Press. Available at: <http://www.oed.com/view/Entry/111424> (last accessed 1 June 2011). Entries 3 and 4 give 'full of desire, desirous' and 'full of lust, sexual desire', respectively. The fifth entry, which cites Shakespeare's *Richard II* among its sources, defines the term as 'full of healthy vigor'.

5. 'Petruchio's tactics of positive reinforcement in his unconventional wooing of Katherine allow her, in turn, to create a private space for herself within her marriage.' See Corinne S. Abate, 'Neither a Tamer Nor a Shrew Be: A Defense of Petruchio and Katherine', 31.

6. Joel Fineman provides an insightful account of the couple's similarities in speech and temperament. See Fineman, 'The Turn of the Shrew'. Frances E. Dolan emphasises the prominence of language and speech in the pair's mutual shrewish behaviour: 'Petruchio is also a shrew in that he dominates through speech' (Dolan, *The Taming of the Shrew: Texts and Contexts*, 18–19).

7. The metaphors that follow his initial description of the 'two raging fires' all attempt to distinguish Petruchio from Kate, presumably establishing Petruchio's authority as the stronger force of nature. But the images that he chooses unwittingly draw them closer together. His first shift, in portraying himself as the wind, is belied by the second, which identifies Kate with the very same element. Petruchio's efforts to best his own metaphors apparently get the best of him; the lovers merge even where they are described in polarising language.

8. According to Lena Cowen Orlin, 'public and private did not sort themselves for early moderns in precisely the same way they do for us, but this is not to deny that a sorting process was engaged in the period' (Orlin, *Private Matters and*

Public Culture in Post-Reformation England, 89). Literature, in particular, enacted this 'sorting process', notes Orlin: 'literature nonetheless gives us glimpses of interpersonal relations, forbidden pleasures, shared jokes, small tragedies, personal triumphs, and private miracles that defied doctrine' (Orlin, 'Chronicles of Private Life', 260).

9. Speech act theory dictates that a successful declarative utterance must have a double direction of fit, from the world to the word *and* word to world: 'the world is altered to fit the propositional content by representing the world as being so altered' (Searle and Vanderveken, *Foundations*, 53). Petruchio's creation of a new world might give his declarative statements enough illocutionary force to make them successful.

10. I am grateful to Tobias Gregory for pointing out Cleese's performance as a sleep-deprived Petruchio in the BBC production of the play.

11. When Petruchio first hears of Kate, he describes his eagerness to meet her in similar terms: 'I will not sleep, Hortensio, till I see her' (I, ii, 102).

12. Abate, *Privacy, Domesticity, and Women*, 35–6. My argument about Petruchio's marriage-making techniques diverges from Abate's in degree rather than in kind. For example, Abate continues, '*anything* Petruchio asks of Katherine, *any* sacrifice or *any* perceived maltreatment she may experience, he subjects himself to as well' (36, emphasis added). I believe that this overstates the degree of reciprocity and balance in the couple's mutual suffering. Since Petruchio clearly inflicts the suffering upon Kate, it is difficult to consider her 'perceived maltreatment' as equally shared. As I have suggested elsewhere (particularly the discussion of *Endymion* in Chapter 3), mutual erotic experiences are not necessarily equal or symmetrical.

13. Laurie E. Maguire writes that Petruchio's domestic life offers glimpses of his private self: 'Petruchio will distinguish between public and private behaviour in his wife's life, as he apparently does in his own. This blustering, military boor in public

Padua is domestic in his country house, enquiring about his dog and his cousin Ferdinand, calling for his slippers, and expressing uncertainty rather than confidence in his private moments ("And 'tis my *hope* to end successfully": IV.i.189; emphasis added)' (Maguire, '"Household Kates"', 140).

14. Deprivation is an embodied and an affective experience that the couple shares but it is also Petruchio's response to Kate's *linguistic* withholding. Having dressed her meat, he asks for 'thanks' (41). She utters 'not a word' (42) and he responds by removing the dish from the table. Although we might expect Petruchio to silence Kate as part of his shrew-taming agenda, here he reveals a desire for her speech. Such a desire is not Petruchio's alone; Kate complains that Bianca's 'silence flouts me' (II, i, 29) and even comes to blows with her sister as a result of Bianca's unwillingness to engage in conversation. For Kate, no less than for Petruchio, then, an unwillingness to engage in speech (or to say the *right* things) signals a profound refusal of affective, not to mention social, engagement. That both Kate and Petruchio crave verbal intercourse testifies to their mirroring need for conversation partners who can confirm the truths they assert.

15. See John C. Bean, 'Comic Structure and the Humanizing of Kate in *The Taming of the Shrew*', 72.

16. John C. Bean observes that 'Kate herself notes the sexual humor' in the scene (73).

17. Ibid., 72. Kate's creative agency in this scene complicates Dolan's reading of the couple's 'relationship as person and mirror' (Dolan, *The Taming of the Shrew*, 31).

18. Maguire, '"Household Kates"', 135.

19. In a wordless 2012 production of the play in Washington, DC, the Synetic Theater Company cast their Petruchio as a painter, who realises and explores his desire for Kate by creating her portrait. In the painting scene, Petruchio is surrounded by a group of dancers, each of whom represents a pigment. The pigments dance between him and Kate, using their bodies and hands to block Petruchio's access to Kate, even as they present her to him.

20. Frances E. Dolan also comments on Kate's embellishments: 'Katherine even goes the game one farther, elaborating on the identification of the old man as a young woman, and blaming her "mistake" on the sun' (*The Taming of the Shrew*, 30).

21. Scholars continue to disagree about Kate's last speech. David Daniell imagines that the couple has reached a private understanding: 'A special quality of mutuality grew between Katherine and Petruchio as the play progressed, something invisible to all the others in the play and sealed for them both by Kate's last speech' (Daniell, 'The Good Marriage of Katherine and Petruchio', 71–84, 76). John C. Bean also emphasises the qualities of reciprocity and mutuality in Kate's final speech, especially when it is compared to its corollary in the earlier anonymous play, *The Taming of a Shrew* (published in 1594). In contrast to the harsh tone of the speech in *A Shrew*, in which Kate blames women for original sin, Kate's speech in *The Shrew* focuses on 'reciprocity of duties in marriage, based on complementary natures of man and woman' (Bean, 'Comic Structure', 68).

22. The play's complex theatrical history is marked by such experimentations with Kate's final speech. Citing the 1929 Columbia Pictures *Taming of the Shrew*, where Kate 'winks as she advocates a woman's submission to her husband', Dana Aspinall attributes this tradition to the 'feelings of vexation regarding *Shrew*' in the twentieth century (see Aspinall, 'The Play and the Critics', 30–1).

METAPHORICAL CONSTRAINTS: MAKING 'FRENZY . . . FINE'

Conceiving Desire in Lyly and Shakespeare has explored the capacity of language to create, to transform and to dramatise the erotic experiences of Lyly's and Shakespeare's characters. I have argued that, on the early modern English stage, metaphorical language constitutes the inner experience that it reveals. Characters such as Lyly's Apelles and Campaspe, and Shakespeare's Kate and Petruchio employ their metaphors deliberately and self-consciously, collaboratively *making* their erotic relations. Other characters' metaphors are less intentional and so more a product of a fundamental or prior erotic orientation. In Othello's 'stops' (II, i, 196) that propel him into frenzied motion, in Endymion's self-effacing exposure and in Antony and Cleopatra's erotics of bounded loss, we find metaphors that are more cognitive than calculated, more self-making than self-made. Their metaphors create but also constrain their erotic experiences. Othello's erotic process consists of the collision between the domains of stillness and experience; Valentine's language of banishment gives way to the more flexible domain of permeability; and Endymion's metaphors of exposure produce a form of erotic intimacy that paradoxically feeds on solitude and distance. Erotic language can be extraordinarily fruitful – active, dynamic, *dramatic* – even if it takes the failure of one metaphor to spark another.

Having emphasised the creative potential of erotic language, I conclude by reflecting on the consequences of its limits. Exemplary are the nymphs in *Galatea*, whose inability to express and understand their desire comprises their erotic experience, even defines their very selves.[1] Still more common is the inability of any single metaphor to dramatise eros in all of its complexity. Lakoff and Johnson note that complex concepts often require a combination of two metaphors 'because there is no one metaphor that will do the job . . . Thus we get instances of impermissible mixed metaphors resulting from the impossibility of a single clearly delineated metaphor that satisfies both purposes at once.'[2] This helps us to understand why the language of desire is marked by inconsistency and change, by a shifting and layering of different conceptual domains that make erotic experience both coherent and incoherent. Metaphors sometimes overlap, sometimes contradict one another; they open up new erotic possibilities as quickly as they cordon off others. Each linguistic shift creates friction that is a form of erotic action in its own right. Some inconsistencies between metaphors are relatively subtle, such as Claudio's shift from the language of scope and restraint to the image of the ratsbane in *Measure for Measure*, but others produce large and decisive breaks between domains of experience. We saw this in Apelles's sharp turn from metaphors of portraiture to those of sculpture. As the span between metaphors stretches, erotic and dramatic tension intensifies: it takes more and more effort to make the world cohere across gaps between conceptual domains. But, as if in response, Lyly, Shakespeare and their characters manage these widening gaps with a linguistic augmentation that, in turn, creates an even broader erotic scope.

Needless to say, a broad erotic scope is itself hard to manage. Just ask Claudio, for whom 'too much liberty' produces 'restraint' (I, ii, 105), or Antony and Cleopatra, whose erotic relationship thrives on borders and boundaries that 'chain'

(IV, viii, 14) the infinite void of 'oblivion' (I, iii, 90). Erotic scope is no less daunting for Lyly's Endymion and Campaspe, both of whom diminish themselves, as microcosm or model, in order to grasp 'things unpossible' (*Campaspe* III, v, 50–1). If metaphors provide what I have been calling shape or structure for the erotic experiences of Lyly's and Shakespeare's characters, does this mean that their metaphors constrict eros? Yes, in a way they do. Cognitive linguists write about metaphorical 'constraints' and 'entailments' because even the most capacious metaphors are rule-bound. Their constraints are what give eros 'distinction' (III, ii, 25), to use Troilus's word. For Troilus, any limitations on eros are intolerable, even monstrous: 'this is the monstruousity in love, lady, that the will is infinite and the execution confined; that the desire is boundless and the act a slave to limit' (III, ii, 75–7). But for others – Antony and Cleopatra, along with a robust kink community – being 'a slave to limit' is sexually exciting.[3] Being confined – in ropes, in words, in a lover's embrace – is a way of being *defined*, being shaped and made singular by another person's desire.[4]

I want to suggest, perhaps a bit perversely, that this kind of eroticism extends to metaphor itself. Like a lover's embrace, metaphors impart 'to airy nothing' what Theseus calls 'a local habitation and a name' (V, i, 16–17). To make love 'local' and habitable is also to make it conceivable. If this account of language appears somewhat static – in Theseus's description, words are where 'things unknown' (15) are housed, where they are fixed, captured and pinned down – the ensuing story of how poetic language is produced is extraordinarily dynamic: 'The poet's eye', claims Theseus, 'in fine frenzy rolling, / Doth glance from heaven to earth, from earth to heaven' (12–13). Throughout *Conceiving Desire in Lyly and Shakespeare*, we have seen eros itself travel a path similar to that of 'the poet's eye', and not only when Cupid drops down from above. From heaven to earth Angelo imagines his erotic decline – 'heaven in my mouth, / As if I did but only chew his name' (II, iv, 4–5) – as he dreams of bringing Isabella down to the earth with him. From earth to heaven, Endymion reaches for the moon and Cleopatra makes herself 'fire and air' (V, ii, 289) in order to 'come' to 'husband' (287) Antony. The process of constraining and limning eros through metaphor makes both love and lovers singular. Erotic experiences as vast and chaotic as 'frenzy' are made 'fine'.

This account of limits and constraints is itself structured by the conceptual metaphors I have explored in this book, most notably Part II's investigation of spatial containment. Like the experience of being 'in love', being 'tied down', whether to a bedpost or to a conceptual domain, is a way of inhabiting that place more fully, plumbing its erotic potential. A passage from Rilke's *Notebooks of Malte Laurids Brigge* describes the ecstatic pleasures that can emerge from what Gaston Bachelard calls 'the very fact of concentration in the most restricted intimate space'. Here is Rilke on the overabundant scope that can come from restraint:

> And there is almost no space here; and you feel almost calm at the thought that it is impossible for anything very large to hold in this narrowness . . . But, outside, everything is immeasurable. And when the level rises outside, it also rises in you, not in the vessels that are partially controlled by you, or in the phlegm of your most unimpressionable organs: but it grows in the capillary veins, drawn upward into the furthermost branches of your infinitely ramified existence. This is where it rises, where it overflows from you, higher than your respiration, and as a final resort, you take refuge, as though on the tip of your breath. Ah! where, where next? Your heart banishes you from yourself, your heart pursues you, and you are already almost beside yourself, and you can't stand it any longer. Like a beetle that has been stepped on, you flow from yourself, and your lack of hardness or elasticity means nothing any more.[5]

For Bachelard, this passage exemplifies the dialectics of inside and outside, but it also illustrates the erotic potential of 'narrowness', its capacity to produce experiences like rapture. Lyly's and Shakespeare's metaphors exploit this potential. Their narrow confines elicit sublime erotic experiences, even when a character is alone. Thus some of Lyly's and Shakespeare's most charged erotic language is spoken in the intervals that separate lovers (Juliet, Endymion, Galatea), in their private recollections and ruminations (Cleopatra, Angelo, Diana's nymphs), or before they meet a beloved, as in Troilus's soliloquy anticipating Cressida's arrival. Although Troilus laments the constraints and limits of 'the act', we have seen how metaphors can constitute erotic acts by giving them meaning.

What will happen when Troilus finally does 'taste indeed Love's thrice-repurèd nectar' (III, ii, 19–20) once Cressida arrives in the orchard? Whatever he is physically doing (and it is, of course, impossible to know), Troilus will also be deciding what those physical acts mean, and that mental activity fills the 'monstrous' gap between 'boundless desire' and 'the act' toward which it bounds. The body may be limited, but the act is enriched by the capaciousness of the fantasy, by the 'subtle[ty]' (III, ii, 22) of Troilus's imagination, which confirms the capacity of language, in its limits no less than its liberties, to unleash possibilities that amplify a character's erotic imagination and create erotic scope. Throughout this book, we have seen how metaphors offer characters a way of accessing even the most elusive aspects of erotic experience. Levinas conceptualises these as alterity, a relation with the future and with mystery. For Bachelard, they signal immensity and grandeur. Aristotle has recourse to entelechy. Most of Lyly's and Shakespeare's characters are afraid or unable to name this experience at all, and those who 'dare . . . describe it' (*Galatea* III, i, 88) find that only the language of infinity is sufficient to the task. Our erotic metaphors allow us to grasp something like immensity by reframing it as intimacy; they locate for us a corner of that vast cosmos that we may possess and inhabit. Such metaphors bind even the inconceivable void by bringing it down to earth, into the desiring body, where lovers can share in the pleasures of oblivion and *make* eros out of the terror of nothingness.

It is, then, the particularity of language that enables erotic scope. And only a capacious erotic imagination can create and contain an infinite variety of metaphors, linguistic registers, modes of speech and the complex interplay among them. The language of desire can be cosmic in scale and extend infinitely outward, but it also turns inward, magnifying a distinct moment in time, plumbing the depths of a single entelechial action. That such wildly expansive, richly textured and infinitely various erotic experiences emerge from basic conceptual domains testifies to the ability of dramatic language to animate even the most prosaic metaphors, to exploit their unavoidable spatiality and stubborn corporeality. For all of the conventionality of metaphor – and of early modern poetic metaphors in particular, shaped as they are by Petrarchan and prescribed conceits – Lyly's and Shakespeare's language makes erotic experience remarkably new. The scope of their erotic metaphors makes the ordinary extraordinary: it turns a soldier into a colossus, a painter into a god, a queen into the moon. Behold Endymion, falling in love with the moon – the same moon that has sparked centuries' worth of familiar verse. Reaching up to the night sky, suddenly he can touch her.

Notes

1. Diana's nymph claims, 'Thou hast *told* what I am in *uttering* what thyself is' (III, i, 57; emphasis added).
2. George Lakoff and Mark Johnson, *Metaphors We Live By*, 95.

3. Troilus is likely to be referring to the limits of his body rather than his sexual imagination, as Cora Fox observes in Troilus's critique of 'the failures of will and desire, which are constrained by the actions of the material body' ('Blazons of Desire and War in Shakespeare's *Troilus and Cressida*', 195). But as we have seen throughout this book, conceptual metaphors, too, are 'constrained by the actions of the material body'.

4. Jean-Luc Marion writes that desire itself establishes this 'radical individuation' of the lover: 'I become myself and recognize myself in my singularity when I discover and finally admit the one that I desire' (*The Erotic Phenomenon*, 108).

5. Qtd in Bachelard, *The Poetics of Space*, 229–30. (From Rilke's *Les Cahiers de Malte Laurids Brigge*, 106.)

BIBLIOGRAPHY

Abate, Corinne S. 'Neither a Tamer Nor a Shrew Be: A Defense of Petruchio and Katherine'. In *Privacy, Domesticity, and Women in Early Modern England*, edited by Corinne S. Abate, pp. 31–44. Aldershot: Ashgate, 2003.

Adelman, Janet. *Suffocating Mothers: Fantasies of Maternal Origin in Shakespeare's Plays, Hamlet to The Tempest*. New York: Routledge, 1992.

—. *The Common Liar: An Essay on Antony and Cleopatra*. New Haven, CT: Yale University Press, 1973.

Agamben, Giorgio. *Potentialities: Collected Essays in Philosophy*. Stanford: Stanford University Press, 1999.

Aquinas, Thomas. *Commentary on Aristotle's* Physics, *Books 3–8*, translated by Pierre Conway. Columbus, OH: College of St. Mary of the Springs, 1958–62.

Aristotle. *Aristotle's Metaphysics*, translated by Joe Sachs. Santa Fe: Green Lion Press, 1999.

—. *The Complete Works of Aristotle: The Revised Oxford Translation*, translated and edited by Jonathan Barnes. Princeton: Princeton University Press, 1984.

Aspinall, Dana. 'The Play and the Critics'. In *The Taming of the Shrew: Critical Essays*, edited by Dana Aspinall, pp. 3–38. New York: Routledge, 2002.

Austin, J. L. *How to Do Things with Words*. Cambridge, MA: Harvard University Press, 1962.

Bachelard, Gaston. *The Poetics of Space: The Classic Look at How We Experience Intimate Places*, translated by Maria Jolas. Boston: Beacon Press, 1994.

Barish, Jonas A. 'The Prose Style of John Lyly'. *ELH* 23, no. 1 (1956): 14–35.

Barthes, Roland. *Camera Lucida: Reflections on Photography*, translated by Richard Howard. New York: Hill & Wang, 1981.

Bauer, Bridgette L. M. 'The Definite Article in Indo-European: Emergence of a New Grammatical Category?' In *Nominal Determination: Typology, Context, Constraints, and Historical Emergence*, edited by Elisabeth Stark, Elisabeth Leiss and Werner Abraham, pp. 103–40. Amsterdam: John Benjamins, 2007.

Bean, John C. 'Comic Structure and the Humanizing of Kate in *The Taming of the Shrew*'. In *The Woman's Part: Feminist Criticism of Shakespeare*, edited by Carolyn Ruth Swift Lenz, Gayle Greene and Carol Thomas Neely, pp. 65–78. Urbana: University of Illinois Press, 1980.

Beere, Jonathan. *Doing and Being: An Interpretation of Aristotle's* Metaphysics *Theta*, Oxford Aristotle Studies. Oxford: Oxford University Press, 2009.

Belling, Catherine. 'Infectious Rape, Therapeutic Revenge: Bloodletting and the Health of Rome's Body'. In *Disease, Diagnosis, and Cure on the Early Modern Stage*, edited by Stéphanie Moss and Kaara L. Peterson, pp. 113–32. Aldershot: Ashgate, 2004.

Berger, Harry, Jr. *Fictions of the Pose: Rembrandt Against the Italian Renaissance*. Stanford: Stanford University Press, 2000.

Berry, Philippa. *Of Chastity and Power: Elizabethan Literature and the Unmarried Queen*. London: Routledge, 1989.

Bethell, S. L. *Shakespeare and the Popular Dramatic Tradition*. London: Staples, 1944.

Bevington, David. 'Asleep Onstage'. In *From Page to Performance: Essays in Early English Drama*, edited by John A. Alford, pp. 52–83. East Lansing: Michigan State University Press, 1995.

Billing, Christian M. *Masculinity, Corporality and the English Stage, 1580–1635*. Farnham: Ashgate, 2008.

Booth, Michael. *Shakespeare and Conceptual Blending: Cognition, Creativity, Criticism*, Cognitive Studies in Literature and Performance. New York: Palgrave Macmillan, 2017.

Bowin, John. 'Aristotelian Infinity'. *Oxford Studies in Ancient Philosophy* 32 (2007): 233–50.

Brickman, Benjamin. 'On Physical Space: Francesco Patrizi'. *Journal of the History of Ideas* 4, no. 2 (1943): 224–45.

Bromley, James. '"The onely way to be mad, is to bee constant": Defending Heterosexual Nonmonogamy in John Lyly's *Love's Metamorphosis'. Studies in Philology* 106, no. 4 (2009): 420–40.

Bruno, Giordano. *Cause, Principle, and Unity, and Essays on Magic*, edited and translated by Robert de Lucca and Richard J. Blackwell. Cambridge: Cambridge University Press, 1998.

— *On the Infinite Universe and Worlds*. In *Giordano Bruno: His Life and Thought*, translated by D. W. Singer, pp. 225–380. New York: Greenwood, 1958.

Burke, Kenneth. *A Grammar of Motives*. Berkeley: University of California Press, 1969. First published 1945 by Prentice-Hall.

—. *Language as Symbolic Action: Essays on Life, Literature, and Method*. Berkeley: University of California Press, 1966.

Burton, Robert. *The Anatomy of Melancholy*, vol. 3, edited by Thomas C. Faulkner, Nicholas K. Kiessling and Rhonda L. Blair. Oxford: Clarendon Press, 1994.

Butler, Judith. 'Desire'. In *Critical Terms for Literary Study*, 2nd edn, edited by Frank Lentricchia and Thomas McLaughlin, pp. 369–85. Chicago: Chicago University Press, 1990.

Carson, Anne. *Eros the Bittersweet*. Princeton: Princeton University Press, 1986. Reprinted Champaign, IL: Dalkey Archive Press, 2000.

Cartwright, Kent. 'The Confusions of *Gallathea*: John Lyly as Popular Dramatist'. *Comparative Drama* 32 (1998): 207–39.

—. *Shakespearean Tragedy and its Double: The Rhythms of Audience Response*. College Station: Pennsylvania State University Press, 1991.

—. *Theater and Humanism: English Drama in the Sixteenth Century*. Cambridge: Cambridge University Press, 1999.

Casey, Edward. *The Fate of Place: A Philosophical History*. Berkeley: University of California Press, 1997.

Cavell, Stanley. *Disowning Knowledge in Seven Plays of Shakespeare*, updated edn. Cambridge, MA: Harvard University Press, 2003.

Chanter, Tina, ed. *Feminist Interpretations of Emmanuel Levinas*. University Park: Pennsylvania State University Press, 2001.

Chess, Simone. *Male-to-Female Crossdressing in Early Modern English Literature: Gender, Performance, and Queer Relations*, Routledge Studies in Renaissance Literature and Culture. New York: Routledge, 2016.

Cook, Amy. *Shakespearean Neuroplay: Reinvigorating the Study of Dramatic Texts and Performance through Cognitive Science*. New York: Palgrave Macmillan, 2010.

Couliano, Ioan P. *Eros and Magic in the Renaissance*, translated by Margaret Cook. Chicago: University of Chicago Press, 1989.

Crane, Mary Thomas. *Shakespeare's Brain: Reading with Cognitive Theory*. Princeton: Princeton University Press, 2001.

Daniel, Carter. 'Introduction'. In *The Plays of John Lyly*, edited by Carter Daniel, pp. 11–25. Lewisburg: Bucknell University Press, 1988.

Daniell, David. 'The Good Marriage of Katherine and Petruchio'. In *The Taming of the Shrew: Critical Essays*, edited by Dana Aspinall, pp. 71–84. New York: Routledge, 2002.

de Beauvoir, Simone. *The Second Sex*, translated and edited by H. M. Parshley. New York: Vintage, 1989.

Deleuze, Gilles. *Masochism: Coldness and Cruelty*. New York: Zone, 1991.

—. *The Logic of Sense*, edited by Constantin V. Boundas. New York: Columbia University Press, 1990.

Dickinson, Emily. 'Tell all the truth but tell it slant –'. In *The Poems of Emily Dickinson: Reading Edition*, edited by R. W. Franklin, p. 792. Cambridge, MA: Belknap / Harvard University Press, 2005.

Dillon, Janette. *The Language of Space in Court Performance, 1400–1625*. Cambridge: Cambridge University Press, 2010.

Dolan, Frances E., ed. *The Taming of the Shrew: Texts and Contexts*. Boston: Bedford, 1996.

Dooley, Mark. 'The Healthy Body: Desire and Sustenance in John Lyly's *Love's Metamorphosis*'. *Early Modern Literary Studies* 6, no. 2 (2000): 3.1–19, <http://purl.oclc.org/emls/06–2/doollyl.htm> (last accessed 16 September 2019).

Ewbank, Inga-Stina. '"Were man but constant, he were perfect": Constancy and Consistency in *The Two Gentlemen of Verona*'. In *The Two Gentlemen of Verona: Critical Essays*, edited by June Schlueter, pp. 91–132. New York: Garland, 1996.

Fauconnier, Gilles, and Mark Turner. *The Way We Think: Conceptual Blending and the Mind's Hidden Complexity*. NY: Basic Books, 2002.

Fineman, Joel. 'The Turn of the Shrew'. In *Much Ado About Nothing and The Taming of the Shrew: Contemporary Critical Essays*, edited by Marion Wynne-Davies, pp. 123–47. Houndmills: Palgrave, 2001.

Fletcher, Angus. *Time, Space, and Motion in the Age of Shakespeare*. Cambridge, MA: Harvard University Press, 2007.

Fox, Cora. 'Blazons of Desire and War in Shakespeare's *Troilus and Cressida*'. In *Staging the Blazon in Early Modern English Theater*, edited by Deborah Uman and Sara Morrison, pp. 189–200. Studies in Performance in Early Modern Drama. Farnham: Ashgate, 2013.

Freeman, Donald C. '"The rack dislimns": Schema and Metaphorical Pattern in *Antony and Cleopatra*'. *Poetics Today* 20, no. 3 (1999): 443–60.

Freeman, Elizabeth. *Time Binds: Queer Temporalities, Queer Histories*. Durham, NC: Duke University Press, 2010.

Frege, Gottlob. 'On Sense and Reference'. In *Meaning: Blackwell Readings in Philosophy*, edited by Mark Richard, pp. 36–56. Malden, MA: Blackwell, 2003.

Freud, Sigmund. 'Medusa's Head'. In *Sexuality and the Psychology of Love*, edited by Phillip Rieff, pp. 202–3. New York: Simon & Schuster, 1963.

Gannon, C. C. 'Lyly's *Endimion*: From Myth to Allegory'. *ELR* 6 (1976): 220–43.

Garber, Marjorie. *Dream in Shakespeare: From Metaphor to Metamorphosis*. New Haven, CT: Yale University Press, 1974.

Gil, Daniel Juan. *Before Intimacy: Asocial Sexuality in Early Modern England*. Minneapolis: University of Minnesota Press, 2006.

Gillies, John. *Shakespeare and the Geography of Difference*. Cambridge: Cambridge University Press, 1994.

Gombrich, E. H. *The Heritage of Apelles: Studies in the Art of the Renaissance*. Ithaca, NY: Cornell University Press, 1976.

Grady, Joseph. 'Primary Metaphors as Inputs to Conceptual Integration'. *Journal of Pragmatics* 37 (2005): 1595–614.

Grady, Joseph E., Todd Oakley and Seana Coulson. 'Blending and Metaphor', <http://markturner.org/blendaphor.html> (last accessed 4 April 2019).

Grant, Edward. *Much Ado About Nothing: Theories of Space and Vacuum from the Middle Ages to the Scientific Revolution*. Cambridge: Cambridge University Press, 1981.

Greenblatt, Stephen. *Renaissance Self-Fashioning from More to Shakespeare*. Chicago: University of Chicago Press, 1980.

—. *Shakespearean Negotiations: The Circulation of Social Energy in Renaissance England*. Oxford: Oxford University Press, 1988.

Hallet, Charles A. '"Metamorphising" Proteus: Reversal Strategies in *The Two Gentlemen of Verona*'. In *The Two Gentlemen of Verona: Critical Essays*, edited by June Schlueter, pp. 153–77. New York: Garland, 1996.

Harris, Jonathan Gil. '"Narcissus in thy Face": Roman Desire and the Difference It Fakes in *Antony and Cleopatra*'. *Shakespeare Quarterly* 45, no. 4 (1994): 408–25.

Heidegger, Martin. *Aristotle's Metaphysics Θ 1–3: The Essence and Actuality of Force*, translated by Walter Brogan and Peter Warnek. Bloomington: Indiana University Press, 1995.

—. 'Building Dwelling Thinking'. In *Poetry, Language, Thought*, translated by A. Hofstadter. New York: Harper & Row, 1971.

Hillman, David. '"If it be love indeed": Transference, Love, and *Anthony and Cleopatra*'. *Shakespeare Quarterly* 64, no. 3 (2013): 301–33.

—. 'The Gastric Epic: *Troilus and Cressida*'. *Shakespeare Quarterly* 48, no. 3 (1997): 295–313.

Hunter, G. K. *John Lyly: The Humanist as Courtier*. Cambridge: Cambridge University Press, 1962.

Irigaray, Luce. 'The Envelope: A Reading of Spinoza, *Ethics*, "Of God"'. In *An Ethics of Sexual Difference*, translated by C. Burke and G. C. Gill, p. 93. Ithaca, NY: Cornell University Press, 1993.

—. 'Place, Interval: A Reading of Aristotle, *Physics* IV'. In *An Ethics of Sexual Difference*, translated by C. Burke and G. C. Gill, pp. 31–48. Ithaca, NY: Cornell University Press, 1993.

Jordan, Tina. 'Guilt, Jealousy, Empathy: Your Dog Has the Same Emotions You Do'. *The New York Times*, 22 March 2019, <https://www.nytimes.com/2019/03/22/books/review/frans-de-waal-laurie-halse-anderson-best-sellers.html> (last accessed 16 September 2019).

Kahn, Coppélia. *Man's Estate: Masculine Identity in Shakespeare*. Berkeley: University of California Press, 1981.

Kermode, Frank. 'Experiencing the Place and Space of Early Modern Theater'. *Journal of Medieval and Early Modern Studies* 43, no. 1 (2013): 1–24.

Kesson, Andy. *John Lyly and Early Modern Authorship*, The Revels Plays Companion Library. Manchester: Manchester University Press, 2014.

—. Lucy Munro and Callan Davies, eds. *Before Shakespeare* (blog), <https://beforeshakespeare.com> (last accessed 1 April 2019).

Khomenko, Natalia. '"Between You and Her No Comparison": Witches, Healers, and Elizabeth I in John Lyly's *Endymion*'. *Early Theatre* 13, no. 1 (2010): 37–63.

Knights, L. C. *Some Shakespearean Themes*. London: Chatto and Windus, 1959.

Kövecses, Zoltán. *Metaphor and Emotion: Language, Culture, and Body in Human Feeling*. Cambridge: Cambridge University Press, 2000.

Lakoff, George. 'The Contemporary Theory of Metaphor'. In *Metaphor and Thought*, 2nd edn, edited by Andrew Ortony. Cambridge: Cambridge University Press, 1993.

—. 'Sorry, I'm Not Myself Today: The Metaphor System for Conceptualizing the Self'. In *Spaces, Worlds, and Grammar*, edited by Gilles Fauconnier and Eve Sweetser, pp. 91–123. Chicago: University of Chicago Press, 1996.

—, and Mark Johnson. *Metaphors We Live By*. Chicago: University of Chicago Press, 1980.

—, and Mark Johnson. *Philosophy in the Flesh: The Embodied Mind and its Challenge to Western Thought*. New York: Basic Books, 1999.

—, and Mark Turner. *More Than Cool Reason: A Field Guide to Poetic Metaphor*. Chicago: University of Chicago Press, 1989.

Leinwand, Theodore. 'Shakespeare against Doctrine'. *Literature Compass* 3 (March 2006): 513–28.

—. 'The Shakespearean Perverse'. *The Yale Review* 100, no. 4 (2012): 118–28.

Levinas, Emmanuel. *Ethics and Infinity: Conversations with Philippe Nemo*, translated by Richard A. Cohen. Pittsburgh: Duquesne University Press, 1985.

—. *Totality and Infinity: An Essay on Exteriority*, translated by Alphonso Lingis. Pittsburgh: Duquesne University Press, 1969.

Levy-Strauss, Claude. *The Raw and the Cooked*, translated by John and Doreen Weightman. New York: Harper & Row, 1970.

Love, Heather L. 'Milk'. In *Shakesqueer: A Queer Companion to the Complete Works of Shakespeare*, edited by Madhavi Menon. Durham, NC: Duke University Press, 2011.

Lunney, Ruth, ed. *John Lyly*, The University Wits Series. Farnham: Ashgate, 2011.

Lupton, Julia Reinhard. 'Creature Caliban'. *Shakespeare Quarterly* 50, no. 1 (2000): 1–23.

Lyly, John. *Euphues: The Anatomy of Wit* and *Euphues and His England*, edited by Leah Scragg. Manchester: Manchester University Press, 2003.

—. *The Revels Plays, John Lyly: Campaspe* and *Sappho and Phao*, edited by G. K. Hunter and David Bevington. Manchester: Manchester University Press, 1991.

—. *The Revels Plays, John Lyly: Endymion*, edited by David Bevington. Manchester: Manchester University Press, 1996.

—. *The Revels Plays, John Lyly: Galatea and Midas*, edited by G. K. Hunter and David Bevington. Manchester: Manchester University Press, 2000.

—. *The Revels Plays, John Lyly: Love's Metamorphosis*, edited by Leah Scragg. Manchester: Manchester University Press, 2008.

—. *The Revels Plays, John Lyly: Mother Bombie*, edited by Leah Scragg. Manchester: Manchester University Press, 2010.

—. *The Revels Plays, John Lyly: The Woman in the Moon*, edited by Leah Scragg. Manchester: Manchester University Press, 2006.

Lyne, Rafael. *Shakespeare, Rhetoric and Cognition*. Cambridge: Cambridge University Press, 2011.

Madelaine, Richard, ed. *Antony and Cleopatra*, Shakespeare in Production. Cambridge: Cambridge University Press, 1998.

Maguire, Laurie E. '"Household Kates": Chez Petruchio, Percy, and Plantagenet'. In *Gloriana's Face: Women, Public and Private, in the English Renaissance*, edited by S. P. Cerasano and Marion Wynne-Davies, pp. 129–65. Detroit: Wayne State University Press, 1992.

Marion, Jean-Luc. *The Erotic Phenomenon*, translated by Stephen E. Lewis. Chicago: University of Chicago Press, 2007.

Masten, Jeffrey. *Queer Philologies: Sex, Language, and Affect in Shakespeare's Time*. Philadelphia: University of Pennsylvania Press, 2016.

Maus, Katherine Eisaman. *Inwardness and Theater in the English Renaissance*. Chicago: University of Chicago Press, 1995.

Mavromatis, Andreas. *Hypnagogia: The Unique State of Consciousness Between Wakefulness and Sleep*. London: Routledge & Kegan Paul, 1987.

Menon, Madhavi, ed. *Shakesqueer: A Queer Companion to the Complete Works of Shakespeare*. Durham, NC: Duke University Press, 2011.

Merleau-Ponty, Maurice. *Phenomenology of Perception*, translated by Colin Smith. Delhi: Motilal Banarsidass, 1996.

Mooney, Michael. *Shakespeare's Dramatic Transactions*. Durham, NC: Duke University Press, 1990.

Neufeld, Christine M. 'Lyly's Chimerical Vision: Witchcraft in Endymion'. *Forum for Modern Language Studies* 43, no. 4 (2007): 351–69.

Orlin, Lena Cowen. 'Chronicles of Private Life'. In *The Cambridge Companion to English Literature 1500–1600*, edited by Arthur Kinney, pp. 241–64. Cambridge: Cambridge University Press, 2000.

—. *Private Matters and Public Culture in Post-Reformation England*. Ithaca, NY: Cornell University Press, 1994.

Parker, Patricia. 'Shakespeare and Rhetoric: "Dilation" and "Delation" in *Othello*'. In *Shakespeare and the Question of Theory*, edited by Patricia Parker and Geoffrey Hartman, pp. 54–74. New York: Methuen, 1985.

Paster, Gail Kern. *Humoring the Body: Emotions and the Shakespearean Stage*. Chicago: University of Chicago Press, 2004.

Pechter, Edward. '"Have you not read of some such thing?": Sex and Sexual Stories in *Othello*'. *Annual Survey of Shakespearean Study and Production* 49 (1996): 201–16.

Pincombe, Michael. *The Plays of John Lyly: Eros and Eliza*. Manchester: Manchester University Press, 1996.

Porter, Chloe. 'Idolatry, Iconoclasm, and Visual Experience in Works by Shakespeare and Lyly'. *Literature and History* 18, no. 1 (2009): 1–15.

Proclus. *A Commentary on the First Book of Euclid's Elements*, edited and translated by Glen R. Morrow. Princeton: Princeton University Press, 1970.

Purnis, Jan. 'Bodies and Selves: Autoscopy, Out-of-Body Experiences, Mind-Wandering and Early Modern Consciousness'. In *Shakespeare and Consciousness*, Cognitive Studies in Literature and Performance, edited by Paul Budra and Clifford Werier, pp. 191–214. New York: Palgrave Macmillan, 2016.

Rawson, Claude. 'I Could Eat You Up: The Life and Adventures of a Metaphor'. *The Yale Review* 97, no. 1 (2009): 82–112.

Rose, Mary Beth. *The Expense of Spirit: Love and Sexuality in English Renaissance Drama*. Ithaca, NY: Cornell University Press, 1988.

Sanchez, Melissa. '"In My Selfe the Smart I Try": Female Promiscuity in *Astrophil and Stella*'. *ELH* 81, no. 1 (2013): 1–27.

—. '"Use Me But as Your Spaniel": Feminism, Queer Theory, and Early Modern Sexualities'. *PMLA* 127, no. 3 (2012): 493–511.

Sartre, Jean-Paul. *Being and Nothingness: An Essay on Phenomenological Ontology*, translated by Hazel E. Barnes. New York: Citadel Press, 1969.

—. *The Psychology of Imagination*. London: Methuen, 1978.

Sawday, Jonathan. *The Body Emblazoned: Dissection and the Human Body in Renaissance Culture*. London: Routledge, 1995.

Schalkwyk, David. *Shakespeare, Love and Language*. Cambridge: Cambridge University Press, 2018.

Scragg, Leah. *The Metamorphosis of Gallathea: A Study in Creative Adaptation*. Washington, DC: University Press of America, 1982.

Searle, John R., and Daniel Vanderveken. *Foundations of Illocutionary Logic*. Cambridge: Cambridge University Press, 1985.

Sentesy, Mark. 'Are Potency and Actuality Compatible in Aristotle?' *Epoché: A Journal for the History of Philosophy* 22, no. 2 (2018): 239–70.

—. 'On the Many Senses of Potency According to Aristotle'. In *Sources of Desire: Essays on Aristotle's Theoretical Works*, edited by James Oldfield, pp. 63–93. Newcastle upon Tyne: Cambridge Scholars, 2012.

Shakespeare, William. *Antony and Cleopatra*, edited by Michael Neill. Oxford: Oxford University Press, 1994.

—. *The Complete Pelican Shakespeare*, edited by Stephen Orgel and A. R. Braunmuller. New York: Penguin, 2002.

—. *Troilus and Cressida*, RSC Shakespeare, edited by Jonathan Bate and Eric Rasmussen. London: Red Globe Press, 2010.

Sharp, Jane. *The Midwives Book, Or the Whole Art of Midwifery Discovered*, edited by Elaine Hobby. Oxford: Oxford University Press, 1999.

Sherman, William. 'Revisiting the House of Sleep'. Paper presented at the Annual Meeting of the Shakespeare Association of America, Washington, DC, April 2009.

Skantze, P. A. *Stillness in Motion in the Seventeenth-Century Theatre*. London: Routledge, 2003.

Sloterdijk, Peter. *Bubbles: Spheres I*, Semiotext(e) Foreign Agents Series, translated by Wieland Hoban. Los Angeles: Semiotext(e), 2011.

Snow, Edward. 'Language and Sexual Difference in *Romeo and Juliet*'. In *Shakespeare's 'Rough Magic:' Renaissance Essays in Honor of C. L. Barber*, edited by Peter Erickson and Coppélia Kahn, pp. 168–92. Newark: University of Delaware Press, 1986.

—. 'Sexual Anxiety and the Male Order of Things in *Othello*'. *ELR* 10, no. 3 (1980): 384–412.

Sogunle, Kenny. 'The Difference Between Falling in Love and Loving Someone'. *Huffington Post*, 27 June 2016, <https://www.huffpost.com/entry/falling-in-love-vs-loving-someone_n_57709758e4b0fa01a14049fa> (last accessed 11 April 2019).

Sorabji, Richard, and Norman Kretzmann. 'Aristotle on the Instant of Change'. *Proceedings of the Aristotelian Society, Supplementary Volumes* 50 (1976): 69–89, 91–114.

Stallybrass, Peter. 'Transvestism and the "Body Beneath": Speculating on the Boy Actor'. In *Erotic Politics: Desire on the Renaissance Stage*, edited by Susan Zimmerman, pp. 64–83. London: Routledge, 1992.

Stanivukovic, Goran. '"Two lips, indifferent red": Queer Styles in *Twelfth Night*'. In *Queer Shakespeare: Desire and Sexuality*, ed. Goran Stanivukovic, pp. 154–76. London: Bloomsbury, 2017.

Starks, Lisa S. 'Immortal Longings: The Erotics of Death in *Antony and Cleopatra*'. In *Antony and Cleopatra: New Critical Essays*, edited by Sara Munson Deats, pp. 243–58. New York: Routledge, 2005.

Steber, Carolyn. '9 Differences Between Loving Your Partner and Being in Love with Them, According to Experts'. *Bustle*, 30 March 2018, <https://www.bustle.com/p/9-differences-between-loving-your-partner-being-in-love-with-them-according-to-experts-8613384> (last accessed 11 April 2019).

Steiner, Wendy. *The Real Real Thing: The Model in the Mirror of Art*. Chicago: University of Chicago Press, 2010.

Stoichita, Victor I. *The Pygmalion Effect: From Ovid to Hitchcock*, translated by Alison Anderson. Chicago: University of Chicago Press, 2008.

Sullivan, Garrett A., Jr. *Sleep, Romance and Human Embodiment: Vitality from Spenser to Milton*. Cambridge: Cambridge University Press, 2012.

Traub, Valerie. *Desire and Anxiety: Circulations in Sexuality in Shakespearean Drama*. New York: Routledge, 1992.

—. *The Renaissance of Lesbianism in Early Modern England*, Cambridge Studies in Renaissance Literature and Culture. Cambridge: Cambridge University Press, 2002.

—. *Thinking Sex with the Early Moderns*. Philadelphia: University of Pennsylvania Press, 2015.

Tribble, Evelyn. *Cognition in the Globe: Attention and Memory in Shakespeare's Theatre*. Basingstoke: Palgrave, 2011.

—. 'Pretty and Apt: Boy Actors, Skill, and Embodiment'. In *The Oxford Handbook of Shakespeare and Embodiment: Gender, Sexuality, and Race*, edited by Valerie Traub, pp. 628–40. Oxford: Oxford University Press, 2016.

Turner, Mark. *Death is the Mother of Beauty: Mind, Metaphor, Criticism*. Chicago: University of Chicago Press, 1987.

Turner, Robert Y. 'Some Dialogues of Love in Lyly's Comedies'. *ELH* 29, no. 3 (1962): 276–88.

Vanhoutte, Jacqueline. 'Age in Lust: Lyly's *Endymion* and the Court of Elizabeth I'. *Explorations in Renaissance Culture* 37, no. 1 (2011): 51–70.

Varnado, Christine. 'Getting Used, and Liking It: Erotic Instrumentality in *Philaster*'. *Renaissance Drama* 44, no. 1 (2016): 25–52.

Wack, Mary Frances. *Lovesickness in the Middle Ages: The Viaticum and its Commentaries*. Philadelphia: University of Pennsylvania Press, 1990.

Walen, Denise A. 'Constructions of Female Homoerotics in Early Modern Drama'. *Theatre Journal* 54, no. 3 (2002): 411–30.

Weimann, Robert. *Shakespeare and the Popular Tradition in the Theater: Studies in the Social Dimension of Dramatic Form and Function*, edited by Robert Schwartz. Baltimore: Johns Hopkins University Press, 1978.

Wells, Stanley. 'The Failure of *The Two Gentlemen of Verona*'. *Shakespeare Jahrbuch* 99 (1963): 161–73.

'What Is Edging and Why Might It Be Employed?' International Society for Sexual Medicine, <https://www.issm.info/sexual-health-qa/what-is-edging-and-why-might-it-be-employed> (last accessed 7 April 2019).

Witt, Charlotte. *Ways of Being: Potentiality and Actuality in Aristotle's Metaphysics*. Ithaca, NY: Cornell University Press, 2003.

INDEX

Abate, Corinne S., 222, 228
action see *entelecheia* (action/
 actuality)
Adelman, Janet, 88
Anatomia, 122–3
Antony and Cleopatra
 bondage in, 136, 140, 151–3,
  157–8
 Cleopatra on her barge,
  140–4
 Cleopatra's erotic agency,
  86, 90–1, 142–3, 151
 the container schema and,
  138, 149, 153
 gaps in nature and time,
  143–4
 identity loss in, 148–9,
  150–1, 153–62
 imagery of death in, 149–50
 language of sexual bondage,
  139, 141–2, 157, 160,
  162, 243
 paradox in, 88

place and displacement in,
 136–41, 148–9
spatial significance of the
 monument, 136, 139,
 155–6
void spaces in, 139, 144,
 145–9, 150, 154, 155
Aristotle
 action/actuality
  (*entelecheia*), 36, 37–8, 49,
  82, 89–90
 'Causation Is Action to
  Achieve a Purpose'
  metaphor, 38–9, 73
 concept of place, 86, 139–40
 Metaphysics, 36, 39, 69
 motion (*kinesis*), 38
 movement towards *telos*,
  38, 49
 Physics, 44, 90, 139
 potentiality (*dunamis*), 43,
  44, 63, 68–9
As You Like It, 99–100

cognitive linguistics
  conceptions of amorous emotions, 32–3
  the event structure metaphor and, 32, 38
  metaphorical 'constraints,' 243
  physical and spatial orientation, 9
  and Shakespeare scholarship, 12–13
  see also conceptual metaphor theory; metaphor
cognitive theory
  erotic desire and, 7–8
  mind-body continuum in, 9
  scholarship on Shakespeare, 12
conceptual metaphor theory
  applied to erotic desire, 11–13
  blending theory and, 12–13
container schema, 105–6, 138, 153
Cook, Amy, 12
Couliano, Ioan, 198–9, 203

Deleuze, Gilles, 142
dreams
  daydreams, 125
  the erotic imagination in *Endymion*, 120, 121–2
  erotic language of dreams in *Sappho and Phao*, 46–7, 48
  permeability of, 122–3

dunamis (potentiality)
  defined, 43, 44, 63
  dunamis/entelecheia continuum, 36, 37–8, 82, 89–90
  two forms of, 68–9
  see also potentiality

edging
  entelechial desire as, 38
  term, 54
embodiment
  and the container schema, 105–6
  early modern notions of, 8–9, 106
  of erotic attraction, 32–3, 74
  permeability of the body, 8, 21, 106
emotions
  in event structure metaphors, 32, 33
  metaphors of temperature for, 11, 31
  in relation to motion, 29–30, 32
Endymion
  dreams in, 120–3
  Endymion's desire for the moon, 15–16, 113–16
  Endymion's exposure of self, 118–19, 120–1, 122, 123, 124
  fantasy of self-containment, 112–13, 129